The Future of International Organization

The Future of International Organization

edited by Rüdiger Jütte and Annemarie Grosse-Jütte

St Martin's Press
New York

A Publication of the Institute of Peace Research and
Security Policy at the University of Hamburg

All rights reserved. For information, write:
St. Martin's Press, Inc., 175 Fifth Avenue, New York, NY 10010
Printed in Great Britain
First published in the United States of America in 1981

ISBN 0-312-31476-0

Library of Congress Cataloging in Publication Data

Main entry under title:

The Future of international organization.

    1. United Nations—Addresses, essays, lectures.
2. International agencies—Addresses, essays, lectures.
3. International organization—Addresses, essays,
lectures.   I. Jutte, Rudiger.
JX1977.F85   1981   341.2   80-21735
ISBN 0-312-31476-0

CONTENTS

PREFACE

This book is about the role and capacity of international organization in the management of a growing complexity of international conflicts and global development problems. The contributions in this volume address specifically, though not exclusively, the development of the United Nations and its potential to exercise regulatory and problem-solving tasks which become increasingly complicated by the interaction of intra-societal and international factors.

These perspectives form the general framework for the particular problems which are presented in the four parts. The introductory section on *Growth and Change of International Organization* evaluates the UN's changing role in the East–West and North–South conflict settings, and the growth of structures of international organization in general. The institutional growth *within* the UN system is interpreted as a specific phase in the development of the organization. Jütte suggests that the expansion of the institutional structure helped to overcome the general stalemate into which the organization was driven under the East–West conflict, and which had also paralysed institutions designed to promote co-operation in the fields of economic and social development. While the system could thereby constructively influence the course of the North–South *conflict*, it may require another institutional development to meet the needs of the further development of North–South *relations* at operational levels. This will probably encourage institutional growth beyond the inner circle of UN bodies. Hoefnagels' analysis of whether or not the quantitative and qualitative growth of the network of international organizations has contributed to their independence as international actors, provides some insight into the suggestion that their regulatory capacity remains within the constraints of the sovereignty-based system of nation states.

The second section *Changing Issues and Decision Structures* focuses on the UN's response to problems of socio-economic development, stressing the organization's role as an infrastructure for the articulation and negotiation of political demands in the North–South context, and to advance more egalitarian decision structures. Rajan traces the history of the issue of sovereignty over natural resources, showing the gradual accommodation of conflicting positions up to the point where a principle consensus has been reached, but more is required for turning general principles into day-to-day practice. The merits and limitations of present arrangements for the conduct of negotiations and decision-making are discussed under this perspective by Gregg, who derives seven 'lessons' from the operation of the present system. While the UN cannot be bypassed in the future process of making a NIEO viable, it probably needs help to make the deficiencies which are at present visible vanish. The creation of additional forums should be carefully considered, and the modes of representation of states as well as the group system should be re-examined so as to maintain their advantages while restricting their less desirable implications. Finally, the design of new decision-structures should not be overshadowed by unfounded ideological fears as to the opponents' political aspirations.

The NIEO programme as it developed within the UN is subject to many criticisms. Bielawski presents the position of socialist states, and suggests that the programme is not sufficiently future-orientated since its main premises leave untouched the continued zero-sum character of international economic relations, do not adequately account for external conditions of underdevelopment, and are based on a false North–South dichotomy by disregarding the difference between capitalist and socialist developed countries. The role of socialist countries as partners in development is then discussed within an 'open' conception of restructuring international economic relations. The inadequacy of the North–South formula is further extended by Chandisingh to the southern side. He stresses domestic socio-economic boundary conditions of developing societies, rather than the differentiation in less- and least-developed countries, as a basis for suggesting more complex patterns of political and economic relations between industrialized capitalist and socialist countries on the one hand, and developing countries following alternative paths of development on the other.

Non-alignment has been an outstanding political factor in formulating the programmatic level of those interests which challenged the established international regimes. Grosse-Jütte describes how the UN system was gradually instrumentalized in attempts to restructure general rules of international behaviour and principles of economic relations. Recent institutional and procedural innovations in disarmament activities are considered against this background, though one may be sceptical whether they, alone, are sufficiently influential to compensate the specific substantive factors and relations characteristic of this field. While her analysis suggests that the 'institutional strategy' of non-aligned countries proved a successful instrument to induce a number of significant changes in both normative orientations and specific principles, Burri correlates this level of action with the level of bilateral relations of non-aligned states with the USSR and the USA, asking whether the relative autonomy achieved by the former reflects on the latter. Though the non-aligned tradition of a country seems to influence positively attempts to diminish and/or balance material dependencies, the over-all picture is not too promising if one goes beyond relative differences.

All these results underline the continuing gap between the general agreement over new general principles and their translation into operational rules and norms actually governing what Rajan refers to as day-to-day practice. This is the focus of the third part *Adjusting Normative Standards for International Behaviour*. Beyond the necessity for more adequate forums for negotiation, this process will eventually touch the core of substantive interests. Some, though certainly not all, obstacles may be a matter of adjusting and/or extending formal legal instruments. Tomaševski describes the legal implications of the NIEO for the structure of international law — at the level of doctrine and as to specific norms — and discusses how legal thinking might contribute to shape political conceptions into more precise legal terms. Processes generating and redefining legal standards are analysed by Weber. In the context of some substantive problems dealt with in UN conferences or specialized bodies, the consensus-building capacity of bargaining processes is stressed as a means to increase the degree of acceptance for new solutions. One such attempt to give more precision to legal principles in the light of new needs has been undertaken by the work of the Committee on Principles of Friendly Relations and Co-operation among States, which was later adopted in a Declaration by the General Assembly.

The latter aspect is particularly relevant for the regulation of international situations of violent and non-violent crises. (Section Four — *Management and Resolution of Conflicts*). While the regulation of international conflicts is traditionally a major task of the UN, it becomes increasingly involved in situations where the modes of intervention available to it prove insufficient. Empirical data presented by Jütte show the discrepancy between the tendency to refer conflicts to international institutions, particularly to the UN, and the actual impact of the organization in the control of conflicts. Problems that arise from new types of conflict situations, involving such factors as non-state actors or essentially domestic conflicts that arouse international concern, become obvious in Ansprenger's study of the UN actions in the case of South Africa and the Namibia dispute. What becomes clear is the dependence of effective UN actions on the initiative of a strong coalition and the likelihood that actions lose their momentum whenever the original support can no longer be maintained. Obaseki's interpretation of the role of the Organization of African Unity (OAU) contains the consequences of the UN's limitations for the regional African context. The analysis underlines the need to rely on explicitly consensual procedures in mediatory attempts and to exclude any elements favouring forced solutions to conflicts and relying on 'external' influences which are unacceptable to the conflicting parties. While this strategy by no means guarantees major successes, it at least precludes seemingly effective resolutions to conflicts which often tend to produce only new, and then still more intractable, conflict situations.

The editors would like to express their gratitude to those individuals and institutions whose assistance and support helped in the preparation of this volume.

A seminar on 'International Organization' and a colloquium on 'Non-aligned Policies in International Organizations', which were held simultaneously in the Inter-University Centre of Postgraduate Studies (IUC), Dubrovnik during the academic year 1978/9, provided an opportunity for all the contributors to meet and discuss together problems of international organization. Both seminar and colloquium were concerned with a much broader range of topics than is reflected in this collection. The present volume is therefore not intended as a representative presentation of the work of either event, neither formally nor in substance. Grants by the University of Hamburg and the IUC (for the seminar) and the Deutsche Gesellschaft für Friedens- und Konfliktforschung, Bonn (for the colloquium), are gratefully acknowledged. We are especially indebted to Dr. Hermann Weissenborn, then of the Office of the President of the University of Hamburg, for valuable assistance in planning the project. Berta Dragicević, IUC Executive Secretary, was responsible for making the Centre a friendly environment to work in. Our thanks for preparing parts of the final manuscripts go to Jeanette Allam and Helga Borman, and to Marion Joergensen for her efficient assistance during earlier phases of the project.

Hamburg, March 1980   R. J.
                                                          A.G.-J.

PART I

GROWTH AND CHANGE OF INTERNATIONAL ORGANIZATION

1 INTRODUCTION

RÜDIGER JÜTTE
Institute of Peace Research and Security Policy, at the University
of Hamburg

The UN of 1980 no longer has much similarity with the institution that came into being in 1945/6. The growth of the international system by newly independent states has dramatically increased the complexity of international relations: an expansion of issues and problems with new patterns of conflict and co-operation has not only affected the internal decision structures of international organizations and their modes of operation, but — still more important — the tasks to be pursued and their role as regulatory elements in the present-day world.

If we look at the UN's institutions we are still confronted with the well-known bodies that in the past have attracted so much attention and shaped the image of the organization: the Security Council (SC), the General Assembly (GA), and — although less well known — the Economic and Social Council (ECOSOC). But they are no longer the institutional 'corner-stones' as originally provided for by the Charter.

Until the end of the sixties, the series of spectacular conflicts and crises — e.g. the Greek Question, Korea, Hungary, Suez, Goa, Cuba, Congo, and Cyprus — dominated the agenda of the UN, and hopes for maintaining or restoring peaceful relations time and again turned to the capacity of both the SC and the GA. The over-all results are well known: the UN's record in 'maintaining international peace and security' presents itself as a history of predominant failures, and the few out-standing roles that the organization could play were indeed exceptions to the rule rather than evidence that it functions as a reliable instrument to safeguard the elements of a rudimentary peace.

Today, there are no fewer international conflicts, but many of them show a combination of characteristics which poses additional problems for the organization in attempts to cope with them. The heterogeneous character of international relations has in practice invalidated the dichotomy of 'domestic' and 'international' affairs. One of the consequences is that both the SC and the GA have to deal increasingly with situations where the domestic policies of a government (repressions, unequal treatment of minorities, violation of individual or collective human rights) raise such international concern as to 'internationalize' intra-state situations and conflicts, with conflicts between or within newly independent states (territorial integrity v. self-determination as a result of artificial boundaries), or with the involvement of non-state actors as major parties in a conflict. Such cases constitute particularly intractable conflict constellations, and the mere consideration of, let alone intervention in, conflict situations of this type invariably challenges the traditional formal hierarchy of the Charter principles and their interpretation. Although 'there is a developing consensus that values at stake . . . should be related to social consequences rather than to outmoded formal criteria',[1] it is indeed less developed or even lacking when it comes to interventionary competences for the organization, and even more so as to procedures and instruments both permissible and likely to be effective to accommodate conflicting values in these situations.

There is, then, a need to go beyond the mere regulation of *conflict behaviour* between international actors towards greater attention for *conflict-generating structures*, not only between states but also within and across those national boundaries which traditionally demarcate the domains of exclusive domestic jurisdiction and limit the interventionist authority of international organizations. However, the practical implications of orientations to modify this limit are extremely far-reaching, a fact which may explain that, despite a general awareness of these problems and verbal invocation of new interpretations, the actual practice has so far been highly restrictive and selective.

Though situations of international crisis placed the UN into the centre of attention, its image and the concentration of its activities have over the years been increasingly influenced by issues related to economic and social development. Over a decade ago, in 1969, U Thant, then Secretary-General of the UN, anticipated the necessity for the organization to decisively broaden and intensify its commitments for effective action and reminded its members:

> I do not wish to seem overdramatic, but I can only conclude from the information that is available to me as Secretary-General, that the Members of the United Nations have perhaps ten years left in which to subordinate their ancient quarrels and launch a global partnership to curb the arms race, to improve the human environment, to defuse the population explosion, and to supply the required momentum to development efforts. If such global partnership is not forged within the next decade, then I very much fear that the problems I have mentioned will have reached such staggering proportions that they will be beyond our capacity to control.[2]

With the 10 years having passed, the substantive core of the Secretary-General's prediction has become the undeniable essence of growing concerns within and across national societies throughout the world. Only very recently, the report of the North-South Commission, entitled 'North-South: A Programme for Survival', emphasized in political terms and even more definitely that any delay in coping with these problems would increasingly diminish the chances of eventually getting them under control.[3]

The response of the UN has been manifold. None of the problems has been actually resolved, nor are there clear solutions in sight. But very clearly they have since then 'captured' the organization by more or less absorbing large portions of its attention and organizational energy. A glance at some major agenda items of the UN between 1978 and 1980 demonstrates the changes in priorities:[4]

Special Session of the GA on Disarmament (1978)
Special Session of the GA on Namibia (1978)
Special Session of the GA on the New International Economic Order
(1980)
UN Conference on Technological Co-operation among Developing Countries (1978)
UN Conference on an International Code of Conduct on the Transfer of Technology (1978)
UN Conference on the Establishment of a UN Industrial Development Organization — to transform the existing UNIDO body into a special organization of the UN (1978)
UN Conference on Science and Technology for Development (1979)
Fifth UN Conference on Trade and Development/UNCTAD V (1979)
UN Conference on the Establishment of a Common Fund — as part of the Integrated Raw Material Programme (1979)
Proclamation of a Transport and Communication Decade for Africa
World Conference against Racism and Racial Discrimination (1978)
World Conference on the UN's Decade of Women (1980)
Continuation of the Third UN Conference on the Law of the Seas
UN Conference on Sea Transport (1978)
UN Conference on State Succession in International Treaties (1978)
UN Conference on Basic Health Care (1978).

This list though by no means complete illustrates and underlines two contours of the organization's profile: first, by the end of the seventies the UN is on a course to restructure comprehensively the vast spectrum of economic and social conditions and relations. The approach transcends the narrow scope of 'international relations'; broadly based programmes for the development of human and social affairs extend to the global level, and a typical instrument to remedy inequalities in the distribution of resources — material as well as immaterial — and to change patterns of the international division of labour is the attempt to define a variety of 'new international orders'. Secondly, in institutional terms, there is a marked shift to consider problems in newly created special and specialized bodies under the leadership of the GA. It was thus not, as one might have expected, the ECOSOC which initiated and further promoted the transformation of by now central issues into strategy and action.

Both task expansion and institutional innovations reflect the significant changes in the international balance of forces, majority configurations within the organization and substantive priorities. However, as a result of these adjustments, the state of the organization is also marked by discrepancies between decisions taken and capacities for their implementation, with serious implications for the credibility of the organization as a whole. Two factors, among others, account for this weakness. G. Myrdal made the observation that 'the United Nations system of intergovernmental institutions has become less and less effective as matrices of international cooperation . . . because an entirely disproportionate part of the energy is concerned with coordination as an escape and a substitute for action'.[5] Evidence of such deficiencies negatively affects the 'external' credibility of the organization, but it endangers, too, the 'internal' credibility. While Myrdal's comment in part applies primarily to the level of programme administration,[6] it should also be seen in connection with the non-acceptability of certain decisions[7] for a number of members. A considerable part of those decisions which shaped, since the beginning of the seventies, the new directions in the organization's commitments, notably in relation to the establishment of the New International Economic Order, were initiated and taken by the GA's 'new majority' of Third World countries against the strong opposition or even, in a number of cases, outright rejection by Western countries. An open confrontation occured in 1974, when the United States in particular seriously questioned the acceptability of the rule of the 'new majority' (by majority, one might add) and threatened to reduce its participation in and support of the organization.[8] Since each of these decisions created in some way or other new institutional machinery, while at the same time resources necessary for the implementation of decisions were withheld, the decision/implementation gap with a myriad of new institutions engaging in increasing amounts of co-ordination also occurs at this level.

The confrontative style of decision making emerging and prevailing in the early seventies and institutional proliferation with negative consequences for the capacity to implement decisions are related. The negative evaluation of the implications is not the only option, however, at least if one is interested in the prospects for the potential resolution of conflicts of interest. After all, conflicts of interest — unsolved — constitute the background for both institutional proliferation and the withholding of resources. The former strategy may in fact serve to resolve a confrontative stalemate without prejudice to the eventual outcome in substantive terms, though the status quo-orientated side will maintain the argument of inefficiency. The further elaboration of the relation between conflict, including its confrontative phase, and decisions involving institutional growth may thus clarify the political 'logic' of much of what is typical for the UN and help to define in more precise terms both the past role of the organization as well as types of potential contributions in the development of new patterns of relations.

Such perspective is not necessarily identical with arguments often found to the effect that the organization, although having failed to meet its primary tasks, nevertheless fulfills a variety of useful 'secondary functions', e.g. by providing a 'meeting place for mutual communication'. Instead, it can be argued that as a result of the dramatic changes of the international system crucial operational purposes have also changed, or been enlarged, so that the organization is no longer primarily an international structure of co-operation, but rather an institutional framework to carry out conflicts over issues which by their very substance have global dimensions and unprecedented complexity. This view rejects an assumption explicitly or implicitly contained in most of the doctrinal thinking about the role of international organizations in the international system. It has been postulated again and again that the collective participation of states in structures of international organization will generate enlightened attitudes and decisions which transcend irresponsible forms of international behaviour by states acting as individual entities. But such a role has never been the case, and it is unlikely to be so long as the classical principle of sovereignty continues to exist as a matter to which nation-states may refer, although their problem-solving capacity is no longer equally 'sovereign' *vis-à-vis* problems that transcend their national boundaries. International organizations in general, and the UN in particular, are '*center(s) for harmonizing* the actions of nations in the attainment of . . . common ends' (Art. 1(4) UNCh),[9] but this should not be equated with claiming them to be *centres of harmony*.

The UN has in fact been a platform of conflict rather than co-operation and co-ordination from the very beginning. Two general empirical rules determining the development of international institutions may explain why this is so. The first rule was formulated by Inis L. Claude, saying that the foundation of international organizations is often characterized by

> a general tendency . . . to exhibit a retrospective mentality, . . . the great organizational endeavours of the modern world have been parts of the aftermath of great wars, and it is possible to argue that they tended to produce instruments better adapted to prevent recently concluded tragedy than dealing with the momentous issues of the future . . . There is a real danger that newly created international organizations may not be simply too little, but also already out of date.[10]

This does not only apply to the UN as to lessons drawn from the failure of the League of Nations and the still lasting war when planning for the organization was begun. It may be likewise a valid perspective to other organizational attempts even if the motivations and models adopted must not necessarily depend on the experience of war.

The UN faced consequences of this kind immediately after its foundation when the structure of the international system with the evolving bipolar superpower antagonism moved in a direction in direct opposition to assumptions and operational principles of the Charter's system of a qualified collective security mechanism.

The second rule pertains to the definition of goals and instruments to fulfil them. Whether one takes the formulation of purposes and principles of the Charter's first two articles or specific provisions on socio-economic matters in Art. 55 as well as related instruments specified in Chapters VI and VII or Art. 60, respectively, one will find that they are both general and ambiguous. The goals set forth are, as has often been repeated, shared by all members, but their general language makes them non-operational. In order to compare alternative courses of action and relate them to concrete measures it becomes necessary to have more specific sub-goals. Unfortunately it regularly turns out that while the shared goals are non-operational, operational sub-goals are no longer shared.

The former aspect, i.e. the incompatibility of the Charter model with the actual international environment, confronted the organization with the problem of adjusting its decision processes. It was aggravated and further complicated by the second aspect in that the element of conflict over goals became a dominant feature so as to preclude the solution of the first imperative. The subsequent globalization of the East–West conflict paralysed the organization not only in the field of maintaining peace and security. As a competition of antagonistic political and socio-economic conceptions, it prevented any significant growth of organizational activities in the field of social and economic co-operation which, as must be recalled, constituted the second pillar of the Charter's conception of peace. The organization – to be more specific and accurate: the then dominating 'old' majority of member-states – essentially neglected the activation of the ECOSOC system, favouring instead the economic reconstruction within the GATT framework. On balance, the conditions of the East–West conflict effected an institutional *de*volution of the organization in the light of the original responsibilities entrusted to it.

The subsequent operation of the ECOSOC system under the control of its decision machinery by Western industrialized countries resulted in a prevailing unresponsiveness to the imperative of formulating effective development policies. Initially, i.e. as long as aid for development was still conceived primarily as an instrument in the East–West competition, development efforts were largely channelled through the institutions that had been established outside the UN framework under the control of western countries to strengthen liberal trade and free market conditions. Demands by developing countries which were advanced through ECOSOC met resistance whenever they were at variance with these maxims. This situation persisted even when the failure of the First Development Decade became obvious, such that demands for a greater commitment for development efforts in terms of both an increase in the transfer of material resources and revised conceptions for development were at best marginally successful. It was in part this deadlock which caused a retreat of planning for development into the regional substructures of the system, but also motivating the Third World countries to formulate to some extent independently elements of alternative development strategies. It is not without a certain irony that the earlier practice to respond to demands for increased material resources for development (capital assistance) with various forms of (comparatively cheaper) transfer of information (technical assistance) now proved counter-productive in that its effects only led to increased demands. These were gradually introduced again into the centralized part of the system in a further elaborated and also 'politicized' form when Third World countries emerged as the 'new majority'. The GA as the only egalitarian decision organ was increasingly used as an instrument, since the mid-sixties, to not only advance specific demands but also to propose and claim the revision of normative standards.

The established rules and structures of the existing international division of labour, exchange relations, and standards of international behaviour were challenged in all those fields where they functioned, in the eyes of the developing countries, to perpetuate the exploitative dominance of the North over the South, giving rise to what is by now the well-known North–South conflict.

The next step towards a further instrumentalization of the GA was, then, only logical. Claims, even if transformed into programmatic declarations, do not by themselves initiate action, and the less so if they touch established privileges. Thus, in order to promote their consideration in operational terms, a strategy was pursued of creating specialized bodies, in particular of the global conference type, with assigned tasks to negotiate operational standards, action programmes, and machinery for implementation.

We have reached again the point where the argument started. The development as it has been traced so far naturally did not have the clear-cut scheme of actions and reactions as it may appear from the condensed format of the preceding retrospective summary. But it seems sufficiently accurate to show the constellation of conflict and institutional growth as a particular stage of a process of *regime change*,[11] i.e. conflict over and the attempt to replace or modify the network of (operational) rules, norms, and procedures governing behaviour and controlling its effects. The two rules introduced earlier provide us, now, with two perspectives to assess the results of this process towards general conclusions about the role and performance of the organization.

The first perspective is how effectively the organization has contributed, in substantive terms, to the process of adjusting conflicting interpretations of international regimes in various issue areas. The evaluation depends on what criteria of effectivity are adopted. In *political terms* effectivity can hardly be denied. To be politically effective always means having one's own definition prevail. The original hierarchical structure of the UN's councils privileged the developed countries to do so with considerable exclusivity and thereby to maintain the status quo in their favour, or at least to minimize its modification. The developments and processes briefly characterized have definitely undermined this prerogative. Both the shift in the definition of issues and the (re-)definition of normative standards to guide problem-solutions, as well as the consideration of operational working arrangements, has brought about a de-hierarchization of the organization's decision-structures to the effect that demands for changes in international regimes can no longer be bypassed. The diminishing unity in opposition against programmatic resolutions on the part of the developed countries as well as the on-going discussion about the legal significance of the GA's resolutions are expressions of this constellation and indicate the actual pressures exercised and perceived.

In *technical-functional terms*, i.e. the achievement of working problem-solutions and machinery for implementation, the balance of effectiveness is less favourable. Three reasons are particularly relevant. First, the inherent complexity of the problems under consideration. It must be recalled that in an unprecendented manner the universality of the organization — so far mostly considered as a formal principle of representation — has been transformed into a substantive quality in that problem-solutions sought for have to take into account a multitude of diverging needs and interests. Secondly, much of the conflict potential is reactivated at this level of operational decisions, and greater care also taken of the fact that decisions to be viable need a minimum of acceptability to ensure practical support in their implementation. This imperative is clearly reflected in the decision-structure of the negotiating bodies. Although they duplicate the egalitarian character of the GA as far as the representation is concerned, their decision rules are based either formally or informally on the principle of consensus rather than the Assembly's majority rule. The most visible result of these factors is consumption of time rather than a production of tangible results. Again, this must not be by necessity an exclusively negative property of the process. Delay is not only the result of a perpetuation of the conflicts over the redefinition of principles since, thirdly, the bargaining at this level also produces a differentiation in the operational objectives among those initially in agreement about principle changes.

The second perspective derives from the combination of both rules and leads to the question of the organization's development as a function of and in response to the changes in its international environment. A comparison of the organization's role in both the East–West and the North–South conflicts seems to be particularly suggestive to conclude our interpretative analysis. The joint effect of the two rules suggests three problems and associated critical phases in the life of international organizations:

— The *first phase* is characterized by the initial spirit of *co-operation*, which underlies the foundation of an organization. Discrepancies between the formalized institutional process of a comparatively static character and the changing state of its environment will, sooner or later, lead to

— a *second phase*, primarily characterized by *conflict processes* with a view to both necessary institutional adjustments to the power relations of its environment and transforming the general goals *of* the organization into operational sub-goals which are compatible with the diverging goals *for* the organization pursued by its individual members. While an organization may not survive this stage if such adjustment is not achieved, success in resolving this problem will then lead to a

— *third phase*, where in a continuous political process varied tasks have to be performed as regards the substantive *accommodation of competing values*, related *re-definitions of behavioral and distributive norms*, and the eventual *re-distribution* of resources in accordance with these norms.

In the development of the UN we can identify a very similar pattern. The *initial co-operative approach* to the solution of international problems as reflected in the charter model was based on a *conception of peace* that comprised *two elements*: first, the maintenance of international peace and security (Chs. VI, VII UNCh) to contain threats to peace, violent and non-violent, and, secondly, international economic and social co-operation to create those conditions necessary for peaceful and friendly relations among nations, including conditions of economic and social progress and development (Ch. IX, Art. 55 UNCh). While both purposes assumed patterns of co-operation in general, and between the major powers in particular, the first task was essentially of a regulatory, the second of a developmental and (re-)distributive nature. This model was already invalidated in an early stage under the influence of the East–West conflict and replaced by a *conflictual constellation*. During this second phase the organization was driven into a marginal role as to the tasks of maintaining peace and security since a basic consensus regarding standards for exercising the regulatory function did not exist to a sufficient degree. In addition, however, the exclusive definition of problems in power-political terms, which characterized the East–West conflict, inhibited any future-orientated co-operation and 'institutional development in relation to the tasks of economic and social development. It can, in fact, be argued with good reasons that the neglect of this aspect aggravated those structural conflicts that were to come into the foreground to the extent that the process of decolonization progressed. At the time when the majority of newly independent states had become members of the UN and gradually developed both their individual identity as well as a certain common identity, the organization was essentially unprepared, conceptually and institutionally, to respond adequately to the needs and demands of these countries. The growing discrepancy between new demands and defensive attempts on the side of the advanced, mostly Western, states to maintain established international structures produced a North–South conflict constellation which gradually replaced the East–West conflict axis. Under the East–West conflict constellation the organization not only remained in a stalemate, but was still further driven into a situation where the exercise of basic functions was seriously threatened (financial crisis; 'Troika'-proposals), with incompatible goal conceptions remaining unresolved. Under the North–South conflict constellation we find a much greater degree of flexibility and effective adjustment. For the increasingly conflictive aspirations, the organization provided a forum to articulate interests and demands. Considering the number of newly independent states this also implied a process of international socialization of remarkable dimensions. The aggregation of interests challenging the existing regimes intensified conflicts, but the institutional growth opened ways and means to reduce the confrontation of goals. A variety of functional subsystems channelled conflicts by fractionating them and breaking up general demands into specific issues amenable to negotiation and bargaining.

In the course of such processes, in varying institutional and functional settings, the understanding of development has itself undergone a process of development. The specific institutional response thus not only moderated the initial confrontation by an active reaction to demands, but produced a number of positive effects. Speaking of positive effects, it should be recalled that in this second phase the critical review of prior conceptions, previously unknown demands, and their transformation into an approach with if not fully shared then at least accepted principles, constituted the primary issue. These effects are related to certain general characteristics of institutional processes which may vary in their concrete forms. Depending on given institutional and procedural. arrangements, each will tend into the 'positive' (+) or 'negative' (−) directions indicated in Table 1. The positive effects with respect to the North–South Conflict are shown in the first column: (1) the instruments of the GA and global conferences contributed during this phase to the evolution of a comprehensive view of development problems, paving the way for a conception taking into account factors so far more or less neglected, political, economic, social, cultural, and especially their interplay. Closely related are (2) the effects of continuity and periodicity of the process as a basis for re-examining initial confrontational positions as well as inconsistent demands and proposals. (3) The forum function assisted the

Table 1. Characteristics of Institutional Processes

Positive Effects N/S Conflict	(+) General Characteristics		(−)
Comprehensive view of Development Problem	Bringing together various issue-areas	(1)	Isolated consideration of issues
Continuous adjustment of Development conceptions	Continuity/ Periodicity	(2)	Routine/ Bureaucratization
Mobilization of public awareness	Forum Function/ Publicity/ Information source	(3)	Technocratic/ Non-public
Tendency towards balance of interests	Consensual decision practices	(4)	Decisions following power status of parties
Co-ordination of activities	Overview function	(5)	Specialization/ duplication

articulation of demands by actors otherwise without voice, and participation in the process has also the further function of disseminating information and improving expertise among the parties concerned. Finally, mobilization of public awareness and concern acts as one of the elements influencing the formulation of official policy positions. (4) Trends towards consensual decision practices support a balancing of interests towards a broader acceptability of decisions. (5) International organization is an instrument particularly suited to exercise overview functions to ensure continued integration of different fields of activity, both in substantive terms and to co-ordinate actions.

These effects indeed form the base that the organization is likely to maintain — different than under the East–West conflict — a constructive role during the third phase. It would certainly be too simple to draw, by some criteria, a clear-cut line between these phases. What can be said, though, is that the second phase has been 'exhausted' and that problem definitions and principles to guide actions now have to be transformed into working arrangements with operational rules and norms.[12] This process has been initiated in various issue areas with more or less visible progress so far. The more recent meetings of UNCTAD have left feelings of disappointment, the UN Conference on the Law of the Seas is a tedious process, and conferences on more specialized, but still all but narrow issues (see p. 3), showed limited results. This gives reason to ask whether the operational problems of the third phase are likely to be solved with the institutional instruments that proved reasonably successful in the second phase. It has been convincingly argued both by participants and observers that the practice of conferences with universal participation and comprehensive agendas is no longer suitable to work out differentiated problem solutions — one of the major reasons being the technique of the Third World countries to 'add' their demands to maintain unity despite increasingly divergent interests if it comes to detailed regulations and actions. It is in this stage that both proliferation and form of the institutional arrangements become an issue. The report of the North–South Commission already quoted suggests, while recognizing the dynamic role of the unified Group of 77 in the past, that mechanisms of negotiations should be strengthened by more structured agendas, a greater role for more differentiated groups with specific interests in the preparatory phases of conferences, and the deliberate use of the committee principle to increase the decision capacity.[13] Bergsten observed *institutional waves*,[14] the first being the foundation of the UN system itself, the second occurring during the sixties and showing strong regional-integrative traits, and the third in terms of the system of UN conferences. The prospects of the UN's third phase will very likely depend on its capacity to initiate a fourth wave of institutional innovation.

Notes

1. Moore, John Morton (1974). 'Toward an Applied Theory of the Regulation of Intervention' in Moore, John Morton, ed. (1974). *Law and Civil War in the Modern World* (Baltimore: Johns Hopkins Univ. Press), 18.
2. Quoted in Meadows, D. H. *et al.* (1972). *The Limits to Growth. A Report for the Club of Rome's Project on the Predicament of Mankind* (New York: Universe Books), 17.
3. *North-South: A Programme for Survival* (1980). Report of the Independent Commission on International Development Issues (London: Pan Books).
4. Information extracted from United Nations (1978). *The United Nations 1978. — United Nations' Day, 24 October 1978* (in German) (Geneva: UN Information Service), 25.
5. Myrdal, Gunnar (1973). 'Foreword' to Elmandjra, Mahdi (1973). *The United Nations' System: An Analysis* (London: Faber and Faber), 13.
6. For a critical discussion of co-ordination within the UN see the review essay by McLaren, Robert I. (1980). 'The UN System and its Quixotic Quest for Co-ordination.' *International Organization*, XXXIV. 1 (Winter): 139–48.
7. Throughout the text we refer to 'decisions' irrespective of whether or not they have a legally binding character for the organization's members. In particular, the resolutions of the GA are only recommendations as far as the 'external' effect is concerned.
8. See the statements by the US Ambassador Scali about the 'tyranny of the majority' during the Twenty-ninth Session of the GA, *United Nations, General Assembly*, A/PV. 2307 (6 Dec. 1974), 47–56.
9. Emphasis added.
10. Claude, Inis L., Jr. (^{2}1973). *Swords into Plowshares* (New York: Random House), 49.
11. For the concept of (international) *regime* and modes of change, see Keohane, Robert O. and Nye, Joseph S. (1977). *Power and Independence. World Politics*

in Transition (Boston: Little, Brown), 19 ff. and Ch. 2, esp. 54 ff. for *regime change* by and within international organizations. It appears that the concept is very similar to that of 'international order' as used within the UN, the difference being that in the UN context reference is usually to a '*new* international order' (economic, information, etc.).

12. A complete format of Table 1 would have to include also the negative effects with respect to the North–South Conflict. These have been omitted here since they appear less relevant for the initial phase of the UN's role. See however the concluding observations as to possible shifts in this direction if institutions and procedures will not be continually adjusted, as well as R. W. Gregg's analysis in this volume.

13. North–South: A Programme for Survival (1980) (*n. 3*), ch. 16.

14. Bergsten, C. F. (1976). *Interdependence and International Institutions* (Madison: University of Wisconsin Press).

2 GROWTH OF INTERNATIONAL ORGANIZATIONS SINCE 1945: INTERPRETATIONS OF QUANTITATIVE AND QUALITATIVE EVIDENCE

MARJO HOEFNAGELS
Polemological Institute, Free University of Brussels

1. Introduction

What is the role of the International Governmental Organizations (IGOs) in the international political system? This question has long been haunting students of international relations, and it is, in fact, still the focal point of every academic discussion on the subject. Where do these IGOs fit in? Do they merely serve to perpetuate the existing nation-state centred international system, or are they indeed 'new actors', stepping-stones to a new and different era in world politics?

Both of these points of view find adherence, and they are reflected in two different theories. On the one hand, there are the 'traditionalists'. As proponents of the state-centric approach to international relations, they are receptive to the first point of view. 'Modernists', on the other hand, favour a transnational model of world politics and opt for the second possibility. Let us have a brief look at each of these theories, and at their evolution during the past few decades.

Traditionalists, who strongly believe that international relations are synonymous with the mutual relations of sovereign nation-states, originally had little faith in 'parliamentary diplomacy'. Morgenthau, who is regarded as the main spokesman for the traditionalists, and who expresses his approval of bilateral diplomacy in almost lyrical terms, did not have one good word for its multilateral counterpart:

> The new parliamentary diplomacy . . . tends to aggravate rather than mitigate international conflicts and leaves the prospects for peace dimmed rather than brightened.[1]

When he wrote these lines in 1948, he could not foresee the rapid growth in the number of international organizations in the decades to come. But even after it had become clear that international organizations were to become permanent aspects of the international system, traditionalists remained convinced that nation-states, even if they might no longer be the only actors in world politics, nevertheless remained *determinant* factors.

Hoffmann describes this situation in a more recent evaluation of the UN:

> The basic unit remains the state, but in order to be able to play an effective role in discharging such functions as the maintenance of peace, the settlement of disputes, the emancipation of non-self-governing territories, the protection of human rights, or the promotion of economic cooperation, the organization should dispose of some real political power over the states, i.e., enjoy a modicum of autonomy and supremacy. In reality, however, decisions within the organization are made by the states. Hence, a contradiction: the basis of action and obligation is supposed to be an emergent community spirit, *as if* the states were no more than agents of this international community, *as if* the organization expressed a general will no longer divided into separate and antagonistic wills, no longer confiscated by governmental interests, which remain most frequently divergent, and which, even when they converge on the organization, tend to use it as an instrument, and to exploit the community fiction for their own purposes.[2]

In the traditionalists' view, then, international organizations are at best new instruments of national diplomacy.

Modernists, on the other hand, show more optimism and more faith in international organizations:

> The very existence of international organizations has injected a new force into the world community and has altered the configuration of world politics. Regardless of the fact that the states which created international organizations have usually intended that they should remain simply instruments for inter-nation collaboration, they have inevitably become something more. They have acquired lives of their own and a distinctive international personality, which has been manifested both symbolically and legally.[3]

Modernists' theories on international relations as a complex network of transnational relations, which include both governmental and nongovernmental interactions, are based on the premise that technology and science have changed our planet into an interdependent world, in which the position of the sovereign nation-state has been seriously affected. During the fifties and early sixties there was a considerable amount of what was later called 'interdependence optimism'. The generally accepted idea was that the increase in personal contacts, via communication and travel, and an increasing linkage of issues and institutions across national boundaries, would make an anachronism of the independent sovereign nation-state. The demise of the nation-state would only be a matter of time, so it was thought, and with it would disappear the phenomenon of international war, which, after all, was nothing but the result of the very existence of separate sovereign states.

The first significant post-war act of international co-operation — the creation of the UN as a renewed effort to achieve world peace through international organization — gave no reason at all for assuming that such co-operation would lead to an erosion of the sovereignty of nation-states. On the contrary, the Charter explicitly endorses the principle of sovereign equality of all the UN's members.

It was rather the regional inter-state co-operation, and particularly the growth of the European Common Market, which inspired political scientists to develop several theories of integration. The then prevailing optimism about the peace-promoting possibilities of international co-operation is clearly visible in these theories:

- In regional integration theory, for instance, which intended to 'explain how and why states cease to be fully sovereign, how and why they voluntarily mingle, merge, and mix with their neighbors, so as to lose the factual attributes of sovereignty, while acquiring new techniques for resolving conflicts between themselves'.[4]
- In functionalism, whose leading thought is that 'the position and legitimacy of the nation-state ultimately rest with the functions it fulfills in satisfying the needs for its population, needs for prosperity and material welfare'.[5] Interdependence creates new social needs which cannot be provided for on a national scale, so that states are forced to co-operate, and to transfer some of their (important) functions to inter- or supranational institutions.
- In communications theory, which does not foresee the obsolescence of the nation-state, but adheres to the general optimism when it is stated that 'an integrated political community is a system of independent states, which, while not governed by a supra-national institution, is characterized by such an intensity of mutual friendship, communication and interaction as to render war obsolete as a means to resolve conflicts'.[6]

IGOs played a central role in these theories. It was understood that in order to participate in international organizations, member-states would have to give up a part of their sovereign power, but the benefits that they would derive from international co-operation seemed large enough to warrant the costs of participation. It was even expected that over time the member-states of an international organization would increase their co-operation to such an extent as to form a fully integrated international community, where sovereignty would lose its national character and be transferred to the international organization. IGOs would thus eventually replace the allegedly obsolete institution of the nation-state.

Gradually, however, when it became obvious that nation-states were not about to disappear, and that IGOs were not about to become the powerful autonomous units that had been foreseen, modernists grew more moderate in their outlook and more careful in their predicitions. They began to regard IGOs as new actors 'next to', rather than 'in lieu of' nation-states. IGOs were no longer thought of as the potential driving forces of world politics:

> It had become clear that international institutions in their political processes and in their functions reflect, and to some extent magnify or modify, the dominant features of the international system.[7]

In an international system governed by power politics, the role of international organizations would be minor, limited by state-power and the importance of military power. In a system of complex interdependence, however, IGOs could play an important role:

> Organizations will set agendas, induce coalition formation and act as arenas for political action by weak states. Ability to choose the organization forum for an issue and to mobilize votes will be an important resource.[8]

Put side by side, the more recent, less extreme, opinions about the role of IGOs might be summarized in the following questions: Are IGOs, as the traditionalists believe, mere instruments of national diplomacy, platforms for furthering national interests, *or* are they something more, do they acquire a certain degree of independence *vis-à-vis* their constituent parts? Are IGOs more than the sum of their member-states, do they have sufficient autonomy to pursue their 'own' policies, and if so, do such policies show concerns which are different from those pursued by individual nation-states?

This article deals with the specific question of the role of IGOs in the international system, and examines its evolution as evidenced by the extension of the IGO network during the last few decades. In Section 2 we shall examine patterns of quantitive growth of IGOs. Section 3 will show the reflection of the international power structure in IGO participation, after which we continue our analysis of growth patterns along both 'horizontal' and 'vertical' lines (Section 4). Further aspects of qualitative growth in terms of the functional scope of IGOs will be the subject of Section 5. The concluding Section 6 will advance some interpretations to summarize the findings.

2. Patterns of Quantitative Growth

It is an undeniable fact that IGOs have grown considerably in number, especially since the end of the Second World War. When it comes to citing actual numbers, however, one should proceed cautiously. Which organizations have to be counted, in other words, which organizations qualify as IGOs? The *Yearbook of International Organizations*, from which data here presented have been derived, defines such bodies as:

(a)   being based on a formal instrument of agreement between the governments of nation-states

(b)   including three or more nation-states as parties to the agreement

(c)   possessing a permanent secretariat performing ongoing tasks.[9]

The seventeenth (1978/9) edition of the *Yearbook* lists a total of 305 international governmental organizations. Roughly half of these, a total of 144, were founded after 1960, with diminishing rates of growth as time went on (Table 1).

Table 1.   Increase in number of IGOs 1960–1975

Year of foundation	Number of IGOs founded
1960–1965	62
1966–1970	49
1971–1975	33
Total	144

These organizations can be ordered in two dimensions:

(1)   *Level* — indicating whether their membership is universal or regional, the latter category again subdivided into four-, three-, two-, one-regional;[10] and

(2)   *Scope* — indicating whether the organization's activities are of a general or of a specialized nature;[11] which leads to the following pattern (Table 2):

Table 2.   Increase in number of IGOs 1960–1975 — classified according to level and scope of organization

	General	Specialized	Total
Universal	—	17	17
Regional			
4-R	—	8	8
3-R	—	6	6
2-R	3	26	29
1-R	9	75	84
Total	12	132	144

As far as *scope* is concerned, the emphasis is definitely on specialized organizations. This category accounts for 132 (92%) of the 144 organizations created in the period 1960–75. As far as *level* is concerned, it is the one-regional level which shows the largest increase in number of IGOs.

This pattern of growth and spread of IGOs remains practically unchanged through the observed 15-year period. When the total period is divided into three separate 5-year periods, the result is not highly fluctuating percentages, but rather a confirmation of a general on-going trend: the largest increase constantly occurs in specialized organizations, and of these most are on the one-regional level (Table 3).

Table 3.   Increase in number of IGOs per 5-year periods (in %)

	1960–65	1966–70	1971–75	Total 1960–1975
Level/Scope				
1-R/S	58 %	43 %	56 %	52.5 %
2-R/S	20	25	10	18
3-R/S	2	8	3	4
4-R/S	3	10	3	5.5
Universal/S	11	8	18	12
General	6	6	10	8
Total	100 %	100 %	100 %	100 %
(N=)	(62)	(49)	(33)	(144)

R: Regional   S: Specialized

It would seem that the evolution of the numerical growth of IGOs broadly follows shifts in the international political situation. In the 1960s the circumstance that a large number of African countries became independent is reflected in the fact that 34 out of 75 newly founded one-regional specialized organizations (45%) are organizations among African states, and almost half of them were created in the period between 1960 and 1965.

On the two-regional level, for instance, the 'Arab Renaissance' clearly has had an influence on the founding of organizations. This relatively restricted area (it is two-regional because the Arab countries are spread over the African and the Asian continents) accounts for 14 out of the 26 new two-regional specialized IGOs (54%), most of them founded in the 1965–70 period.

3. Reflection of Power Structure in IGO Participation

Does this suggest a direct connection between political power and IGO participation? In other words, are the most powerful nations also the ones who participate most in international organizations?

In their study on the structure of systems of international organizations, Alger and Hoovler[12] mention that IGO membership is highly related to the wealth of a nation. When we compare the wealth of nations with their degree of IGO participation (see Table 4), this supposition does

Table 4.   Ranking of nation-states according to GNP and IGO-memberships (20 leading states)

GNP[13]	IGO-memberships[14]
United States	France
Soviet Union	Netherlands
Germany, Fed. Rep.	United Kingdom
United Kingdom	Belgium
France	Italy
Japan	Germany, Fed. Rep.
P.R. China	Denmark
Italy	Norway
India	Austria
Canada	Spain
Poland	United States
Australia	Luxembourg
Czechoslovakia	Sweden
Brasil	Switzerland
German Dem. Rep.	Brazil
Sweden	Mexico
Mexico	Greece
Netherlands	Argentina
Spain	India
Argentina	Portugal

'Western' states in *italics*

not seem to be confirmed, unless we add 'Western' to 'wealthy'. The Western countries in the 'top twenty' of the world's richest nations are well represented in the column listing the highest number of IGO memberships, and in this column we find also a majority of Western nations.

A further indication of Western preponderance in the IGO network is the fact that members of the group of socialist states which belong to the list of the twenty wealthiest nations are conspicuously absent from the listing of intensive IGO participation. The USSR, e.g., the second richest country in the world, ranks only sixtieth in IGO participation.[15] Szwalowski ascribes the realtive scarcity of IGOs within the socialist group of countries to the fact that 'the lead in the field of institutionalized regionalism was taken by the Western countries, and the "socialist commonwealth", as they like to call themselves, only hesitantly followed suit'. Szwalowski continues:

This may be well illustrated by just comparing the respective dates: the OEEC was created in 1948, and the Council for Mutual Economic Assistance (Comecon) followed in 1949; the Western Union Defence Organization, NATO, SEATO, and the WEU were created in 1948, 1949, and 1954 respectively, and the Warsaw Treaty Organization followed in 1955; the European Organization for Nuclear Research (CERN) was created in 1953, and the communist Joint Institute for

Nuclear Research followed in 1956; the European Investment Bank and the Inter-American Development Bank were created in 1957 and 1959 respectively (several similar non-communist regional intergovernmental banks may also be mentioned), and the International Investment Bank of Comecon followed in 1970; finally, the European Launcher Development Organization (ELDO), the European Space Research Organization (ESRO), and the International Telecommunications Satellite Consortium (INTELSAT) were created during the early sixties and were followed by 'Intercosmos' (not a full-fledged international organization) at the end of the sixties, and 'Intersputnik' in 1971. Communist commentators like to lay great stress on the fact that it was the West that first created the military and political regional organizations (especially NATO), which had to be countered by the peace-loving Soviet Union and her allies by the creation of the Warsaw Treaty Organization. They would never admit that it was, in fact, the 'socialist camp' that actually copied the West, during a period of over twenty-six years, in respect of literally all kinds of regional international organizations.[16]

The picture of Western preponderance on the over-all IGO network has been a rather stable one. There has been no major shift in the ranking of IGO participation in the last 15 years, since all states have maintained their status as member of the 'top twenty'. Nevertheless, there have been indications that their dominant position is being affected in two ways.

First, a growing number of IGOs is founded by states which are neither highly industrialized nor all liberal in their economic structure. The figures on new African and Arab IGOs mentioned at the end of the previous section serve as an illustration in this respect.

Secondly, *within* certain IGOs there is a growing influence from countries which are neither 'Western' nor 'wealthy', e.g. the so-called 'Group of 77' in UNCTAD. Within the UN system this has apparently reached such dimensions that in 1975 the then US Secretary of State, Henry Kissinger, thought it necessary to 'reprimand' Third World UN members by saying that those who try to use the UN as a forum for their national aspirations 'may well inherit an empty shell.'[17] That was not all. In an article which was published in the *International Herald Tribune*, Leslie Gelb described the action that followed

Secretary of State Henry Kissinger has formally initiated a policy of singling out for cutbacks in U.S. aid those nations that have sided against the United States in votes in the United Nations. In some cases, the cutbacks involve food and humanitarian relief. The official who disclosed this information to *The Times* called the policy no more than a 'zap list' to punish small countries that were voting against the United States. State Department officials, who confirmed the policy, spoke of it as simply a way of showing developing nations that their behavior in international organizations would affect their direct relations with the United States. It was acknowledged, among other things, that nations whose aid programs have been delayed or cancelled are not explicitly being told why, although as one official said, 'When our ambassador comes to them and complains about their votes in the U.N., and a few weeks later an aid transaction falls through, they get the picture.'[18]

Historically, of course, the dominance of the US in international organizations dates back to the Second World War and the central role they played in post-war international relations. Early in the war the US started their post-war planning under the guidance of Cordell Hull.

Before the war, Hull's foreign policy had been aimed at eliminating trade barriers and protection, and at creating multilateral trade relations. This policy, set up to make the free world accessible for American goods and capital, was supplemented during the war with plans to guarantee such accessibility and stability, through the creation of international organizations, such as the International Monetary Fund and the United Nations. After Hull's departure, his policy was continued until the conclusion of GATT in 1947, whereafter changes began to occur during the Truman administration.[19]

Cox/Jacobson, who studied decision-making processes within eight specialized agencies of the UN and noticed that 'many states may look upon IGOs principally as instruments for preserving their hegemony or improve their status,'[20] also found this to be particularly true for the US:

United States enthusiasm, though, did not carry with it a willingness to cede any significant degree of sovereignty. On the contrary, international organizations were never viewed as something that would seriously hamper American freedom of action, and whenever this came to be, the United States drew back.[21]

A concrete example of the truth of their statement was provided on 5 November 1977 when (after a two-years' notice period had expired) the US indeed withdrew also *formally* from the International Labour Organization (ILO). It is worth having a closer look at this event since it provides a clear example of hegemony within IGOs and of what might happen when such dominance can no longer be maintained. Cox, who has the advantage of possessing both personal experience from within the organization (having been associated with ILO from 1948 to 1972) and the necessary distance acquired as an outside observer since 1972, has analysed the situation in detail:

ILO has been the expression of a global hegemony in production relations. At its origins in the making of the Versailles Treaty in 1919, the ILO was the response of the victorious powers to the menace of Bolshevism. By creating the ILO, they offered organized labor participation in social and industrial reform within an accepted framework of capitalism. During the interwar period, the ILO was nourished by the spirit of reformist social democracy, yet ever heedful of the practical limits imposed by dominant conservative forces.

The United States' rejection of the Versailles Treaty precluded US membership in the ILO. In 1934, however, the Roosevelt administration passed over this obstacle and joined the ILO. The government's initiative sought to give an international dimension to the New Deal. From that moment on, the United States took the lead in shaping the hegemonic consensus in the ILO. In 1944, by sponsoring a major conference in Philadelphia, the Roosevelt administration appeared to encourage the organization to take on a prominent role in post-war international social policy. During the Cold War years, the ILO's emphasis on trade union freedom and collective bargaining expressed one ideological facet of America's dominant world position.

At present, the ILO lies under a cloud, because the erstwhile hegemonic consensus seems to have come undone. There is no longer any firm cohesion among the more powerful forces (American, West European, and now Soviet as well), and no agreement on the concessions that can be made to those less powerful but of growing effectiveness (the Third and Fourth Worlds). The voice of American organized labor in particular has questioned whether a consensus acceptable to it can be put together again through the ILO, and by implication, whether some alternative institutionalizing of hegemony in world production relations might be possible and preferable. That is the meaning of the U.S. withdrawal'.

But what about the effects of the US withdrawal? Let us listen to Cox once more:

The tripartite structure of representation has given the ILO a western bias, despite its universal membership. The ILO was never able to gain support in Third World countries comparable to that which made UNCTAD and UNIDO *their* organizations. Experience suggests that an option of Third World political support is effectively closed out. Nor can executive leadership and the ILO bureaucracy be counted upon as a possible source of innovation and renewal. The myth of Soviet influence, alive in the imagination of American delegates, must also be discounted. This leaves the countries of western Europe as the mainstay of the ILO. From them came the original impetus and sustaining support for the organization. There is every indication that western Europe, and particularly the Federal Republic of Germany and the Deutsche Gewerkschaftsbund (German Confederation of Trade Unions, or DGB), are ready to assume the mantle of leadership, but the broader political structures would remain largely unaffected by such an outcome. Hegemony, reconstructed a little on the surface, would remain substantially undisturbed. Even American influence, so potent during the period of withdrawal notice, would seem likely to remain effective since the ILO would continue to court American reaffiliation. Such influence far outweighs the formal voting rights of a member in good standing.[22]

Another, less drastic, example is the case of the Food and Agricultural Organization (FAO):

As the global food regime of the post-war era has become subject to increasing challenge, stress and deviation, political leaders in the United States and other industrialized countries have sought to protect their states' very large stake in the traditional status quo. Part of their strategy has been to deflate universal multilateral bodies, and hence to dampen 'populist' pressures by circumventing forums controlled by Third World majorities. Alternatively, these countries' spokespersons have sought to create new specialized institutions with built-in veto opportunities, weighted voting, limited membership or limited authority, and to propose bilateral alternatives to multilateral programs where one-on-one rather than one-against-many bargaining conditions would prevail.[23]

4. Horizontal and Vertical Growth Patterns

The establishment of IGOs, be it by the already dominant group of states, or by relative newcomers on the international scene, shows one particular aspect, which, at least at first sight, seems to cast doubt upon the preponderant role of the nation-state in the IGO network, and to point towards a certain independence of IGOs *vis-à-vis* the nation-state.

IGOs are based on a formal instrument of agreement between the governments of nation-states. This does not necessarily mean that the initiative to create an IGO always originates with the governments who will be members of the organization-to-be. On some occasions international institution-building is the outcome of *ad hoc* conferences. Such was the case with the World Food Council for example, which was one of several new institutions set up to continue the work of the World Food Conference held in 1974. Yet another way in which IGOs are created is by or through existing IGOs. A surprisingly high number of IGOs was founded either through the initiative, sponsorship, or support from other international organizations. Of the 144 new IGOs established in the 1960–75 period, 83 (58%) were founded at the initiative of national governments, while 61 (42%) originated from other IGOs.

If more than 40% of these organizations owe their existence to other international organizations, a further investigation into this reproduction from within the IGO network is warranted. Using the two-dimensional division that was described in Section 2, Fig. 1 gives a more detailed picture.

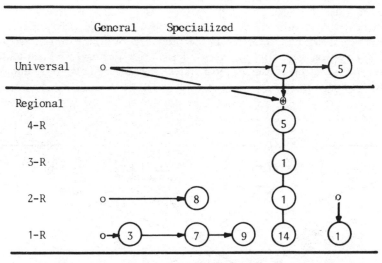

N = 61 organizations   θ: Often by joint initiative of general and specialized IGOs

Fig. 1.   Structure of the establishment of new IGOs at the initiative of other IGOs, 1960–1975

The direction in which these new organizations are created is clear:

— As far as *scope* is concerned: organizations of a general nature create specialized organizations; specialized organizations set up new specialized organizations, generally in their own field of activity. The over-all tendency is *not* from specialized to general organizations.
— As far as *level* is concerned: the direction is either from higher to lower level (when universal organizations set up regional ones), or horizontal, e.g. when one-regional organizations create new one-regional organizations. The over-all tendency is definitely *not* from lower to higher level.

When such a high percentage of international organizations emanates from within the IGO system, would that not be an indication that at least some IGOs, i.e. those which take the initiative of setting up new organizations, are more or less independent actors, and not mere 'instrumentalities through which the states of the world could further some aspects of their respective national interests'?[24] It is doubtful that this is indeed a valid indication. International organizations are set up by national governments as a method of self-preservation. Through the creation of IGOs, states can keep control over those new activities which, due to their complexity, technical characteristics, or international aspects, would acquire other than purely national treatment and would thus be taken out of their sovereign power. When these IGOs, which are mostly of the general type, in turn create specialized organizations in various fields of activities, it can be interpreted as the formation of a kind of 'subsystem', with a vertical structure, in which all elements ultimately remain under the joint control of the member-states. Fig. 2 attempts to symbolize such a structure.

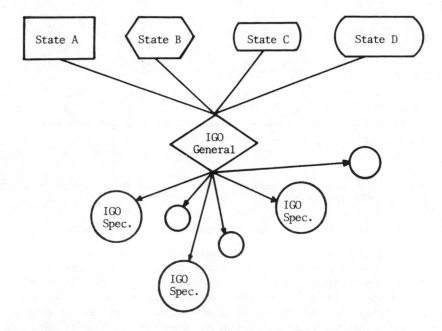

Fig. 2.   Vertical structure of IGO-'subsystem'

The total IGO network contains several of these 'subsystems', each consisting of a 'head organization', with its own number of specialized organizations. The UN is the most obvious example, but we could also think of the Commonwealth, the Organization of American States, the European Communities, etc.

The UN system is definitely the leader in this field. Of the 61 IGOs which were founded by other international organizations in the 1960-75 period, 34 (56%) were to a greater or lesser extent sponsored by organizations belonging to the UN system.

The regional economic commissions of the UN have been particularly active in helping to create such new organizations. The Transafrican Highway Co-ordinating Committee, for instance, which was founded in 1971 in Addis Ababa, sees its secretariat financially and administratively supported by the UN Economic Commission for Africa, and the latter's Executive Secretary, or his representative, is a member of the Committee together with representatives of each member-state. Another example is the Latin American Free Trade Association (LAFTA), established in 1960 as a result of preliminary conferences held under the auspices of the UN Economic Commission for Latin America.

The specialized agencies of the UN have also been active in establishing new IGOs, each in their own domain; UNESCO helped create organizations in the fields of art, science, and education. FAO actively stimulated organization-building in the fields of agriculture, environment protection, etc.; thus the International Commission for the Conservation of Atlantic Tunas, established in 1969, is the result of an international convention drafted at a conference convened by the FAO. The Universal Postal Union, to give another example, has its own 'sub-organizations', which are in fact independent regional IGOs, created in accordance with Art. 8 of the Universal Postal Convention as 'restricted postal unions', in every continent of the world — (Nordic Postal Union, 1896; Postal Union of the Americas and Spain, 1911; Arab Postal Union, 1946; European Conference of Postal and Telecommunications Administration, 1959; African Postal Union, 1961; Asian-Oceanic Postal Union, 1962).

To some extent, the tendency towards the creation of new IGOs along the lines described above, i.e. from general to specialized organizations and from higher to lower level, might be the result of the manner in which the IGO network is composed. There is in fact only one truly universal organization — the UN. It is in itself a large and complex system of organizations with widespread activities in every part of the world. It is so immense and so complex that co-ordination of activities within the UN system has become a major problem, and a variety of proposals for structural changes have been put forward and are discussed.

A number of leading regional organizations are intimately related to the UN, especially through their permanent observer status with the General Assembly. Under this special status they are entitled, among other things, to participate in the work of the UN Economic and Social Council (ECOSOC) on an on-going basis. There are some six 'head organizations', each representing a specific area of the world:

Organization of American States (OAS)
League of Arab States (LAS)
Organization of African Unity (OAU)
European Community (EC)
Council for Mutual Economic Assistance (CMEA)
Organization of the Islamic Conference (OIC).

Each of these regional 'head organizations' again forms a system in itself, with its own organs and a number of more or less independent 'specialized agencies'. As an example of how such a regional organization system is built up, we will take a closer look at the CMEA as one of the above-mentioned IGOs (sometimes also referred to as Comecon).

CMEA was created in January 1949, most probably as a countermove to the Marshall Plan and the creation of the OEEC in 1948. Original members were Bulgaria, Czechoslovakia, Poland, Rumania, Hungary, and the USSR. It was to be an 'open' organization, which could be joined by other countries of Europe adhering to the CMEA principles and wishing to participate in broad economic co-operation with its member countries. Membership now includes, in addition to the original members, Cuba, Mongolia, Albania (which has not participated since 1961), the German Democratic Republic, and Vietnam; North Korea has the status of observer.

The organizational structure of the CMEA can be described in terms of three levels. On the *first level* there are the organs of the organization proper:

— The *Session of the Council* is the supreme organ. Sessions are held at least once a year and consist of delegations led by the heads of governments of all member-countries.
— The *Executive Committee* is the main executive organ in which all member-countries are represented at the level of deputy heads of governments.
— The *Secretariat* is the economic, executive, and administrative body. It is headed by a Secretary, who is appointed by the Session of the Council, and Assistant Secretaries, who are appointed by the Executive Committee.
— *Standing Commissions* (at present some twenty-two in number), in which each member-country is represented, generally at the ministerial level. They deal with specific fields of activity such as energy, agriculture, transport, foreign trade, etc.

In the seventies three new bodies were created in order to streamline the functioning of the above-mentioned organs:

— *Committee for Co-operation in the Field of Planning* (1971). It has the Bureau for Integrated Questions of Economic Planning as its working organ. National delegations to the Committee are headed by the Chairman of the State Planning Committees.

- *Committee for Scientific and Technical Co-operation* (1971). National delegations are headed by the Chairmen of state organs for science and technology.
- *Committee for Co-operation in the Field of Material and Technical Supplies.*

Apart from the Session of the Council, the Executive Committee, the Secretariat, the Standing Commissions, and the three Committees, yet another type of organ (not provided in the CMEA's Charter) has developed: the so-called *Conferences.* In 1974, for example, there was the Conference of the Member Countries of the CMEA for Legal Problems, the Conference of Ministers of Internal Trade, and the Conference of the Chiefs of the Water Resources Authorities.

The *second level* is represented by three semi-autonomous bodies within the CMEA.

The Institute for Standardization.
The Bureau for the Co-ordination of Ship Freighting.
The International Institute for the Economic Problems of the World Socialist System.

These institutions are financed out of the budget of the CMEA Secretariat.

A *third level* is formed by a growing group of smaller international organizations which complement the activities of the CMEA itself and function, in a way, as the CMEA's 'specialized agencies'. This group of officially independent organizations is so closely related to the CMEA that Szawlowski includes them in what he calls the 'CMEA family', mainly on the following grounds:

- The initiative to set up these organizations was taken at various CMEA meetings and the CMEA is *expressis verbis* referred to in most of the founding agreements.
- The constituting documents of some of these organizations have been deposited with the CMEA secretariat, rather than with the government of one of the member-states.
- The 1971 Comprehensive Programme foresees closer co-operation and co-ordination of the activities of these organizations with those of the CMEA. In fact, certain actions have already been undertaken to bring all these smaller organizations under more formal co-ordination, if not *de facto* supervision by CMEA.[25]

Altogether, the 'family' accounts for twenty-one of the total of thirty international governmental organizations in the Eastern European countries, which makes it, together with the Warsaw Treaty Organization (WTO), the nucleus of international co-operation in that area.

What is already visible in the structure outlined above, becomes obvious from Szawlowski's comprehensive study on 'the system of international organizations in the communist countries'. The CMEA is definitely the head of the twenty, more or less associated, formally independent members of the 'family'. Moreover, the structure of the CMEA, as well as the WTO, is such that their leading member, the USSR, has reserved for itself all the commanding positions. The USSR not only makes the largest financial contribution (figures available for the CMEA in 1969 assess the contribution of the USSR at 64.5%),[26] but it is also the predominant power in every phase and aspect of the organization's activities.

It may be argued, of course, that the situation in the Eastern European organizations, and especially in the CMEA, is different from that of other organizations due to the state-controlled economies of the member-states. And yet the situation in other regional systems of organizations seems to be more or less similar. The former Secretary-General of NATO, Manlio Brosio, writes about that organization that there is an 'unquestionable supremacy of the United States', which, however, 'does not result in obedience and subservience to the directives and interests of Washington', and adds the general observation that 'politically, in all international organizations the weight of the more powerful states will always prevail, regardless of the juridical equality guaranteed by their statuses'.[27]

It is, therefore, plausible to assume that the extension of the IGO network through the creation of new IGOs by already existing organizations tends to strengthen the position of the founding organization, and, with it, that of the leading member(s) within that organization.

5. Patterns of Qualitative Growth

The several aspects of the growth of the IGO network so far examined provide little or no evidence that a quantitative extension of the IGO network would be a step in the direction of the demise of the nation-state. On the contrary, in a world consisting of nation-states, IGOs seem to be reflecting the interests of the dominant states in the international system. In the absence of any significant indication of a relative independence of the IGO network in the quantitative data, we will now look at some further qualitative aspects of its extension. What are the most relevant subjects that IGOs deal with, and in which area(s) have most of the new IGOs been established?

Table 5 shows the number of specialized organizations in various fields of activities mentioned in the *Yearbook of International Organizations*, and the increase in the number of organizations in these fields during the 1960–75 period.[28]

The listing in Table 5 shows that there is a cluster of relatively few subjects which are of importance to the IGO network, while others seem to have comparatively little relevance. The activities in which IGOs seem to be most involved have remained virtually unchanged over the last

Table 5.   Classification of specialized IGOs according to field activity

Field of Activity	IGOs founded before 1960	IGOs founded 1960–75	Total number of IGOs existing in 1975
Bibliography, Documentation, Press	–	2	2
Religion, Ethics	–	–	–
Social Sciences, Humanistic Studies	–	–	–
International Relations	2	1	3
Politics	–	–	–
Law, Administration	15	8	23
Social Welfare	9	2	11
Professions, Employers	–	1	1
Trade Unions	–	1	1
Economics, Finance	17	34	51
Commerce, Industry	13	12	25
Agriculture	29	15	44
Transport, Travel	18	8	26
Technology	6	5	11
Science	13	8	21
Health, Medicine	5	6	11
Education, Youth	3	8	11
Arts, Literature, Radio, T.V.	3	3	6
Sport, Recreation	–	–	–
Environment	1	3	4
Development	1	6	7
Women	1	–	1
Communications	10	8	18
Military	5	1	6
Total/Specialized IGOs	151	132	283

15 years. These most significant subjects are listed in Table 6, in order of the number of organizations related to these subjects.

There are almost no IGOs in the fields of religion and ethics, social sciences and humanistic studies, politics, sport and recreation. This may suggest that there is a kind of 'division of labour' in the international organizational system, since the categories in which there is little or no IGO involvement mostly rank high on the list of INGO (International Non-Governmental Organization) activities.

Could it be said then, that the fields of activity in which IGOs are most active concern typical 'governmental' activities? And would it be logical to conclude that IGOs are, thus, mere extensions of national governments? This would indeed be a hastily drawn conclusion, to say the least, yet it has some heuristic value. One might look for instance, at the group of most important IGO subjects with Morgan's theory of

Table 6. Most relevant fields of activity in sequence of number of IGOs

1960	1975
Agriculture	Economics, Finance
Transport, Travel	Agriculture
Economics, Finance	Transport, Travel
Law, Administration	Commerce, Industry
Commerce, Industry	Law, Administration
Science	Science
Communications	Communications

high politics vs. low politics in mind. Morgan, who studied possibilities of a common foreign policy for the European Community, set up a theoretical framework as follows:

> It is tempting, and to a certain degree useful, to distinguish between the concepts of 'foreign policy' and 'external relations', by arguing that 'foreign policy' as traditionally practised by nation-states through their foreign offices and diplomatic agents, concerns such matters of 'high politics' as prestige, political influence, national security, and the pursuit of diplomatic objectives, whereas 'external relations' cover more mundane activities such as the regulation of international trade, migration across frontiers, and other issues which might not unfairly be characterized as 'low politics'.[29]

He argues that it is 'foreign policy' which is kept in the hands of national governments, whilst 'external relations' or 'low politics' are more or less handed over to the Community.

> The European Community is very actively involved in a wide variety of external relations, but it can hardly be said to be conducting a foreign policy. High politics, it might appear, remain the prerogative of the governments in Paris, Bonn, or London, rather than the Community's institutions in Brussels.[30]

When the present findings on the qualitative extension of the IGO network are placed within Morgan's theoretical framework — which he presented, it is true, with some reservations — a picture emerges resembling a number of concentric circles. The centre represents the nation-state firmly in control of issue areas and policies considered most vital for its survival; the next, wider, circle would contain areas of 'low politics', which could partly be delegated to IGOs; and IGOs would be placed in a third, even wider circle, with subjects of little political relevance, subjects which are considered peripheral to the nation-state system.

6. Some Inferences

It is hardly justifiable to draw far-reaching general conclusions from the altogether limited evidence presented here. There are numerous other elements which are of importance and would have to be taken into account in assessing the role of IGOs.

There is, for instance, the down-to-earth factor of the *power of the purse*. Most IGOs are simply dependent on national governments for financial support. They are also, to a large extent, dependent on national governments for their personnel.

We have looked primarily at vertical structures within IGO sub-systems and at the existence of several such sub-systems parallel to each other, but we have not looked at IGO–IGO contacts. We could ask whether the existing horizontal ties among IGOs are significant enough for IGOs to form a closely knit network, parallel to, or even 'above', the nation-state system, and strong enough to allow them to act more or less independently from that system. Certainly there are horizontal ties among IGOs, but these interactions generally seem to have a purely consultative or informative character. Thus, Cox and Jacobson, who included such IGO–IGO relationships in their study on decision-making in IGOs, came to the conclusion that 'representatives of other international organizations have played a relatively limited role in the eight organizations.[31]

The realm of organizations considered here only refers to the Western model. The question of whether there would be other forms of organizations, equivalents of IGOs, in non-Western cultural contexts, was brought up in the *Yearbook of International Organizations*. Specific reference was made to the Chinese situation, where associations came into existence between widely dispersed Chinese populations based on the family name or the ancestral province. The intra-Chinese development had 'nourished' for some time reflections on alternative organizational patterns. Whether organizational forms currently emerging from the Chinese experiment could be employed at the international level remains a matter for attention, but there seems to be no evidence of any use of such a distinct form. The discussion in the *Yearbook* on possible functional alternatives for IGOs thus ended with the observation that 'the regional organizations in non-Western societies tend to differ very little, organizationally, from the Western model'.[32] And when they do so there is little evidence that such different forms will be copied on a large scale.

IGOs cannot exist without member-states, but nation-states can and do function without IGOs. Governments have various ways and means to bypass international organizations. They can, for example, communicate through the traditional, bilateral diplomatic channels, or, if the institutionalized co-operation through IGOs becomes less advantageous for a certain member-state or a group of member-states, their governments can choose to hold other, less formalized meetings, or come together in smaller forums. In the previously cited study on ILO, Cox refers to one such possibility:

> There is much current evidence that United States policy is tending to limit commitment to existing universal international organizations and to move selectively toward the use of agencies (old, new or *ad hoc*) more effectively under US-control. The World Bank is a case of an old agency still substantially controlled by the United States, the International Energy Agency is an example of a new one.[33]

On the European scene, the EEC summit meetings are almost classical examples. From the very beginning of the EEC, the heads of government of the member-states felt it necessary to hold summit meetings 'on important questions regarding the Community's institutions. Such meetings were held from 1960 on, at first on an irregular basis, but then more regularly, until in 1974 the decision was made to institutionalize them. According to Tindemans there were two reasons for this institutionalization:

> Until the decision of the Paris summit meeting, the institutional system of the Community did not possess a real instrument for political decision-making. Undoubtedly, the Council of Ministers could have played this role; it was actually its vocation, and strengthening of its tasks, at the expense of the Commission, could have led to it . . . but that would have meant that the governments of the member-states would agree to the Council of Ministers taking up such a responsibility. The step taken in December 1974 was not a *coup de force* meant to bring the institutional system out of balance; it was an attempt to fill a void in the heart of an organism suffering from a dangerous lack of dynamism.[34]

A second reason for the institutionalization of the EEC summit meetings was the crisis in decision-making in the Community. 'Despite the summit meetings in The Hague (1969) and in Paris (1972), which had been convened to give a new impetus to the Community', wrote Tindemans, 'we are faced with a very hesitant Europe.' Why this hesitancy? It is not because there would be an absence of political will to forge a united Europe, but rather 'because this abstract will cannot be translated into daily reality. The institutional machinery of the Community shows an increasing impotence. It is not the political will which is lacking, but the possibility to arrive at deeds'.[35]

And for that purpose, 'to arrive at deeds', the governments of the member-states found a way around the EEC organization by transferring the political decision-making for the Community to secret summit meetings, which will, admittedly, 'adversely affect the role of the Community's institutions'.[36]

Keeping in mind the above-mentioned reservations, it can be said with some authority that the present review has produced no signs of IGOs weakening the central position of the nation-states in the contemporary political system, despite their rapid growth in the last few decades. The results seem to support the thesis that IGOs reflect, rather than moderate, the existing power structures. Those who were, or are, optimistic about the role of IGOs as locomotives for change into a better world are likely to be disappointed.

Notes

1. Morgenthau, Hans J. (^{5}1973). *Politics Among Nations* (New York: Knopf), 532.
2. Hoffmann, Stanley (1971). 'An Evaluation of the United Nations' in Wood, Robert S., ed. (1971). *The Process of International Organization* (New York: Random House), 71–2.
3. Rothwell, Charles E. (1973). 'International Organization and World Politics' in Goodrich, L. M. and Kay, D.A., eds. (1973). *International Organizations: Politics and Process* (Madison: University of Wisconsin Press), 30.
4. Haas, Ernst B. (1971). 'The Study of Regional Integration' in Lindberg, J. N. and Scheingold, S. A., eds. (1971). *Regional Integration. Theory and Research* (Cambridge, Ma.: Harvard University Press), 6.
5. De Vree, J. K. (1976). 'Politieke integratie en desintegratie' in Van Schendelen, M. P. C. M., ed. (1976). *Kernthema's van de politicologie* (Meppel: Boom/ Intermediair), 204.
6. Deutsch, K. W. *et al.* (1957). *Political Community and the North Atlantic Area* (Princeton, N.J.: Princeton University Press).
7. Hoffmann, Stanley (1973). 'International Organization and the International System' in Goodrich and Kay, eds., (1973) (*n. 3*), 49–50.
8. Keohane, Robert O. and Nye, Joseph S. (1977). *Power and Interdependence* (Boston-Toronto: Little, Brown & Co.), 37.
9. *Yearbook of International Organizations 1978–1979* (^{17}1978). (Brussels: Union of International Associations.) While there remain certain problems in classifying international organizations due to borderline categories, organizational substitutes, and alternative styles of organization, the organizations included in the present study all belong to the *Yearbook's* category A, which means they fully qualify as IGO according to the criteria listed above.
10. Following the *Yearbook's* procedure, 'regions' are the same as continents: Africa, America, Asia, Australia, and Europe. 'Universal' are those IGOs which include member-states from all five continents.
11. An organization was classified as 'general' when it stated as its aims the over-all purpose of close co-operation, e.g. 'to discuss all matters of common concern and interest', and covered a number of different fields of activity.
12. Alger, Chadwick F. and Hoovler, David (1975). 'The Feudal Structure of Systems of International Organizations.' *Proceedings of the Vth International Peace Research Association (IPRA) General Conference*, Varansi, India, 1974 (Oslo: International Peace Research Association), 145–82.
13. For the GNP-ranking see Taylor, Charles L. and Hudson, Michael C. (^{2}1972). *World Handbook of Political and Social Indicators* (New Haven-London: Yale Univ. Press), 306 (Table 5.4).
14. For the ranking of IGO-membership see Taylor and Hudson (^{2}1972) (*n. 13*), 354 (Table 6.2).
15. Taylor and Hudson (^{2}1972) (*n. 13*), 355 (Table 6.2).

16. Szawlowski, Richard (1976). *The System of International Organizations of the Communist Countries* (Leyden: A. W. Sitjhoff), xxii.
17. From a speech by Henry Kissinger, 14 July 1975.
18. Gelb, Leslie H. (1976). 'U.S. will cut aid to nations voting against stance in U.N.' *International Herald Tribune* (Paris edition), 10/11 January 1976, 1.
19. Hellema, Duco (1979). 'De Duitse Herbewapening 1945-1954.' *Tijdschrift voor Diplomatie* (Brussels), VI. 2 (October): 115.
20. Cox, Robert W. and Jacobson, Harold K. (1973). *The Anatomy of Influence. Decision-making in International Organizations* (New Haven–London: Yale University Press), 5.
21. Cox/Jacobson, (1973) (*n. 20*), 411.
22. Cox, Robert W. (1977). 'Labor and Hegemony.' *International Organization* XXXI. 3: 386 ff.
23. Hopkins, Raymond F. and Puchala, Donald J. 'Perspectives on the International Relations of Food.' *International Organization* XXXII. 3: 613.
24. Rothwell (1973) (*n. 3*), 28.
25. Szawlowski (1976) (*n. 16*), 103-5.
26. Ibid. 68.
27. Brosio, Manlio (1976). Preface to Szawlowski (1976) (*n. 16*).
28. Each organization was classified according to the 'secondary reference' in the *Yearbook of International Organizations 1978-1979* ([17] 1978). Two classifications were added, however, since they appeared to be of some importance to the IGO system: 'military' and 'communications'. Where organizations were classified under more than one secondary reference in the *Yearbook*, the subject that seemed most relevant was chosen.
29. Morgan, Roger P. (1973). *High Politics–Low Politics. Toward a Foreign Policy for Western Europe*. The Washington Papers No. 11 (Beverly Hills–London: Sage Publications), 8.
30. Ibid. 9.
31. Cox/Jacobson (1973) (*n. 20*), 400.
32. *Yearbook of International Organizations 1978-1979* ([17] 1978) (*n. 9*).
33. Cox (1977) (*n. 22*), 422.
34. Tindemans, Leo (1978). 'Van Top Conferentie tot Europese Raad' in *Belgisch Buitenlands Beleid en Internationale Betrekkingen*, Liber Amicorum voor Prof. Omer de Raeymaeker (Leuven: Leuven University Press), 387-8.
35. Ibid. 388.
36. Ibid. 397.

PART II

CHANGING ISSUES AND STRUCTURES

3 THE UNITED NATIONS AND SOVEREIGNTY OVER NATURAL RESOURCES

M. S. RAJAN
School of International Studies, Jawaharlal Nehru University, New Delhi

1. Introduction

The demand for recognition and/or proclamation of permanent sovereignty over natural resources is one of the more important questions within the forum of the UN in which the efforts of the vast majority of members of the Organization — who also happen to be the newly-independent members — were directed towards their gaining fuller sovereignty and equality in the Community of Nations. Somewhat curiously, however, the question did not arise as a straightforward political issue. It arose in the context of the efforts of the UN for some years before 1952 to promote the economic development of underdeveloped countries — even though political arguments were used mostly by the spokesmen of the developing countries for recognition/proclamation of what they called 'permanent' sovereignty over their natural resources. And the even wider context in which the question was often posed — mostly by the old, developed states — was international economic co-operation. It was argued that the efforts of the UN to promote the economic development of the underdeveloped countries, mostly the newly-independent, sovereignty-conscious, states, called for the widest measure of international economic co-operation, including especially the developed states whose assistance and co-operation were essential for the success of the UN programmes and activities. It is a clear case of differing (not necessarily conflicting, because both groups claimed to stand for international co-operation) national interests of two groups of members which were, however, seen by some members in both groups as a case of conflict of interests. It is instructive that the question was brought up before, and discussed in, the widest and the largest forum of the UN, obviously with a view to 'harmonizing the actions of nations in the attainment of [their] common ends' (Art. 1 (4) UNCh) — in this case, the protection and/or promotion of their mutual economic interests/development.

2. The Nature of the Problem

The question of, what later became, 'permanent sovereignty over national resources' was first brought up by the representative of Uruguay before the Seventh Session (1952) of the UN General Assembly in the context of discussion on the economic development of the developing countries.[1] The draft resolution he moved on the occasion sought to recommend that member-states respect the right of each country to nationalize and freely exploit their national wealth as an essential factor of economic independence.[2] In introducing the draft resolution, the Uruguayan representative said that the right of each country to exploit its wealth freely was directly related to the problem of financing economic development; that the usual forms of aid, loans, private investment, were a valuable factor, but not the ideal solution. The ideal solution, in his view, was to attain economic independence, to dispose freely of its own resources, and to obtain foreign exchange by selling those resources to buyers of its own choice. Technical assistance (which the UN organs had been giving) was, according to him, only a temporary solution.[3]

Thus was launched a subject which is still, 27 years later, on the agenda of the UN organs. The one change (in recent years) is the context in which the question continues to be discussed; from that of the economic development of developing countries, it is now discussed as an issue under the rubric 'The Use and Development of Natural (Non-agricultural) Resources'. There has also been a change in the political framework in which it is presently discussed — from what seemed initially to be a confrontational stance between the developing and the developed states to one of co-operation between the two groups of states. This altered framework recognizes the interdependence of states for their economic development (as for other purposes), mutuality of interests and benefits, a rough equality of bargaining strength and, since 1974, the need to conform to the Declaration on the 'New International Economic Order'.

The debates and actions on the subject have largely taken place in the General Assembly, the ECOSOC, and the UNCTAD. The demand for recognition/proclamation of sovereignty over natural resources has been based (explicitly or implicitly) on the *Purposes and Principles* of the Charter (Arts. 1 (1)-(4); 2 (1), (7) UNCh), some other related provisions (Arts. 56, 57 UNCh), and also the large number of resolutions of UN organs on the economic development of the developing countries. It is interesting to note that these Charter provisions have been cited by the spokesmen of both the developed and the developing states — sometimes in support of their differing stands.

In the beginning, as pointed out earlier, the focus of the debate was on the promotion of economic development of the developing countries. But as the debate became prolonged, the focus appeared to be shifting intermittently and alternatively to the legal and political issues, so that it sometimes appeared as though the question under discussion was: how can member-states exercise sovereignty/equality consistently with the desire for international economic co-operation? In other words, it was not always clear which was the end and which the means: economic development or sovereignty/equality or, perhaps, both were ends and means simultaneously reinforcing or promoting each other.

This ambivalence of the debate has its origins in the nature of the problem being debated: the inequitable distribution of natural resources among member-states, deriving from monopolies based on geography, geology, or special advantages deriving from economic environment. Obviously, without a world-wide arrangement for a more balanced development of different parts of the world, situations of geographical monopoly or advantages deriving from economic environment cannot be exploited in full — for those states which have abundant natural resources might not be in a position to exploit them by themselves; and those which have the trained personnel, technological and capital resources and need the natural resources, are starved of them. The location of the natural resources is obviously arbitrary. It has no relation to the needs, interests, technological development, and financial resources. Of course, the developing and the developed are not two clear-cut groups of members; they are only in different stages of the process of development to which, obviously, there is no limit because of the 'revolution of raising expectations'. Some states (e.g. Canada and Australia) straddle both groups. What is more, within each group, there is a great deal of differentiation; some are developed in relation to the others in the same group. And beyond these groups there is another — the so-called 'Fourth World' — which has no resources whatsoever which could ever help it to become reasonably developed. However, *all* of them aspire to higher and higher standards of living.

This unevenness of resources and development among member-states has far-reaching political and economic implications for international relationships. It reinforces the traditional hierarchical structure and relationships among the sovereign nation-states, to which the vast majority of members are stridently opposed. They are seeking to establish a more egalitarian, democratic international structure and relationships, as otherwise the 'sovereign equality' as the basis of membership of the UN would be rendered unsubstantial.

3. The Nature of UN Action

What has been the role of the UN system of institutions in seeking to remedy the present situation in respect of one aspect of the existing situation — namely, the physical location of natural resources in a country, on the one hand, and the ownership and/or exploitation of these resources by another country or an external agency?

The General Assembly and some other organs have affirmed, by over-whelming majorities, the principle/right of sovereignty over national resources located in one's own territory; that this includes the right to the state concerned to dispose of its resources in conformity with the rights and duties of states under international law and the Charter of the state concerned to dispose of its resources in conformity with New International Economic Order. Few members opposed or abstained on these propositions. Whenever there were divisions of option, they were mostly between the large majority of the developing states which supported them, and the small minority of the developed.

UN organs have not only affirmed the simple principle/right of sovereignty over natural resources, but have also gone into the positive and negative implications thereof. At the very first (the Seventh) Session of the Assembly which discussed the subject, it was elaborated that the right should be exercised 'with due regard, consistently with their sover-eignty, to the need for maintaining the flow of capital in conditions of security, mutual confidence, and economic co-operation among nations'; it also asked members to refrain from acts designed to impede the exercise of that right (GA Res. 626/VII). In other words, the Assembly balanced the right with a duty towards other members. Likewise, when the Fifteenth Session unanimously affirmed the right, it did so with the qualification 'in conformity with the rights and duties of states under international law' (GA Res. 515/XV). When the Seventeenth Session made a far-reaching contribution towards implementation by affirming the right of national-ization (by GA Res. 1803/XVII),[4] it made it clear that it should be based on grounds of public utility, security, or national interests and on 'appro-priate' compensation in accordance with, however, *national* legislation and in accordance with international law. In case of dispute, the national jurisdiction of the state nationalizing should first be exhausted, but 'upon agreement by sovereign states and other parties concerned' the settle-ment of the dispute should be made through arbitration or international adjudication. A decade later, the Twenty-seventh Session in effect modi-fied the above recommendation by omitting the conditions justifying nationalization and by asserting that nationalization was 'the expression of sovereign power . . . in virtue of which it is for each state to fix the amount of compensation and the procedure for these measures . . .' and any dispute was to fall 'within the sole jurisdiction of its [the national-izing country's] courts'.[5] It is worth noting that this resolution was voted by an even greater majority than the earlier one (121 votes against 87 for resolution 1803/XVII). In respect of the many resolutions passed on the subject during the last 27 years, there were few negative votes (even by the developed states) and very few abstentions. When members were divided in their votes, the divisions often cut across the two groups of members. The socialist states usually supported the stand of the developing states; when occasionally they did not, the reason was that the proposal voted upon was not radical enough or that it adversely affected their vital interests.

From the Twenty-first Session onwards, UN organs have spelt out the measures of implementation of the principle/right of sovereignty over the natural resources. These include: (1) an increased share in the administration and profits of foreign enterprises; (2) not only freedom to decide the manner of exploitation and marketing of resources, but also the acquiring of the capability to do so by, for example, the training of indigenous personnel; (3) the Committee on Natural Resources[6] was asked to give periodic reports on the advantages derived from the exercise of the right by the developing states, especially by way of increased mobilization of financial resources; (4) prohibition of coercion against the exercise of the right of sovereignty on natural resources, on the plea that such coercion is a violation of the UN Charter and the International Strategy for the Second Development Decade. An UNCTAD resolution (46/III) reinforced the prohibition by adding that any form of coercion would constitute a threat to international peace and security.

Apart from the large number of General Assembly resolutions, there have been equally large numbers of reports by the Secretary-General and resolutions by UNCTAD and ECOSOC. The Sixth (1974) and the Seventh (1975) Special Sessions of the General Assembly spelt out further the implications and consequential actions of the various resolutions.[7]

From the Twenty-eighth (1973) Session of the Assembly onwards, the principle/right of sovereignty over natural resources has been geographically extended to the Israeli-occupied Arab territories *and* all others occupied by alien regimes (i.e. colonial territories) or those covered by *apartheid*.[9] Spokesmen of many developing countries have sought to extend in their statements to UN organs the scope of categories of natural resources, such as selling non-commercial (or so-called strategic) reserves of primary products, marine resources of coastal states, forests and their products, and the marketing of products of nationalized concerns. The spokesmen of Panama have even claimed their geographical location as a 'natural resource'.

A redeeming feature of the UN debates on the question is that among both groups of the developing and the developed states, there were many who avoided extreme, partisan positions and confrontationist attitudes; they sought to keep down emotional, chauvinist, or rhetorical arguments which were often provoked in discussions on issues involving 'sovereign equality' of states. Rather, they based their arguments on 'realistic' reasons of economic interdependence and the mutual needs of both groups of states — and those of the states which straddled both groups — for co-operation and co-ordination. For, what was involved in the question was not only, and obviously, the interests of the developing states, but also, though less obviously, those of the developed states. And, for a variety of reasons and circumstances, they needed each other more than they were willing to admit, frankly and openly, for promoting and/or maintaining the standards of living of their peoples. If, for the developing countries, the exploitation and marketing of natural resources primarily for their own benefit are of vital importance, there is no question that they are of equal importance to the developed states which depend on these resources for their industrial economy. Neither group of states can thus do without the other. There are some states which straddle both groups; some of them are partly developed and partly (and still) developing; some of them both export and import foreign capital. Therefore, the interdependence and mutuality of their interests is quite clear, and these were repeatedly brought out in the UN debates.[10] Very likely this co-operative attitude was possible, and encouraged by, the forum in which the question was discussed. Placed in this setting the issue boiled down to the modalities of revising or modifying old agreements on the ownership or mining of natural resources by foreign firms or countries so as to place the mutuality of interests of the two groups of states on a more modern, if different, level.

4. The Significance of UN Actions

Undoubtedly, by now, the principle/right of sovereignty over one's natural resources has been legitimized and sanctified by the UN system of institutions. The Secretary-General, as long ago as 1971, said: 'The principle of sovereignty over natural resources has been proclaimed so frequently and solemnly, that it has by now acquired the weight of a Charter principle.'[11] According to the spokesman of a developing country, the general acceptance of the principle represented 'a virtual revolution in thinking and had [far-reaching] implications for relations between states'. It formed a 'major foundation-stone' of the proposed New International Economic Order.[12]

Without any doubt these views are factually correct, in so far as the mere acceptance of the principle/right is concerned, and as evidence of the UN legitimizing the thinking/approach of the overwhelming majority of members — both the developing and the developed. However, has all this really had any significant impact on the existing inequitable — primarily to the developing states — economic order? Is the mere proclamation — loudly, repeatedly, and on many occasions and in different forums — a substitute for an operative policy or action? Alas, it is not!

The truth of the matter is that the vast majority of the developing states are still struggling to achieve genuine economic independence from the developed states. Many of them are not even substantively (let alone, fully) exercising the rights of sovereignty in the sphere of economic relations. They are not yet able to speed up their economic development by the expected mobilization of additional financial resources, technical know-how, equipment, or marketing facilities.

But then, could this failure be blamed even partially on the UN (and International Organization generally)? Not at all!

For one thing, the UN system of institutions could not have done more or better than it actually did in legitimizing the principle/right within the realm of respective powers and functions. Indeed, in going through the UN records on the subject, one gets the feeling that the institutions have done more than they normally do in respect of similar questions (and *could do* within the limits of their powers) to the extent that the UN debates, reports, and resolutions on the subject are tiresomely and unnecessarily repetitive; that these actions are disproportionately larger than the measures of implementation by member-states. Indeed, a cynic might well come to think that the proportion of the former is much larger than that of the latter, precisely because of lack of progress on the latter; that this situation is simply the result of the need of the developing states for emotional fulfilment in the absence of practical benefits from the implementation of the right/principle by many states, in some respects even by the developing states which voted for the resolutions.

There are, plainly, two glaring limitations to further progress in the realization of the benefits of exercise of the right/principle of sovereignty over natural resources: the limitations of the powers and functions of the UN/International Organization; the sovereignty of member-states itself (paradoxical as it may sound).

5. Limitations of the Role of the UN

So far as the UN is concerned, it is clear that on matters such as this one, it can at best proclaim principles/rights and lay down norms — and do no more. For the UN (like most inter-governmental organizations at present) was set up by the sovereign states as a supplement to, not a substitute for (or to supplant), the multi-state system, and is meant primarily to serve *that* system. The organization is based on 'sovereign equality', and its powers under provisions (other than those of Ch. VII) of the Charter are essentially of a recommendatory or advisory character. It has neither the power nor the institutional mechanism for enforcing any norms, recommendations, or advice against the wishes of member-states, even when they have supported them in the deliberations of UN organs.

Furthermore, the UN, like all international organizations at present, is subject to the limitation of what has been called 'collective colonialism', that is, control by the rich countries of actions directed to the poor.[13] After all, those who benefit from the existing inequitable economic order are also those who mainly control the purse-strings of the UN, and it is too much to expect these nations to readily and willingly permit the Organization to act in support of the norms/recommendations affirmed by it. These nations are beneficiaries of certain legal/political rights acquired in the past, either under a colonial set-up or under duress (in view of their military or political power) *vis-à-vis* the presently developing countries;

and in many cases, the power equation between those rich nations and the present poor nations has remained substantially the same. Apart from the natural (if not legitimate) tendency of such beneficiaries to be reluctant to give up the benefits (at least readily, on demand), there could be (and perhaps there are) vague fears that any sudden sacrifice of these benefits (without some visible *quid pro quo*) might lower the living standards of their own people. This is plausible, especially in a period such as the present one, when many of the developed (non-socialist) countries at least might entertain the sincere belief that many of the developing countries are technologically incapable of exploiting by themselves their natural resources, or alternatively, fear that those which are capable might not continue to supply the resources to the developed countries which need them or seek to dictate the terms of the sales.

All this means that the UN alone cannot implement the principle/ right of sovereignty over natural resources, which is now one of the major principles on which the proposed New International Economic Order is founded. It is not, and was indeed never intended to be, an autonomous organization, independent of its member-states and the sovereign-state system, which is the foundation of the Organization, as of all inter-governmental organizations. The foundational assumption of international organization, which is continually relevant, is that changes in the existing international system can be effected only by (or with the consent/acquiescence of) the sovereign nation-states. The UN, like all other inter-governmental organizations, can only be, for the foreseeable future, a midwife of the New International Economic Order; it cannot itself conceive or beget one. That can only be done, individually or collectively, by member-states alone in a co-operative endeavour.

6. The Role of Member-States

This will come about only if, and when, the developed states realize their long-term interest in co-operating with the developing states to alter the existing economic order (which is in favour of the former) to base it on mutuality of interests. After all, the industrial development and high living standards of the developed states are largely founded on the ready access to, and cheapness of, natural resources in an era when they could control both. With the colonial frontier having receded, and two-thirds of UN members being those who have become independent since the end of the Second World War, the sources of these natural resources are no longer (in most cases, or to the same degree as before) subject to the control of the developed states. On the other hand, the dependence of those states on these resources for their industrial economy has (in most cases at least) increased rather than decreased. Prudence, therefore, demands that they co-operate with these newly-independent and developing countries in assisting them in utilizing these natural resources for mutual benefit. Secondly, the developed states must be both willing and able to make some sacrifices in the short run in favour of the developing states − not as a favour to the latter, but as an investment for long-term benefits. The problem here is not so much of governments not being persuaded of the need for short-term sacrifices for long-term benefit (it is interesting to note that no -developed state is, in principle, opposed to the recognition of the principle/right of sovereignty over natural resources), but of their inability to persuade their respective peoples to do so. By the very nature of the problem, it is both a delicate and difficult one to solve urgently − at least not as urgently as the needs of the developing states. The old historical legacy of the existing inequitable economic order cannot, therefore, be easily or quietly changed, neither in the minds of the peoples nor in physical terms.

Today, the simple issue (and the grievance of the developing states against the developed states) is not that the latter do not recognize the principle/right of sovereignty over natural resources, but that they disregard or violate it whenever the developing states seek to exercise it. The problem is the inability or unwillingness of these states to co-operate in the implementation of the principle/right in the *day-to-day conduct of international relations*. Apart from the difficulty of persuading their respective societies to make sacrifices in order to help the people of the less-developed states, this could be partly due to the lack of understanding and appreciation of the precise stand of the developing states by the developed states. For instance, the former are not asking for any new or exclusive right of nationalization which is not already sanctified by customary international law (which, by and large, was evolved by the presently developed states with little or no contribution by the developing states); it is not ideologically inspired, as is often suspected. In their search for ways and means of speeding up their economic development and raising the living standards of their peoples, they have found one such instrument in the demand for international recognition and legitimization of the right/principle of sovereignty over natural resources. They have little or no desire to carry out (as suspected or feared by the developed states) immediate or wholesale nationalization as, indeed, demonstrated by experience during the last 27 years, since the question was first raised in the forum of the UN. Finally, since the passing in 1974 of the Declaration on the New International Economic Order, the developing states have sought to fit the principle/right into the framework of the New Order which seeks to balance the rights and obligations of both groups of states (and hence, approved by consensus). All that the developing states − the 'climate' of international relations − for re-negotiation, not states − the 'climate' of international relations − for renegotiation, not necessarily or always termination, of the old treaties/agreements on the exploitation of the natural resources of one state (usually a developing one) by another (usually a developed state or one of its national or multinational corporations) in the light of the altered legal and political context of current international relations. They only desire and seek to *re-establish* (not snap) their existing international economic relations with the developed countries (in many cases, their respective former metro-politan countries) on a new basis, more in tune with the altered needs of the people and the domestic and international contexts.

This patently reasonable and fair attitude of the developing states is rooted not only in straightforward goodwill towards the developed states (which is true in most cases at least), but also in plain self-interest, and for that reason enduring. For many of the developing states presently lack the technological skills required for mining and marketing their natural resources and will be dependent on the developed states for many more years to acquire these (in many cases) from the very states (or their companies) that had owned and/or exploited their natural re-sources. Furthermore, many of the developing states will be dependent for many years on the goodwill and co-operation of the developed states for direct intergovernmental aid and for encouraging private investment. Without both of these the developing states cannot easily or soon make any substantial progress in their economic development, for which (partly) they have been urging, *inter alia*, the international recognition and legiti-mization of the principle/right of sovereignty over their natural resources. Hence, the developing states are as keen to promote economic co-operation with the developed states as they have been to seek international legiti-mization of the principle/right of sovereignty over their natural resources. From the 27 years of debates in the forum of UN organs (and outside), it is crystal clear that the developing states have no intention to pursue — or have not pursued — policies of political chauvinism, economic isola-tionism, or autarchy. Where these appear, as exceptions, they are more cases of political rhetoric rather than the practical policy/action actually followed.

But it is not only the developed states which have to change their attitude and outlook on their economic relations with the developing states, or to make short-term sacrifices in their own long-term interests and the interests of the international community generally; the developing states, too, have to do these things in the process of the implementation of the right/principle of sovereignty over their natural resources. A mere denunciation of the existing international economic order and just 'wishing' the New International Economic Order will not bring in any results. They, too, must be both able and willing to make short-term sacrifices to promote their long-term interests and also those of the inter-national community generally. For example, they need to have the courage to cancel or revise many of the existing treaties/agreements with developed states or their companies in order to bring them into tune with the legal/political realities of the late twentieth century. But many of them are unwilling or unable to do so for a variety of reasons — and have said so openly in the course of the debates in UN organs (and outside also). They could also take some modest steps, such as joint projects with the developed states (or their corporations); they could organize joint producer/consumer forums with other developing states; those of the developing states which are economically more advanced than the others could make investments in other developing countries, and so on. But, while they have been talking about these in UN forums and outside (e.g. in the non-aligned conferences), very few practical steps have been taken by most of them, or those steps taken have not been very significant in the pursuit of economic self-reliance.

7. 'Equitable Redistribution of Resources'?

Above and beyond all these problems and difficulties there is the intractable problem — for the present and the foreseeable future — of any equitable way of redistributing natural resources, viz. financial/technical competence required to exploit the natural resources. In a sovereign nation-state system, with vast variations in the size, resources, population, geographical location, and stages of political/economic/cultural development, neither the state-system nor (much less) international organization has the power or will to undertake this impossible task. The long-term possibility of doing it is not any brighter. Early in 1971 the UN Secretary-General placed the question of sovereignty over natural resources in its widest possible perspective:

> . . . without a more equitable system of international relationships, without a world-wide arrangement for the more balanced development of different parts of the world, it is almost inevitable that these situations of geographical monopoly or advantages deriving from the economic environment will be exploited to the full. The principle of national sovereignty over natural resources has been proclaimed so frequently and solemnly that it has by now acquired the weight of a Charter principle. But, we here [i.e. in the United Nations] know that this principle is not a substitute for the political and philosophical reality into which we must fit a natural resource policy ensuring some degree of organization in the exploitation and utilization of natural resources. The principle of national sovereignty should be considered in conjunction with another principle, that of world solidarity.

In his view, '*it is the combination of these two principles that should gradually find expression in the definition of economic arrangements for this exploitation and distribution of natural resources . . .*'. He insisted that the UN should consider the problem of natural resources from the standpoint of the most far-reaching economic, social, and political co-operation possible and with an approach as universal as possible to the interests and objectives involved.[14]

It is hardly necessary to point out that we do not have — and are not likely to have in the foreseeable future — 'a more equitable system of international relationships', nor a balancing of the principle of 'national sovereignty' with that of 'world solidarity'. Until we achieve this — in other words, until the international system moves beyond the sovereign-state system — it is hard to make any equitable arrangements for the redistribution and/or exploitation of natural resources. The international legitimization of the principle/right of sovereignty would, therefore, remain an academic achievement until and unless the developing states themselves achieve the technological and personnel capacity and acquire the capital investment required for exploiting and marketing their own resources on the basis of rough equality with those of the developed states. This is possible either directly, through the co-operation and assistance of the developed countries on a bilateral basis or, indirectly, through an international agency. In either case, it is a long and slow process to achieve the objective.[15]

The other suggested idea of 'equitable sharing' of resources among the members of the international community — as it is sought to be applied in other fields, the oceans, the antarctics, the atmosphere, and outer space[16] — is either irrelevant or Utopian so far as the natural resources of the sovereign states are concerned — for the simple reason that such uplifting concepts as 'the common heritage of mankind', 'equitable system of international relationships', and 'world solidarity' have little to do with the foundations of international organizations, namely, the sovereign-state system, and the basis of UN membership, 'sovereign equality'. Besides, there is every justification for treating as the 'common heritage of man-kind' the resources of the sea (beyond the 'economic zone') and for seeking to establish for it an international regime. This approach could be equally relevant to the utilization for the benefit of the international community of the antarctica, the arctic region, the atmosphere, and outer space. In respect of both cases, no state has any claims of sover-eignty over them, and no state, for the time being and for the foreseeable future, can lay or sustain any such claim. The case of the territorial sovereign, in which the natural resources are located, is altogether dif-ferent for 'permanent sovereignty' over resources. There is, therefore, simply no question or prospect of it agreeing to 'share' resources with other nations or even to agree to any international regime for their ex-ploitation and marketing.

The only hope for the distant future is the formulation of a treaty that would establish an international companies' law, administered by representatives drawn from signatory countries to govern the conduct of host governments and foreign corporations (or governments) — as suggested by George Ball.[17] But, immediately, the more practical proposal is for a code of conduct for the guidance of multi-national corporations (and governments) with investments abroad and the host countries which is under consideration by the UN. These would, of course, be non-binding and non-enforceable, but to the extent that they represent a consensus between the developing and the developed states, and would be based on mutuality of interests of the two groups of states, they are likely to be respected by both. For the foreseeable future that is all that can be expected to work. But then, at present, that is a way by which international organizations seek to regulate relations among states and which is equally acceptable to the latter.

Notes

1. For a detailed account of the consideration of the issue see the author's monographic study, Rajan, M. A. (1978). *Sovereignty over Natural Resources* (Atlantic Highlands, N.J.: Humanities Press).
2. UN Doc. A/C.2/L.165 and Corr. 1–3.
3. GAOR, VII. Sess., 2nd Cte., 231st Mtg., 253.
4. Entitled *Declaration on Permanent Sovereignty over Natural Resources.*
5. GA Res. 3041/XXVII. The GA thereby adopted a draft resolution submitted by UNCTAD's Trade and Development Board, which clarified that it is for the state nationalizing foreign-owned property to fix the amount of compensation, and that disputes regarding it were solely within the domestic jurisdiction of the state.
6. Established by ECOSOC in 1970.
7. The basic instruments adopted at these sessions are the *Declaration on the Establishment of the New International Economic Order* (GA Res. 3201/S–VI) with the *Programme of Action on the Establishment of a New International Economic Order* (GA Res. 3202/S–VI) and the *Resolution on Development and International Co-operation* (GA Res. 3362/S–VII). Of similar significance, in addition, the *Charter of Economic Rights and Duties of States*, adopted in the regular session following the Sixth Special Session (GA Res. 3281/XXIX).
8. GA Res. 3366/XXIX.
9. See, for example, a resolution passed by the Committee on Natural Resources in 1977 (E/C.7/L.68, Rev.1) asking the Secretary-General to report to the Committee on the exercise of this right in such countries or territories.
10. See Rajan (1978) (*n. 1*), esp. Ch. 5.
11. Statement on behalf of the Secretary-General by the Under Secretary-General for Economic and Social Affairs at the opening of the first session of the Committee on Natural Resources. Committee on Natural Resources. *Report on the First Session*. ESCOR, 51st Sess. (1971), Supp. 1, 51.
12. GAOR, 29th Sess., 1335th Mtg., 263.
13. See Cox, Robert W. and Jacobson, Harold K. (1973). *The Anatomy of Influence. Decision-making in International Organization* (New Haven–London: Yale University Press), 424.
14. Statement on behalf of the Secretary-General (*n. 11*).
15. On the various ways and means of which developing states have sought to exercise permanent sovereignty over natural resources and how international organizations could and did help them, see the three recent Reports of the UN Secretary-General, E/C. 7/66 (17 March 1977), E/C. 7/98 (21 March 1979), and E/C. 7/99 (14 March 1979).

16. See, for example, Schachter, Oscar (1977). *Sharing the World's Resources* (New Delhi: Allied Publisher), 38 ff.
17. Ball, George (1975). 'Proposal for an International Charter' in Ball, George, ed. (1975). *Global Companies* (Englewood Cliffs, N.J.: Prentice Hall Spectrum), 170–1.

3 NEGOTIATING A NEW INTERNATIONAL ECONOMIC ORDER: THE ISSUE OF VENUE

ROBERT W. GREGG
United Nations Institute for Training and Research, New York

Practising politicians and other close observers of the political process know that institutional venue can be important to the success or failure of policy initiatives. Many promising ideas have languished in inhospitable or ineffectual institutions, while others have been speeded on their way to law and practice by nurture in a more favourable forum. Thus, one of the important matters attending the launching of new policy initiatives is frequently the forum question, or what might be termed institutional strategy.

The campaign within the UN for a New International Economic Order (NIEO) provides an instructive case study of this relationship between setting and substance, between process and policy. Whether the NIEO is good or bad economics, and whatever its merits as a prescription for development among Third World countries, it constitutes a significant challenge to the capacity and adaptability of the UN system. And it has stimulated a vigorous debate among governments and international officials about the appropriate institutional context for multilateral economic diplomacy.

This debate did not, of course, begin with the call for a NIEO. Institutional issues have been an important staple of the UN system agenda for many years. Indeed, the proliferation of multilateral institutions — agencies, councils, programmes, funds, and committees, permanent and temporary, intergovernmental and expert — has been as much a reflection of frustration with existing forums as it has a response to newly emergent issues. The United Nations Conference on Trade and Development (UNCTAD) and the United Nations Industrial Development Organization (UNIDO) are the classic examples of institutions which owe their existence to the search (in each case by developing countries) for more congenial and effective forums. Had the UN's Economic and Social Council (ECOSOC) been more responsive to Third World interests, and had its membership been expanded sooner to permit fuller participation by Third World countries, perhaps UNCTAD at least would not have been created and centrifugal tendencies within the UN system would not have reached their present proportions.

In any event, debate over venue is a familiar feature of UN history. It has been especially acute in the period of Third World 'ascendancy', beginning with the massive influx into the UN of newly independent African states in the early 1960s. It has coincided with what Robert Rothstein has characterized as the shift from non-alignment to class war, that is,

> the end of a period . . . in which external relations performed primarily ceremonial functions for the developing countries and the beginning of a period in which the quest for changes in operation of the international aid and trade systems became increasingly prominent.[1]

As multilateral diplomacy took on an increasingly North–South coloration, institutional issues became increasingly important. Developing countries became ever more impatient with the established forums, including ECOSOC, the GATT, the IMF, and the World Bank, as well as some of the UN's specialized agencies and even UNCTAD, whose quadrennial conferences in New Delhi and Santiago in 1968 and 1972 were widely viewed as deeply disappointing. The indictment varied from institution to institution, touching upon membership, decision-making rules and procedures, leadership, organizational ethos, priorities, and, of course, results. Predictably, the developed market economy states were generally more supportive of most of these institutions. When the non-aligned countries, at their 1973 summit in Algiers, opened the campaign for a new order by adopting resolutions calling for a thorough reorganization of the international economic system, the forum question was already salient.[2]

Until the 1970s and the debate over the NIEO, efforts to achieve reform of the international economic system and to relate the functioning of that system to the problems of development in the Third World had largely been fragmented and piecemeal.[3] The NIEO, on the other hand, is a comprehensive programme, claiming the interrelatedness of various economic measures and the need to pursue reforms on a broad front, more or less concurrently. Similarly, institutional issues had earlier been addressed in an *ad hoc* fashion, reflecting specific, if cumulative, frustrations or needs. There was no general comprehensive agenda regarding multilateral institutions or the relationships between substantive economic policies and the institutional setting(s) in which they might best be negotiated and implemented. The NIEO changed that.

I

The documents which together lay out the agenda for a NIEO actually say very little about multilateral institutions and decision-making processes. The emphasis is on the structure of the international economic system, rather than on the structures which serve that system and in which elements of a new order might be negotiated. Some attention is paid to the problem of adequate participation by developing countries in World Bank and IMF decision-making, and the logic of certain other NIEO objectives leads directly to the creation of new multilateral institutions which are favourable to the interests of developing countries.[4] But in the main the explicit focus of the NIEO agenda is economic.

However, the NIEO is as much a political manifesto as it is an economic one, and important elements of the political agenda are institutional reform and influence and control over the decision-making processes of multilateral bodies.[5] The institutional aspects of the NIEO are less explicitly stated, but they are none the less real because of that. Indeed, Sidney Weintraub goes so far as to assert that 'the central issue in the NIEO relates to the process of international decision-making'.[6] If the call for a NIEO is placed in the appropriate historical context, it is unmistakably clear that it is a challenge to the privileged position of the developed market economy states in international economic decision-making. The developing countries

 . . . view the results of the existing international order as unjust and inequitable, hence their demand for a new international economic order. But they also take exception to the processes whereby the results have been arrived at, processes from which they have been largely excluded or in which their role has been substantially less than their numbers and their needs suggest that it should be. Thus the New International Economic Order might more accurately be termed a New International Economic and Political Order; the developing countries seek not only a larger share of the pie, but also control of the knife that cuts the pie.[7]

What emerged from the Sixth and Seventh Special Sessions of the UN General Assembly in 1974 and 1975 was a comprehensive set of negotiated demands called the NIEO; however imperfect the agreement, rough consensus had been reached on 'what to do'.[8] At this point the central question became 'how to do it'. This question inevitably focused attention on institutional strategy. The choice of forum ceased to be a sometime concern of governments and became instead a major preoccupation of governments as the North–South dialogue unfolded. Developing countries ceased to regard more egalitarian decision-making in multilateral institutions as a long-range issue, a desirable but impracticable objective. They began to treat it as a necessary component of the NIEO and to consider its applicability in a number of immediately pending negotiations.

The NIEO thus intensified the perennial debate over which international economic issues should be addressed in which forums, possessing what authority, and observing what decision-making rules. This sharpening of the institutional issue has been attributable (a) to the normative bias of the NIEO in favour of egalitarian decision-making, and (b) to the practical problems of transforming the NIEO from a manifesto into a working reality. The normative quality of the NIEO guarantees that each institutional requirement of the new order will be an occasion for the developing states to demand greater participation and more equity in future international economic problem-solving. But institutional issues are not only important in the new order, they are also important to the creation of that new order. Virtually all governments act as if the content of a new order, the speed with which it comes into being, and the legitimacy it enjoys will be affected by the institutional context within which the NIEO is planned and negotiated.

II

Debate over the NIEO is widely referred to as the North–South dialogue. This characterization contains an element of distortion, of course, because it does not take into account the largely peripheral role of the Eastern European communist states and the Peoples' Republic of China;[9] more over, it overstates the monolithic character of the two major blocs. Nevertheless, it correctly describes the main axis of the debate.

These two principal parties to the NIEO dialogue — the developed market economy states of the North and the developing states of the South — have different institutional agenda. Each has a preferred tier of institutions in which it would like the NIEO to be negotiated. These two tiers of institutions differ from each other in several important respects.

The *South* prefers an institutional context for negotiating the NIEO which is hierarchical, with the UN General Assembly the dominant forum. In this view, the General Assembly, and to a lesser extent UNCTAD, would negotiate regarding the establishment of the NIEO and would create or legitimize other forums for specific tasks associated with the NIEO. The UN's appeal lies in its universality, its egalitarian/majoritarian decision-making rules and practices, and its political character. Ambassador Mohammed Bedjaoui of Algeria summarized the case in a recently published volume:

> In the opinion of the developing countries, international organizations, and especially the United Nations, provide an ideal context for the drafting of a legal new deal with a view to the transformation of the international economic order and the development of all peoples. Through its egalitarian character, its majority basis and hence its democratic origins, the (UN) resolution seems to them to present sufficient guarantees as a method for the elaboration of international norms responding to today's needs.[10]

The primary role of the UN in the creation of a new order follows logically from two convictions voiced by Bedjaoui and shared by many Third World spokesmen that ' "membership" must eclipse the "leadership" of dominant oligarchies'[11] in the elaboration of a new order and that the Third World now possesses a ' "right to the creation of law" (in the more political and egalitarian UN system forums) thanks to the strength of their numbers'.[12]

The *North* has not shared this enthusiasm for the UN, whether it be the General Assembly or UNCTAD (or, for that matter, UNIDO or the Committee of the Whole). The preference of the developed market economy states has been for a pluralistic system, with the negotiation of international economic reforms taking place in what they regard as the appropriate specialized forums such as the IMF, the World Bank, and the GATT. In these institutions leadership takes precedence over membership; decisions have substantive rather than symbolic value, and have been carefully negotiated by experts, not generalists, in an atmosphere conducive to bargaining, not posturing. There is no 'resolution therapy'[13] here, only the sober quest for incremental change, one step at a time, within an agreed framework of international economic co-operation.

Sidney Weintraub says it succinctly: 'Each group of countries will wish to negotiate issues of importance to it in the institutions that it dominates.'[14] And the fact is that the old-order institutions — the Bank, the Fund, the GATT — are controlled by the vested interests, the UN institutions by 'the aspirants to power, influence, and benefits'.[15]

Both groups use both tiers of institutions because they must; they will almost certainly continue to do so. But the NIEO has intensified disagreement over the division of labour between the two tiers. In summarizing this important element in the conflict between North and South over the NIEO, Weintraub observes that 'dialogue is useful, but control is crucial in how different groups view the various international organizations'.[16]

III

The debate over the appropriate venue for negotiating the NIEO has not been an academic exercise. It has been reflected in decisions regarding the choice of forums for the North–South dialogue and for negotiation of new order issues; in vigorous criticism of these forum decisions; and in jockeying for position among multilateral organizations seeking a leading role in the NIEO process. Even when institutional and decision-making issues appear to have been laid to rest, they are never far from the surface; they continue to complicate relations between developed and developing countries and among UN system bodies.

The initial chapter in this debate is by now thoroughly familiar. In 1974 the demands of the developing countries were codified at the Sixth

Special Session of the UN General Assembly into a Declaration and Programme of Action on the Establishment of a New International Economic Order,[17] and later in that same year, at the Twenty-ninth Session of the General Assembly, into a Charter of Economic Rights and Duties of States.[18] The actions of OAPEC in suddenly reducing the flow of crude oil to the West, and of OPEC in dramatically inceasing the price of oil, seemed to herald the opening of a new era in international economic and political relations, and certainly emboldened the developing countries in their confrontation with the developed countries at the UN in 1974. But those actions also produced an energy crisis and prompted the call for an international energy conference. As we know, the eventual result was the Conference on International Economic Co-operation (CIEC), a North–South dialogue with a much broader agenda than energy.

The CIEC took place outside of the UN framework, between December 1975 and June 1977. It was, in the judgement of virtually all participants and observers, a failure.[19] The guarded optimism which had been generated by the Seventh Special Session was dissipated by the altogether unremarkable results of the Paris Conference. But no one was prepared to concede that the NIEO was dead, so soon after its launching. The North–South dialogue continued, in part because the developing countries were deeply committed to the NIEO and determined to press for its implementation, and in part because the developed countries were unwilling to shoulder the blame for burying the NIEO however opposed they were to many of its specific provisions.

In December 1977 the UN General Assembly resolved 'that all negotiations of a global nature relating to the establishment of the New International Economic Order should take place within the framework of the United Nations system';[20] towards that end it created a Committee of the Whole to act as a focal point for a number of NIEO-related tasks, among them:

> Overseeing and monitoring the implementation of decisions and agreements reached in the negotiations on the establishment of the new international economic order in the appropriate bodies of the United Nations system;
> Providing impetus for resolving difficulties in negotiations and for encouraging the continuing work in these bodies;
> Serving, where appropriate, as a forum for facilitating and expediting agreement on the resolution of outstanding issues;
> Exploring and exchanging views on global economic problems and priorities.[21]

In effect there had been a change of venue. The CIEC was to be succeeded by the UN as the central forum for the negotiation of the NIEO. This was not a surprising development. One indictment of the CIEC had been its lack of a formal UN connection, a shortcoming which cost it something in legitimacy.

The precise mandate of the Committee of the Whole was a source of disagreement from the first, a fact reflected in the bland title and its unfortunate acronym. The Group of 77 in New York generally wanted the Committee to possess negotiating authority; opposition to such a role came from such diverse sources as the government of the United States and the UNCTAD Secretariat. The United States was not ready to negotiate across the board on the NIEO agenda, much less to do so in the egalitarian framework of the UN; Secretary-General Corea and his colleagues regarded the Committee as a usurper of UNCTAD's rightful role. In the months that followed, the Committee of the Whole accomplished very little, ultimately assuming the role of a preparatory committee for action-orientated global negotiations, to be launched at the 1980 Special Session of the UN General Assembly. The resolution calling for such negotiations makes clear that they are to take place within the UN system and that the General Assembly is to play the central role.

When the Paris Conference closed, there were some who hoped that the North–South dialogue would gravitate to another small forum (the Development Committee of the IMF and the World Bank was occasionally mentioned, although it was never a realistic alternative);[22] but it is now apparent that moves to circumvent the UN will be unavailing. It is equally clear that the UN General Assembly has now gained ascendancy over UNCTAD in the jurisdictional quarrel within the UN. UNCTAD officials have for some time promoted an expanded role in multilateral economic negotiations for their institution,[23] but the political requirements of the NIEO, together with UNCTAD's deficiencies, have conspired to shift the focus of UN efforts on behalf of the NIEO from Geneva to New York.

While the General Assembly has assumed the central role in the negotiating process, negotiations regarding specific elements of the NIEO agenda are proceeding elsewhere in the UN system. UNCTAD has provided the forum for negotiations on an Integrated Programme for Commodities and a Common Fund. A Code of Conduct for the Transfer of Technology is also being negotiated in UNCTAD. The UN Conference on the Law of the Sea has been the scene of negotiations about one of the quintessential new order issues, a regime for the seabed. Thus far, negotiations regarding trade and protectionism and monetary reform have taken place within Western-dominated institutions (the Tokyo Round of Multilateral Trade Negotiations under GATT's auspices and the IMF, respectively); they have not used NIEO formulations as their working documents, and the results can hardly be said to have contributed to the realization of new order objectives. Negotiations on various other issues will presumably begin in appropriate forums within the UN system or under UN sponsorship when the will exists to move beyond the conceptual phase of the dialogue to serious bargaining.

The venue for negotiation of these specific NIEO issues has frequently been controversial, but it has been less of a problem than the broader, catalytic negotiations which were the rationale for the Seventh Special Session, the Paris Conference, and the Committee of the Whole, as well as for much of UNCTAD IV and V and the 1980 Special Session of the General Assembly. However controversial specific issues may be, negotiations on such issues have usually been preceded by an agreement in principle that the subject is ripe for negotiation and hence negotiable. No such agreement exists across the board on the NIEO as a whole or on many of its more important measures (a good example is redeployment of industry). Given that harsh reality, it is not surprising that there should be strong resistance to the kind of broad, comprehensive negotiations regarding the NIEO which the General Assembly and UNCTAD wish to conduct. The objections of developed market economy states to such negotiations are in no small part due to the institutional setting in which they would take place.

Six years and innumerable meetings after the adoption of the Declaration and Programme of Action on the Establishment of a NIEO, the venue issue is still very much alive. The North and the South still declaim on the merits of their preferred tiers of institutions and try to steer the North–South dialogue into what they regard as more congenial forums. But over this span of years, and as a result of experience acquired in those innumerable meetings, *several lessons have been learned — or may be learned* — which should provide some perspective on the problem of venue for the negotiation of a new order.

IV

(1) The *first* and perhaps least dramatic *lesson* is that *the UN cannot be bypassed*. This is not to say that all negotiations concerning all elements of the NIEO will be conducted directly under the aegis of the UN. But global negotiations concerning the content of the new order and strategy for its implementation will take place within the UN, and principally within the General Assembly. If the venue is other than the General Assembly, those negotiations will have to be legitimized by the Assembly.

This is not the scenario favoured by the developed countries, or at least the more conservative among them. They would prefer to negotiate about the NIEO in more congenial forums, smaller in size, less self-consciously egalitarian, and better insulated from ideological confrontation. They still do not subscribe to the thesis that UN resolutions have 'compulsory value',[24] nor are they likely to in the foreseeable future. As far as they are concerned, the argument that UN resolutions on the new order create legal obligations begs the question, asserting the existence of new order conditions and principles when in fact the establishment of that new order is the objective of still inconclusive UN negotiations. But recognition of the UN's defects and the limits of its authority does not negate the essentiality of the UN to the NIEO exercise. The developing countries are adamant about the UN's role; the developed countries have acquiesced in it.

Had the Paris Conference succeeded in important respects, a more modest role for the UN would probably have been tolerated. But CIEC failed. A careful analysis of that failure might as logically have led to a differently constituted CIEC, functioning under different ground rules, as to the UN; but in the aftermath of the Paris Conference it was no longer possible to bypass the UN. Initial difficulties in implementing the NIEO agenda only served to heighten the symbolic importance of the UN, with its egalitarian/majoritarian ethos which seemed to prefigure the new order.

(2) *The UN may be central to the effort to negotiate a new order into existence, but the UN needs help.* The requirement that the UN must not be bypassed does not necessarily increase the likelihood that the NIEO will be realized. It may, paradoxically, make the NIEO more difficult to achieve. The UN's deficiencies become obstacles to the North–South negotiations to the degree that those negotiations must go forward within the UN framework — unless, of course, measures are adopted which correct or circumvent those deficiencies.[25]

There are *two strategies* which need to be pursued if the UN is to improve its capacity to play the central role in negotiating the NIEO for which it has now been cast. These strategies are not mutually exclusive. In the *first* place, efforts to restructure the UN system should be redoubled; the relevant UN organs must be strengthened. The very existence of the Committee of the Whole is testimony to the UN's weakness. In a more rationally designed and effectively functioning UN system, either UNCTAD or ECOSOC would have been charged with the tasks which were assigned to the Committee of the Whole. But the developed countries lacked confidence in UNCTAD and developing countries were unwilling to entrust the NIEO agenda to ECOSOC. Each of these two bodies and the secretariats which serve them are flawed in important respects.[26] The General Assembly, in spite of its alleged advantages as a forum where political will can more readily be brought to bear, is much better suited to the airing of grievances than it is to bargaining about an economically complex agenda.

The restructuring exercise was to have addressed some of these problems, but it has only scratched the surface, improving the secretariat in New York but not yet reforming ECOSOC or the General Assembly, or even seriously addressing the relationships between New York and Geneva or among the components of the larger UN system.[27] There is renewed interest in Charter reform, meaning the enlargement of ECOSOC;[28] whether such a change is desirable or not, it does not go to the heart of the matter. As Miguel Wionczek has argued so persuasively, the UN system is in crisis.[29] Its institutions are in conflict; their work habits are often appalling; the quality and even the relevance of the substantive work of the international bureaucracies leaves much to be desired; the results of the negotiating process are frequently tortured texts which create the illusion of action when there is none. These are not faults which are easily corrected, but it must be recognized that they complicate the task of launching the NIEO and that they require much more serious and sustained attention from all governments, North and South, than they have had heretofore.

The *second* strategy calls for the creation of a small but politically potent group of officials who would work essentially in camera in a continuing effort to break log-jams which impede the negotiating process. Jahangir Amuzegar, who writes realistically about North–South negotiations, argues that the UN system 'lacks an effective mechanism for a "planetary bargain" at a high political level',[30] and urges a small but representative council to fill this void. Such a council would not be a reconstituted CIEC, or even a more official version of the Brandt Commission. It would surely not replace the UN, but rather function in parallel with it, doing what the UN seems incapable of doing: searching out shared or convergent interests, seeking to define problems in ways acceptable to all, identifying the major elements of solutions to those problems, and determining what requires expert attention and what is ripe for consideration by high-level government authorities.[31] It will not be easy to create such a council. But something very much like it is required to move the dialogue forward in constructive ways.

(3) Although the UN needs the help of a small council, functioning out of the limelight, there are also *risks involved in channelling the NIEO dialogue into additional forums.* This is especially so if some governments view such a council as an alternative forum rather than a complementary one. The problem has been described by one seasoned UN observer as the 'slow train/fast train' phenomenon.[32]

This lesson from North–South negotiations is best illustrated by the experience of UNCTAD and CIEC during the mid-1970s. It will be recalled that the first ministerial meeting of CIEC was held in Paris in December 1975, and that the Conference came to a conclusion in June 1977. UNCTAD IV met in Nairobi in May 1976. Preparatory work for the two conferences was going on concurrently, and UNCTAD's Nairobi session took place during the course of the North–South dialogue in Paris (between the first and second ministerial meetings to be precise). The fate of the two sets of negotiations was linked.

If UNCTAD IV had failed unequivocally, the Paris Conference would have taken on greater significance. In fact, some representatives of developed countries seem to have had that result in mind. But the eleventh-hour 'agreement' on the Common Fund at Nairobi somewhat revived expectations regarding UNCTAD and may have removed some of the urgency from the Paris negotiations. Conversely, the dialogue in Paris deprived a critical UNCTAD session of some of its importance. Although results in one forum may be a catalyst for progress in another, the evidence suggests that governments are just as likely to excuse inaction in forum A by reference to action in forum B, especially when there is a jurisdictional rivalry. Governments will argue, in effect, that there is no point in boarding a slow train when a fast train is coming.

The fragmentation of the UN system and competition among its various institutions contributes to this phenomenon. This competition is especially acute between UNCTAD and the New York UN (the gradual emergence of New York as the centre of gravity for the North–South dialogue has been strongly resisted in Geneva). There are latent conflicts between UNCTAD on the one hand and the IMF and the GATT on the other. The NIEO agenda is broad, and the boundaries between multilateral institutions ill-defined. The constituencies for the activities of different institutions are well established in most capitals. In this situation of institutional competition it is not always clear which are the fast trains.

(4) Another lesson of the NIEO debate thus far has to do with *numbers*. Conventional wisdom has it that negotiation is virtually impossible with so many at the table, and it is demonstrably true that universal *participation* introduces into the negotiating process free riders, the marginally involved, and the under-prepared. But the evidence of several years of North–South dialogue is that when there is a willingness to reach a meeting of minds, numbers do not matter that much. On the other hand, universal participation is invariably a problem when the parties are frozen into rigid and unyielding positions. Given the will to move on the part of key governments, creative chairmen and secretariat officials can usually find ways to reduce the number of active participants in serious bargaining to a small and representative number. They can use such well-established techniques as contact groups and such informal devices as limiting room size to produce an atmosphere conducive to hard bargaining. Negotiations such as those on the Common Fund illustrate both the best and the worst of global bargaining; but when Group B decided to abandon its opposition to the fund and the Group of 77 decided to scale down its expectations, i.e. when the parties got down to real bargaining, numbers ceased to be a serious impediment to progress.[33]

The point that the developing countries have insisted on is not that every state must be present for every stage of the negotiating process, but that every state must have a *right* to participate, directly in many cases and through spokesmen answerable to the group in others. Once that right is acknowledged and the process 'opened up' to all members, such factors as knowledge, interest, stamina, and the confidence of one's peers take hold and reduce the number of participants to more manageable proportions.

The more serious question is how to bring to the negotiating table officials who have authority — officials who are close to the seats of power and who can commit their governments on important matters of substance regarding the NIEO. Few meetings devoted to North–South issues do not produce their share of speeches decrying the absence of ministerial-level representation. But one of the lessons of North–South negotiations is that ministers will not waste valuable time participating in a general, platitudinous debate on a broad, unfocused agenda, or in negotiations on NIEO issues which are not ripe for action. UNCTAD's ministerial-level meeting in 1978 on debt was moderately successful because it had been very carefully prepared and met most of the conditions for constructive action.[34] But the political will which is necessary to advance the NIEO will not be generated at ministerial-level meetings; it is an antecedent, without which there will be few ministerial-level meetings.

(5) Other lessons concern the *group system*, which some would blame for the failure of the negotiating process. It is true that the group system places a premium upon intra-group agreement, often at the expense of intergroup agreement. As Robert Rothstein has argued so cogently, the Group of 77 arrives at its package of demands not by compromise but by addition, with the result that little can be bargained away without hurting some developing states more than others. Serious bargaining with the developed countries leads to an unravelling of the carefully constructed package and threatens the solidarity of the Group of 77.[35]

But the group system is at once better than its reputation and worse. On the positive side, it necessitates collective reflection on the needs of a very diverse group of states; it also requires a division of labour and hence the development of expertise and leadership by states and by individual statesmen, including the emergence of group spokesmen who significantly reduce the babble and confusion which otherwise would characterize the North–South dialogue.

On the other hand, it does encourage group rigidity, especially on the part of the Group of 77, which is often at variance with the interests of some of the members. This is especially true of the more general negotiations, such as those in the Committee of the Whole. Paradoxically, in the case of the developed countries the lack of a firm group position — usually because of Scandinavian and/or Dutch initiatives — sometimes misleads the Group of 77, who interpret disagreement within Group B as a signal that opposition among developed countries is eroding. This can and does encourage inflexibility among the Group of 77 and defers compromise.

Although the group system now flourishes throughout the UN system, neither the Group of 77 nor Group B follows precisely the same script in all institutions. The Group of 77 in the General Assembly and the Group of 77 in UNCTAD are often at odds with each other, as are the institutions in which they function. The developed countries try to operate as a group in Geneva, but group discipline is much less apparent in

New York. Group D, the Eastern European bloc, is a marginal factor in the group system in both places. Ironically, for all of the rigidity which it displays in some institutions on some occasions, the group system is not sufficiently coherent and disciplined across the UN system to provide much of a corrective for the fragmentation and dysfunctional competition which plague the efforts to establish a new order.[36]

However, the most significant flaw in the group system, made painfully clear over the years, is that it is lacking in symmetry. Although the developed countries have not always taken the North–South dialogue as seriously as they might, when they choose to approach the negotiating process in a conscientious manner they can mobilize expertise which the developing countries cannot match. The Group of 77 has been strengthened in its command of the issues and in its bargaining capability by the support of the UNCTAD Secretariat. But the UNCTAD staff has been spread thin by the many demands made upon it, and it has never been able to perform for the Group of 77 the functions which the OECD Secretariat has performed for Group B (not to mention the superior resources which many of the Western market economy states have at their disposal back in their capitals).

Moreover, the cost of UNCTAD's efforts to provide staff support for the Group of 77 has been high in terms of Western distrust of that organization. The trade-union mentality of the UNCTAD Secretariat has seriously compromised its ability to play the role of honest broker in the NIEO negotiations, and has contributed to the weakening of UNCTAD's role in those negotiations relative to the UN in New York. The time is ripe − indeed, it is overdue − for the creation of a separate secretariat for the developing countries, both because negotiations would be improved by more symmetrical capabilities and because UNCTAD needs to be rescued from its slide into irrelevance.

(6) Another lesson of the North–South dialogue concerns *voting*, or rather non-voting, for consensus has become the preferred outcome of NIEO negotiations, rather than divisive votes which record the numerical superiority of the Group of 77. But the lesson is not just that consensus has become a more widely used working method within the UN system since the Sixth and Seventh Special Sessions of the General Assembly, but that consensus, which seems so sensible a practice on matters of such moment, has already been corrupted.[37]

Few would deny that the quest for consensus represents a desirable trend in multilateral decision-making, although some of the more fervent advocates of a more egalitarian international order are uncomfortable with this 'major concession' by the developing countries.[38] The problem, however, is that the preoccupation with consensus often leads to resolutions which create the illusion of progress where little or no progress has occurred. Consensus frequently focuses disproportionate attention on the texts of resolutions rather than on the substantive issues which divide states; it commonly masks profound disagreements. Even more important is the practice of reservation, often on fundamental points, a tactic which devalues consensus and is probably more harmful to the NIEO than more forthright acknowledgement of differences and a conscientious search for institutions and procedures which could help to resolve those differences.[39]

(7) It has frequently been suggested by governments in the developed countries that the Group of 77 behave irrationally, emphasizing the *ideological aspects of the NIEO* even at the expense of their economic interests. This argument has been made with respect to such issues as the mandate of the Committee of the Whole, the regime for the seabed being negotiated in the UN Conference on the Law of the Sea, and some aspects of the UNCTAD negotiations on an Integrated Programme for Commodities and a Common Fund. In effect, the developing countries stand accused of treating the NIEO and the associated institutional issues first and foremost as a political manifesto, rather than as an agenda for their economic development.

The evidence to date does not support this charge. Thus, another lesson of the North–South dialogue is that the developing countries will not allow their political agenda, including their preferences regarding institutions and multilateral decision-making practices, to interfere with the pursuit of their economic objectives when the anticipated economic benefits are relatively substantial, unambiguous, near-term, and widely shared.[40] Conversely, when the perceived economic benefits of NIEO objectives are ambiguous, insubstantial, long-range, or badly distributed, the Group of 77 will tend to be more vigorous in its pursuit of political and institutional objectives.

Illustrations of this proposition are numerous, but the classic case is to be found in the seabed negotiations.

> In this case, the impulse on the part of the Group of 77 to focus on the political and ideological aspects of the issue has not been balanced by the clear prospect of substantial and early economic benefits. Although the mineral wealth of the seabed may well be substantial, there is lack of agreement on the revenue-sharing potential of deep-seabed mining; given the technological problems and costs of extracting those minerals, any economic payoffs are still many years away, at best. In view of these uncertainties, it has not been difficult for the third world countries to concentrate on the politics rather than the economics of the seabed. Not only is there nothing tangible and immediate to lose, but there is something important to gain in the context of the campaign to create a new order: a vitally important precedent for other negotiations now in progress or still to be undertaken.[41]

Therefore, the Group of 77 has in effect rejected what might be regarded as very forthcoming compromise proposals and has instead insisted on a strong international regime, very much under the control of the developing state majority.

The issue of egalitarian/majoritarian decision-making in multilateral institutions is central to the NIEO. But the developing countries have backed away from an ideological position on this issue when insistence upon their agenda would place substantial economic benefits at risk. This has been true in their handling of demands for more participation in IMF and World Bank decision-making, and in the creation of the International Fund for Agricultural Development. It is this evidence of pragmatism which suggests that the developing countries will be flexible on institutional issues if the developed countries are responsive on some of the important matters of economic substance.

V

UN system institutions and decision-making processes have been affected by the campaign to create a NIEO. But while the system has not been inflexible, those adaptations which have occurred are manifestly less than those which are required if the institutional context for negotiating a new order is to facilitate that process rather than impede it.

Six years of negotiating a new order have demonstrated a number of truths and trends about the UN and the problem of venue for the NIEO. They indicate that the UN will indeed be the principal forum for new-order negotiations, and that universal participation in those negotiations need not be the serious impediment which many of the larger developed countries have claimed. They indicate that the Group of 77 will not as a rule try to impose its overwhelming majority upon the developed countries, but will instead seek consensus. More generally, they indicate that the developing countries will be pragmatic in their pursuit of a more egalitarian order, provided that the prospect of economic benefits justifies abandonment of the more ideological aspects of their institutional agenda. In spite of the rhetoric which accompanies the quest for a new order, the UN system will remain pluralistic and international economic reform will continue to be incremental.

On the other hand, the evidence of these six years of faltering negotiations is that progress on the NIEO has been slowed by a number of structural and procedural factors. The UN itself requires a more thoroughgoing restructuring. The UN system is characterized by dysfunctional competition, to which the group system often contributes when it should be helping to link the efforts of various UN bodies. Moreover, the group system tends to rigidity and lacks symmetry with respect to group capabilities for economic analysis. The practice of consensus is frequently misused, and its utility for multilateral decision-making has already been depreciated. Furthermore, it is increasingly apparent that the UN needs the catalytic presence of a relatively small but high-powered council to supply momentum to a bargaining process that is unlikely to be self-starting in the General Assembly or even in UNCTAD.

All of this seems to suggest that the venue issue has been decided in favour of the UN, and that this is not necessarily a bad decision, even from the point of view of developed countries which have traditionally at best been sceptical of the UN. It also suggests that the principal issue now confronting member states is whether they are prepared to address a much more difficult question: Are they willing to undertake a number of controversial reforms which will improve the capacity of the UN system and the UN itself to establish an NIEO?

Unfortunately, measures which some states would regard as institutional reforms are viewed by other states as attempts to undermine structures and processes in which they have confidence. The UN's restructuring exercise illustrates this point. Vested interests, as well as deeply-ingrained organizational habits, have so far blocked the full implementation of the General Assembly's resolution on restructuring.[42] They have made it virtually impossible to consider seriously some of the recommendations of the Group of Experts on restructuring,[43] and that body did not even venture into some areas of reform because they were regarded as too controversial. Developing countries do not want UN reform to weaken the egalitarian/majoritarian principles which they regard as so essential to a new order; nor do they want reform to downgrade 'their' preferred institutions. For these reasons they rejected suggestions by the Experts which (a) would have institutionalized procedures for suspending a vote on divisive issues, and (b) would have reduced UNCTAD's independence. Conversely, the developed countries have feared that restructuring could degenerate into yet another vehicle for extending the reach of NIEO principles. They have not been over enthusiastic, for example, about recommendations that ECOSOC be opened to all UN members.

The kind of small council which might help the UN to break log-jams in the negotiation of the NIEO would meet with profound distrust in many Third World capitals. It would be construed as a device for shifting the real centre of North–South negotiations away from the UN and into a small élite body more readily controlled by the large industrial powers. Its practical value would be outweighed for many by its symbolic liabilities. The creation of a separate secretariat for the Group of 77 would not only threaten UNCTAD's present role and elicit opposition from that quarter, it would also trouble some among the Group B countries who fear its probable domination by the more radical Non-Aligned Movement, and who are none too happy in any event about strengthening the Group of 77's negotiating capacity.[44] In short, institutional reforms will not come easily.

There is much talk in the North–South dialogue about the lack of political will to move forward with the NIEO agenda. Although such charges, usually levelled by the developing against the developed countries, ignore the complexities of the decision-making process in pluralistic democracies, they do provide a crude shorthand description of an unwillingness to treat development problems with the urgency they deserve. But there is a second area in which political will is lacking and for which responsibility is more widely shared by developed and developing countries alike. It is the area of institutional reform. Both parties to the North–South dialogue conspire to slow the pace of reform or to block it altogether. Because they still harbour strong reservations about many of the elements of the new order, developed state governments are loath to support reforms which strengthen the UN's capacity to negotiate meaningfully regarding that new order. Because they attach so much importance to the institutional symbols of an egalitarian order, developing state governments have trouble supporting reforms which will modify and perhaps weaken those features of the UN which most reflect egalitarian values. In effect, the venue issues is still very much alive, festering just beneath the surface of superficial agreement between North and South that global negotiations on the NIEO are to take place in the UN.

Effective multilateral machinery for negotiating a new order is not a sufficient condition for the realization of that new order, but it is very probably a necessary condition. The existing machinery is not now adequate for this large and demanding assignment. It remains to be seen whether the principal parties to this critical dialogue over the future of the international economic order can develop a common institutional strategy.

Notes

1. Rothstein, Robert L. (1977). *The Weak in the World of the Strong* (New York: Columbia Univ. Press), 128.
2. For a thorough treatment of the role of the Non-Aligned Countries in the launching of the NIEO, see Jankowitsch, Odette and Sauvant, Karl P. (forthcoming). 'The Origins of the New International Economic Order: The Role of the Non-Aligned Countries' in Sauvant, Karl P., ed. (forthcoming). *The New International Economic Order: Changing Priorities on the International Agenda* (Oxford: Pergamon Press).
3. The programmes of action for the First and Second UN Development Decades, while fairly ambitious, are of a different order than the NIEO.
4. For example, the NIEO objectives of providing equitable access to the resources of the sea-bed and the ocean floor, and of adopting an integrated approach to commodities have both resulted in important (and controversial) proposals for new multilateral institutions.
5. For a brief discussion of the NIEO as a political manifesto, see Gregg, Robert W. (1979). 'The New International Economic Order as a Political Manifesto', *UNITAR News*, XI.
6. Weintraub, Sidney (1977). 'The Role of the United Nations in Economic Negotiations' in Kay, David A., ed. (1977). *The Changing United Nations* (New York: The Academy of Political Science), 96.
7. Gregg (1979) (*n. 5*), 22.

8.   This point is developed in Gosovic, Branislav and Ruggie, John G. (1976). 'On the Creation of a New International Economic Order: Issue Linkage and the Seventh Special Session of the UN General Assembly', *International Organization*, XXX. 2: 309–45.
9.   Perhaps West–South might be a more appropriate label.
10.   Bedjaoui, Mohammed (1979). *Towards a New International Economic Order* (Paris: UNESCO), 140.
11.   Ibid. 141.
12.   Ibid. 142.
13.   Boyd, Andrew (1976). 'The United Nations Thirty Years On', *International Affairs*, LII (Jan): 67–75.
14.   Weintraub (1977) (*n. 6*), 97.
15.   Ibid.
16.   Ibid. 98.
17.   GA Res. 3201 (S–VI) and 3202 (S–VI), 1 May 1974.
18.   GA Res. 3281 (XXIX), 12 Dec. 1974.
19.   See the analysis of Amuzegar, Jahingir (1977). 'Requiem for the North–South Conference', *Foreign Affairs*, LVI. 1: 136–59.
20.   GA Res. 32/174, 19 Dec. 1977.
21.   Ibid.
22.   See Gregg, Robert W. 'The IMF/IBRD Development Committee', unpublished.
23.   See UNCTAD Doc. TD/B/AC.30/2, 26 Oct. 1979, as well as the reports of the Secretary-General of UNCTAD to UNCTAD IV and UNCTAD V (TD/194 and TD/245, respectively).
24.   The debate over the weight to be accorded UN resolutions is presented in Bedjaoui, 1979 (*n. 10*), esp. Part Two, Ch. I.
25.   The role of the UN as an obstacle to the NIEO is discussed in Gregg, Robert W. (forthcoming, 1980). 'UN Decision-making Structures and Processes and the NIEO' in Laszio, Ervin and Kurtzmann, Joel, eds. (forthcoming, 1980). *Political and Institutional Issues of the New International Economic Order* (New York: Pergamon Press).
26.   For the most thorough dissection of UNCTAD's problems, see Rothstein, Robert (1979). *Global Bargaining* (Princeton, N.J.: Princeton Univ. Press). ECOSOC has not had a recent biographer, but its problems were quite extensively treated in the report of a group of experts on UN restructuring, United Nations (1975). *A New United Nations Structure for Global Economic Co-operation* (New York: United Nations – UN Publ. Sales No. E. 75.II.A.7). An earlier analysis of ECOSOC is contained in Sharp, Walter (1969). *The United Nations Economic and Social Council* (New York: Columbia Univ. Press).
27.   See the report of the *Ad Hoc* Committee on the Restructuring of the Economic and Social Sectors of the United Nations System, *Official Records of the General Assembly, Thirty-second Session, Supplement No. 34* (A/32/34) and *Supplement No. 34A* (A/32/34/Add. 1); see also UN General Assembly Resolution 32/197, 9 Jan. 1978. For a recent analysis of progress under restructuring see Renninger, John P. (1980). 'The Restructuring of the Economic and Social Sectors of the UN System: An Analysis.' Paper presented to the 21st Annual Convention of the International Studies Association, Los Angeles, 19–22 Mar. 1980.
28.   See the draft resolution submitted during the 34th General Assembly by Argentina and Jamaica, UN Doc. A/C.2/34/L.103, 3 Dec. 1979.
29.   Wionczek, Miguel S. (1979). 'The NIEO: A Diagnosis of Past Failures and the Prospects for the Future.' Paper presented to a joint conference of UNITAR and

the Centre for Economic and Social Studies of the Third World, Mexico City, 8–13 Jan. 1979.

30. Amuzegar (1977) (*n. 19*), 158.
31. Jordan, Robert S. and Wilson, Thomas W., Jr. (n.d.). 'North–South Relations and Conference Diplomacy; A Confusion of Postures', unpublished paper.
32. This analogy was suggested to the author by Diego Cordovez, Assistant Secretary-General of the UN, Office of Secretariat Services for Economic and Social Matters.
33. This point has been made by numerous participants in protracted negotiations within the UN system.
34. This sense of accomplishment with respect both to the ministerial character of the meeting and to its results, was manifest at the conclusion of the TDB meeting, and participants invariably commented on the importance of the preparatory work.
35. Rothstein (1979) (*n. 26*) for a detailed analysis of the group system at work.
36. Efforts to establish the Committee of the Whole and to define its mandate provide a good illustration of the problems of communication and co-ordination between the Group of 77 in New York and the Group of 77 in Geneva. The 'two' groups were conspicuously at odds over the COW.
37. Bedjaoui (1979) (*n. 10*), 167–74.
38. Ibid. 167.
39. The United States, in particular, incurred a considerable amount of ill will following UNCTAD IV and the adoption by consensus of resolution 93 (IV) on an Integrated Programme for Commodities, when it seemed to disassociate itself from that consensus during the Preparatory Meeting for the Negotiation of a Common Fund. The United States and other conservative 'hardliners' had made their dissatisfaction with the Common Fund clear at Nairobi, but they did join the consensus, signalling a support in principle about which they held serious reservations. It was not until much later that they really embraced the Common Fund. See Schechter, Michael G . (1979). 'The Common Fund: A Test Case for the New International Economic Order.' Paper presented at the Annual Conference of the International Studies Association/South in Atlanta, Georgia, 5 Oct. 1979.
40. Gregg (1979) (*n. 5*), 23. This same point with respect to the moderation displayed by the Group of 77 is also made in Sewell, John W. (1977). 'The United States and World Development, 1977' in Sewell, John W. and Staff of the Overseas Development Council (1977). *The United States and World Development: Agenda 1977* (New York: Praeger), 15–16, and in a variety of other analyses of the North–South dialogue.
41. Gregg (1979) (*n. 5*), 25–6.
42. GA Res. 32/197, 9 Jan. 1978.
43. United Nations (1975) (*n. 26*).
44. For the case for stronger technical support arrangements for the Group of 77, see Hall, Kenneth O. (1979). *The Group of 77 — Strengthening its Negotiating Capacity*. Third World Forum: Occasional Paper No. 11 (Nyon, Switzerland: Third World Forum).

5 THE SOCIALIST COUNTRIES AND THE NEW INTERNATIONAL ECONOMIC ORDER

JAN BIELAWSKI
School of Planning and Statistics, Warsaw

1. The Failure of International Development Policies

The past two decades have seen an unprecedented upsurge in international negotiations in the field of economics. In the initial phase these negotiations were largely geared towards economic integration on a regional basis. Economic problems of the developing countries becoming independent in the fifties and sixties proved to be of such scope and magnitude that they called for common action.

Multilateral negotiations on global economic issues constantly expanded and deepened, not least through the creation of the specialized machinery by which concrete topics could be tackled. Since the first session of UNCTAD, set up in 1964 with the active support of the socialist countries,[1] the developing countries have gradually realized that political independence did not by itself suffice and would have to be complemented by concrete measures to make their vulnerable economies more viable.

The Group of 77 founded at that time attracted many new members which, gradually influenced by the spectacular performance of the OPEC countries, developed a much greater cohesion, at least as far and as long as their major claims were concerned.

However, there is now widespread recognition that existing international development policies have largely failed to achieve their stated objectives. The hopes that were placed on the International Development Decade[2] have been essentially frustrated.

The strategy was based on two main assumptions: first, that the steady economic growth on the post-war pattern would continue within the market-economy countries and, secondly, that this expansion through mechanisms of trade, transfer of technology, and development finance would be transmitted to the developing countries. Accordingly, the key policy prescriptions of the strategy were focused on measures to be taken to improve access to markets, to promote the transfer of technology on fair conditions, and to achieve a substantial expansion in the flow of financial resources of development. The strategy stressed the quantitative targets, in particular those pertaining to the rate of economic growth, the development of foreign trade of the developing countries, and the flow of financial resources with a separate target for official development assistance.

Both underlying assumptions were completely invalidated in the seventies, which also saw the grave economic recession of the capitalist world, the breakdown of the Bretton Woods System, and other largely unforeseen developments and policies which created an atmosphere of uncertainty about the growth of international trade and world economy.

The central concept of growth transmission proved to be defective. For one thing, the growth rate of the capitalist countries slowed down considerably after 1973, and is likely to remain at a low level in the next decade. As a result, over the entire period of more than two decades of steady economic expansion in the developed areas, ending in the early 1970s, relatively few developing countries benefited from any substantial 'trickle down' of that expansion to their domestic economies.

For the decade 1970–80, the rate of growth of GNP for all developing countries would be about 5.5%, somewhat short of the 6% target established for the Second UN Development Decade. Moreover, for the non-oil exporting countries GNP growth is likely to average only 5.3% per annum. The performance of the least-developed countries is even poorer, as their GNP is expected to show an annual average growth rate of only 3.4%, i.e. no higher than the rate observed during the 1960s.[3]

The failure of international development policies is probably best illustrated by the meagre rate of the *per capita* economic growth in the seventies. In the group of low-income countries, which includes almost two-thirds of the people of the developing countries, the average is below 1.5%.[4] Widening disparities between the developing countries and the developed market-economy countries, must have been an inevitable outcome as shown by the following figures[5] (US prices and rates of exchange prevailing in 1970):

Economic Growth *per capita* 1960–75 (US prices)

	1960	1965	1970	1975
Developing countries	169	190	222	260
Developed market-economies	1988	2403	2846	3123

The ratio of about 12 to 1 between the average *per capita* GNP in the two groups of countries has remained nearly constant over the period, and the absolute gap can be expected to widen in the foreseeable future.

For the developing countries as a whole, the end of the seventies can thus be characterized as a period of inadequate economic growth associated *inter alia* with a loss of dynamism in export earnings and a continued insufficiency of long-term capital inflows.[6] In general, the economies of developing countries have remained highly vulnerable to external economic forces and other sources of instability.

Therefore, an upsurge of protectionist policies in the capitalist countries stemming from their protracted economic difficulties, mostly of a structural character, constitutes one of the most important factors explaining why 'it will be more difficult for the developing countries to expand their economies in the coming decade than it had been in the past 25 years'.[7] Consequently, the over-optimistic World Bank projections of the annual growth of GNP in the developing countries for 1975–85 have already been reduced from 5.7% to 5.2%.[8]

The second main weakness of the Strategy's approach was that it did not adequately take into consideration the fact that development is a multidimensional concept that encompasses various interrelated aspects of a broadly conceived economic and social policy which make up the qualitative side of the whole process.[9]

Thirdly, no sufficient account was taken of the fact that economic relations between developed and developing countries have come to be increasingly dominated by the activities of transnational corporations which control a substantial proportion of the foreign trade of the developing countries and have a major stake in their domestic production.

It can, then, be justifiably argued that the central concept on which the Strategy was founded corresponded only to a limited degree to the institutional realities of the world economy. As pointed out in the report of the Secretary-General of UNCTAD, the main weakness of the strategy as 'assessed from the viewpoint of its influence on the development process can be attributed basically to the fact that its underlying concepts and assumptions were not in keeping with the realities of the world economic system'.[10] It is also belatedly admitted that the existence of the Strategy has had no significant positive impact on the pace of development of the developing countries.[11]

The socialist countries have never shared the view that the economic growth of the developing countries will be automatically stimulated by economic growth in the developed capitalist states. Their official position is that the mechanism of the world capitalist economy 'consistently reproduces relationships of inequality and dependence'.[12]

2. In Search of a NIEO

The failure of the traditional economic order to solve the problems of poverty and economic backwardness and limited results of international development policies, still aggravated by the economic crisis which beset the capitalist world in the seventies with serious repercussions for the developing countries, imparted a sense of urgency to the need to reduce their dependence on the Western countries, and led to the convocation of the Sixth and Seventh Special Sessions of the General Assembly[13] in 1974 and 1975. Noting the continuity of negotiations and the direct links between UNCTAD and General Assembly sessions, the convocation of a large number of UN 'global' conferences as well as the Paris Conference on International Economic Co-operation (inaptly labelled as 'North–South dialogue'), one can legitimately assert that we are faced with a quasi-permanent international conference on development and related issues.[14]

Basic guidelines for changing the existing system of world economic relations have already been laid down by the UN General Assembly in two important decisions in 1974. One of them was the Declaration and the Programme of Action on the Establishment of a New International Economic Order[15] adopted in May by the Sixth Special Session of the General Assembly. The second was the Charter of Economic Rights and Duties of States[16] adopted a few months later by the Twenty-ninth (regular) Session of this body.

Prepared over a seventeen-month period by a working group of representatives from forty member-states, under the auspices of UNCTAD, the Charter spells out fifteen fundamentals which should govern international economic relations, *inter alia*:

Sovereign territorial integrity and political independence of states,
Sovereign equality of all states,
Non-aggression,
Non-intervention,
Mutual and equitable benefits,
Peaceful co-existence.

In turn, the Programme of Action consists of a set of urgent measures which need to be taken effectively by the international community. Although some capitalist countries, including the USA, the Federal Republic of Germany, Great Britain, and Japan, have expressed strong reservations on these documents and voted against their adoption, in the view of the vast majority of the UN member-states they provide a new framework for the UN's International Development Strategies.

The socialist countries' policies were based on the assumption that major changes have become a necessity since the existing mechanisms of international economic co-operation meet neither the interests of the developing countries nor those of the socialist ones and, therefore, no longer conform to the will of the majority of member-states of the UN.[17] The socialist countries, in voting for these documents, expressed their conviction that the progressive principles underlying a NIEO might, if implemented, bring about positive transformations in the world economy.[18]

At its Thirtieth Session held in July 1976, the Council for Mutual Economic Assistance (CMEA) noted in its final communiqué that, in accordance with their socialist principles, the CMEA member-states fully supported the legitimate aspirations of the developing countries for the achievement and strengthening of their political and economic independence and would resolutely contribute to the attainment of the goals set forth in the Declaration on the Establishment of a NIEO, in the Programme of Action and also in other UN decisions on this subject.[19]

In November 1976 the Political Advisory Committee of States Parties to the Warsaw Treaty declared that the participants in the meetings of the Committee were in favour of the restructuring of international economic relations on an equitable and democratic basis and on the basis of the equal rights of all states, large and small, socialist and capitalist, developed and developing. In this connection they supported the guiding principles of the programme for international co-operation proposed by the developing and non-aligned countries.[20] These views have been reiterated on several other occasions.[21]

The socialist countries' attitude towards a NIEO may be examined more broadly in terms of their views on positive transformations in the world economy which would reduce the existing inequilibria and disparities existing among the respective regions. Or, in a more restrictive way, in terms of their attitude towards global structural and institutional transformations proposed by the developing countries, and finally embodied, with rather minor corrections, in the UN documents.

In is interesting to note that the socialist countries, while supporting many ideas incorporated in the documents constituting the conceptual basis of a NIEO, nevertheless made it clear that a new order 'cannot be considered as the only strategy to be accomplished and subject to no change in the future'.[22] They rather preferred to speak about 'the restructuring of international economic relations on an equitable and democratic basis', thus establishing a link with the easing of international tension and asserting that 'we are only at the beginning of the process of restructuring international relations'.[23] They added, however, that 'the progressive resolutions of the Sixth and Seventh Sessions of the General Assembly and the adoption of the Charter of Economic Rights and Duties of States constitute important milestones on the road toward such a restructuring'.[24]

The main goals to be achieved in this process, as officially declared by the socialist countries during the Sixth Session of UNCTAD, are as follows:

Elimination of discrimination and any artificial obstacles in international trade, eradication of all manifestations of inequity, diktat, and exploitation in international economic relations;

Restructuring of the world economy and international trade to promote their future balanced development and, especially, to speed up the industrialization of economically backward regions and to raise the level of living of all peoples;

Consolidation of national sovereignty over natural and economic resources by restrictions on the activities of transnational corporations and the implementation, in conjunction with the restructuring of international economic relations, of progressive domestic changes in the developing countries themselves;

Modification of the existing inequitable machinery of international economic relations towards a democratization of supporting institutions.[25]

The concentration of the struggle for a NIEO on the political forums of universal organs and organizations, where the developing countries have an edge of an undisputed majority, entailed the need to keep up the pressure of the Third World on the other countries.[26] This tactic has already resulted in several concessions and could not be described as entirely unsuccessful. It is also implemented by multiplying the number of meetings devoted to development issues, setting up new bodies or reorientating their priorities, or linking the greatest possible amount of topics discussed within the UN system with a NIEO.

However, recent experience has shown that discussions at the political level have become too general and too repetitive, or even counterproductive, as shown by the deadlocked negotiations in the Preparatory Committee for the New International Development Strategy.[27] This is one of the major factors making for what R. Prebisch at the Fifth Session of UNCTAD in Manila called 'the dynamics of chaos'.

The assessment of the result of UNCTAD V[28] as well as of the last round of multilateral trade negotiations within GATT, indicates that Western countries have neither changed their positions on the basic economic objectives they pursue nor the instrumentalities of international economic organization they prefer. These countries, beset by recently less pronounced but still unmanageable problems such as unemployment and inflation, made a rather feeble attempt to meet the legitimate demands of the developing countries. More annoying still, the capitalist countries increasingly refer to their economic difficulties to reopen issues which appear to have been settled.[29]

It has by now become quite obvious that the mixture of hopes, often conflicting attitudes, and not infrequently half-hearted policies account for the modest progress in international negotiations on the establishment of a NIEO.[30] At the Fifth Session of UNCTAD, the socialist countries officially declared that 'despite the wide range of multilateral economic negotiations held under the auspices of the United Nations the basic requirements of the Declaration and the Program of Action on the Establishment of a New International Economic Order have, in fact, not yet been fulfilled'.[31]

3. The Conceptual Basis of a NIEO

The need to restore justice and equality in international relations constitutes the axiomatically adopted basis of a NIEO and a point of departure for all major claims of the developing countries.

The socialist countries fully recognize the necessity of a proper redistribution of income on a world scale, based on an international division of labour and radically changed patterns of international economic relations.[32] However, the evidently static approach implicit in the postulate of a mechanical transfer of resources is not likely to remedy the present world situation calling for long-term solutions as well as structural and social change. Without undermining the historical responsibility of the former colonial metropoles, the new order embracing all groups of countries cannot be based solely on redressing the injustice of the past, but first and foremost on a new set of principles ensuring universal and mutually beneficial co-operation, allowing for the special needs of the developing countries.

Paradoxically, a NIEO as outlined in the UN documents is not sufficiently future-orientated, as evidenced by its main premises:

— *international economic relations are more or less considered as a zero-sum game* where some partners stand to gain only at the expense of others; accordingly, the main thrust of a NIEO is geared towards income redistribution and a strengthening of the bargaining positions of the developing countries in a thus restructured order;
— the *origin of underdevelopment* lies in the *external conditions* of the Third World, which in turn implies that the way out of backwardness depends upon external factors;
— the *concept of a NIEO* is based on the *false North–South dichotomy*, which blurs the class contradictions of the contemporary world.

3.1. International Economic Relations as a Zero-sum game

In a bold oversimplification, the attainment of a NIEO is to be brought about by means of two groups of measures. The first group, bent on yielding immediate results, encompasses all forms of automatic transfer of resources from the developed countries to the developing countries. Here we can mention changes in terms of trade, indexation of prices, different forms of development or brain-drain taxes, compensation mechanisms and financial aid, especially official development assistance, and the like.

The second group of measures aims at structural changes designed to produce, in the long run, more lasting effects. If the former group of measures was intended to reduce the income gap, the latter was devised to lay firmer foundations for the change in the 'balance of forces'. From among a variety of measures we could mention here the crucial issues of the effective control over natural resources of the developing countries and their resolve to diminish their dependence on transnational corporations. This group also comprises restructuring of the institutional framework which governs the external economic relations of the developing countries and, in particular, changes in the decision-making process in international economic organizations which determine the 'rules of the game' of multilateral co-operation. The main task, however, is to change the place the developing countries occupy in the international division of labour, mainly by a greater diversification of their exports which is in turn contingent on the evolution of the production and consumption patterns.

The economic recession of the capitalist countries in the mid-seventies and its repercussions, such as waning results of the raw materials boom, brought about certain modifications in the developing countries' policies that focused their attention again on activities and mechanisms producing most immediate results.

It follows that the main weakness of a NIEO is that the postulated changes remain exclusively within the framework of the mechanism of the monopoly-dominated world market-economy. The strategy approach outlined above was an attempt to meet the development problem by a series of related measures within the existing institutional framework designed to provide the developing countries with an improved share of benefits of economic expansion in the developed countries. It is often claimed that the Declaration and the Programme of Action offer a fundamentally new approach to development issues, constituting an attempt to restructure the institutional framework itself.[33] But, on closer scrutiny, it becomes evident that 'restructuring' should not be taken at its face value. The main operative concept of the Declaration and the Programme of Action is that the restructuring can result only from increased bargaining power on the part of the developing countries.

Thus, the main contradiction of a NIEO as a collective proposal of the developing countries is that the existing mechanisms based on the existing balance of forces are supposed to change this very balance of forces to the advantage of one — although the most numerous — segment of the world's population. In other words, these countries are trying to dismantle the existing edifice of the present international economic order, rightly assuming that, as stated in the Declaration, it perpetuates a relationship of domination and generates a permanent disequilibrium and waste of resources. Simultaneously, the developing countries are picking up the same elements they had previously discarded and are making an effort to construct a new structure in which they would have much more room for themselves.

Hence, the division of benefits of international co-operation is not seen as an inevitable derivate of the operation of the market forces and other capitalist mechanisms which so far have had the greatest impact on the world economy. It is naïve then to assume that the basically profit-orientated market mechanism which served so well to deepen the economic plight of the developing countries, will prove remedial when a completely different approach is needed.

As a result, the measures considered and already implemented are often mere palliatives, mitigating but not eradicating international exploitation which is deeply rooted in the capitalist method of production itself. This, and other factors, such as the progressing differentiation within the Group of 77, account for the fact that 'the program for a NIEO sponsored by the developing nations, while embodying several progressive ideas, is not always consistent'.[34]

Needless to say, declare the socialist countries, the restructured international economic order, even when it has been attained, 'will not be such as to abolish the inherent defects of capitalism or to guarantee that the development process will be completely immune to their effects'.[35]

A concerted attack on world poverty as well as the stimulation of economic growth in the less-developed regions implies, among other things, structural changes in international relationships among all groups of countries. The socialist countries actively participate in all efforts to elaborate a new framework of institutions and rules to regulate international economic relations. It is imperative to eliminate practices which have been developed essentially by the capitalist countries and to replace them by progressive principles and working mechanisms derived from the global objectives of a NIEO.

While it is impossible to list a full range of demands that will be made upon international economic organizations in the process of building a NIEO, one of the underlying principles should be to encourage the joint-gain situation in which all parties are better off. In other words, the fundamental task for institutionalizing a NIEO is to ensure that this collective joint-gain aspect prevails in international co-operation.

Although it is still difficult to foresee to what extent a major constitutional restructuring of international economic organization will be both necessary and feasible, future efforts should not lead to further institutional proliferation but rather be conducive to adaptations for a better co-ordination of these forms of state behaviour and policies that are essential for the successful management of interdependence.

Acknowledging the obvious truth that the economic interdependence among countries has become a reality which is expressed in increased international co-operation, there are no grounds to use this term, as is often done in the UN forum, solely in a positive sense, i.e. implying that greater interdependence constitutes a fundamental force for better relations among nations. Such oversimplistic application of much more sophisticated theories blurs the obvious fact that interdependence, understood both as a process and an actual state of affairs, is a two-edged sword involving costs as well as benefits.

The costs are mainly connected with the way of functioning of the market-economy countries. They have in fact, helped to release international economic forces which they, like the Wizard's Apprentice, can no longer effectively control. The experience of most of the developing countries has also shown that the benefits, where they can be obtained, are not shared equally; and the greater economic interdependence may indeed be politically and socially detrimental. Thus, 'for most developing countries, their interdependence with developed countries has been a one-sided or asymmetrical relationship characterized by a condition of structural dependence'.[36]

The socialist countries, convinced that the inequality, injustice, domination, and dependence in international relations is brought about by the exploitative character of the capitalist system, reject all attempts to create linkages between 'growing economic interdependence' and 'equal responsibility' of all members of the international community for the state of the world economy.

3.2. External Conditions of Development

Secondly, overemphasis on the external conditions based on a *dependencia* school of thinking leads to the acknowledgement of the power position of the developed capitalist countries which renders ineffective efforts to introduce the structural changes in the world economy and international economic relations. There is a need to stop the development of, and pose an alternative to, the emerging neo-colonial pattern of division of labour, the signs of which are reflected primarily by the shifts in the reallocation and investment policy of international capital.[37]

A NIEO implemented, as the capitalist countries see it, would ensure their access to energy and raw materials, assert their monopoly of technological innovation, consolidate the neo-colonialist distribution of labour and the system of economic ties based on the market mechanisms. Eventually, it would also produce a new type of dependence, the essence of which is that developing countries would no longer be directly subordinated to a particular capitalist economy, but they would continue to depend on the developed capitalist world as a whole.[38] The socialist countries declared that the restructuring of international economic relations based on 'justice and equal rights can become an important factor in accelerating the growth of the developing countries. Nevertheless, their economic progress depends primarily on their own efforts including the mobilization of their internal resources.'[39]

The group of socialist states ('D' in UNCTAD) believes that the external assistance should be complemented with the mobilization of internal resources[40] and carrying out of the progressive socio-economic reforms which might prove decisive in breaking the vicious circle of poverty.[41] Therefore, aid should be rendered so as to promote maximally the indigenous development, making it possible for the developing countries to become, in the long run, genuinely economically independent.[42]

It goes without saying, that internal and international development strategies should be consistent and mutually supportive. It is also self-evident that development is inseparable from social progress since, in contrast to economic growth, it denotes by definition a qualitative change. Subscribing to this philosophy, the socialist countries have time and again emphasized that the struggle for greater equity among states would be greatly strengthened by all measures leading to greater equity also within their societies.

Accordingly, the developing countries should be encouraged to take the road to independent development, eliminating outmoded social relationships, re-establishing and strengthening national sovereignty over their national resources and creating independent national economies.[43] Although many developing countries have not attached sufficient importance to a 'redistribution with growth' development strategy, there is a marked shift of emphasis in favour of measures designed to promote the accelerated development of the developing countries on the basis of the principle of self-reliance.[44]

The socialist countries 'view with sympathy the efforts of developing countries to establish cooperation among themselves in such spheres as trade, production and finance'.[45] They also believe that 'the strengthening and intensification of mutual cooperation among developing countries would not lead to the isolation of those countries, but on the contrary, encourage the creation of new possibilities for the expansion of their trade and economic cooperation with other groups of countries . . .'.[46]

The undertones of certain apprehensions are connected with the so-called 'disassociative policies' often advocated as likely to bring about patterns of development which would be more in keeping with the basic needs of the people and escaping the fatality of *dependencia*. It is far from certain, however, that the proposed 'de-linking' would by itself encourage the desired policies. Social change seems to depend on the nature and structure of power which, as the socialist countries see it, should be examined in terms of class struggle, rather than on the degree of involvement of a given economy in the international division of labour.

Increasing doubts are being expressed about the so-called 'basic needs strategy', which is now considered and apparently orientated to involve certain tasks towards self-evident goals, such as sufficient nutrition, housing, medical care, etc. Apart from the difficulties involved in defining the basic needs, such a 'charity scheme' entails the risk of creating an 'anthropological garden'[47] where the poor as the vast majority could be maintained just above the physical survival line, while the affluent minority could preserve their privileges at little cost. Such a satisfaction of needs would be neither indigenous nor authentic, and serving as a pretext for non-development it could be easily perpetuated.

Development as a major process in the international system cannot be divorced from the over-all political setting. It is self-evident that the formulation and implementation of any far-reaching programmes for restructuring of international economic relations are conceivable only in peace and an atmosphere of genuine trust in relations between states, including countries with different economic and social systems and countries at different levels of development.

The socialist countries have always adhered to the principle that it is only under conditions of *détente*, maintenance of peace, the strengthening of international security, and progress in the field of disarmament that international economic co-operation can be successfuly developed in the interest of all states.[48] However, without coupling political *détente* with military *détente*, further progress towards major structural changes in international economic relations could be extremely difficult, if not entirely impossible. The socialist countries have always held that progress towards general and complete disarmament should release substantial resources to be utilized for the purpose of economic and social development of developing countries. Fully aware that the arms race is incompatible with a NIEO, as it was also stressed by the Special Session of the General Assembly, the socialist countries actively support all efforts 'to beat the swords into ploughshares' which should become an integral part of the New International Development Strategy.

3.3. North–South Dichotomy

Seen in retrospect, a NIEO is by no means an accomplished concept, but rather an evolving body of ideas and mechanisms which are believed to put them into practice. Simultaneously, one should not overlook the fact that the struggle for more just and equitable international economic relations had started much earlier than the term 'a NIEO' was coined.

Accordingly, the socialist countries' support for a NIEO should be seen in a longer perspective than their relentless struggle against colonialism, neo-colonialism, foreign aggression and occupation, racism and apartheid, and all forms of foreign domination and exploitation. The well-known initiatives of the socialist countries, which resulted among other things in a number of UN resolutions, accelerated the process of decolonization. The changing balance of forces due to the very existence and growing strength of the socialist countries, their active support for the newly emerging nations, already independent or still struggling for their national liberation, paved the way for many actions undertaken at a later stage by the developing countries. It is also undeniable that states of the socialist community have helped move the question of restructuring international relations from the level of theoretical discussion to one of practical action.[49]

The socialist countries adhere to the notion that the crisis of the traditional order stems not only from the contradictions among the developed and the developing countries and, consequently, calls for more complex solutions than only those offered by a NIEO. Their support for a NIEO then, is not without certain reservations, the more so as they refuse to be treated on par with the capitalist countries. The socialist countries consider it essential that the reshaping of international economic relations can in no way be based on the arbitrary division of countries into North and South regardless of their socio-economic systems.

In a joint statement of the socialist countries attention is drawn to the fact that there are, and can be, no grounds for holding the socialist countries responsible either for the consequences of colonialism or for the harmful effects on the developing countries of the inequality which still exists in economic relations, or for the heavy burden resulting from the crisis of the capitalist economy.[50]

The socialist states should not be placed indiscriminately on the same footing with imperialist powers and former colonial metropolies because of the contrastingly dissimilar historic responsibility and because of their present distinctly different attitude to the Third World's struggle for full political and economic independence. The development of international economic relations convincingly demonstrates that there exists in the world not only two opposing economic and social systems but also two fundamentally different bases for the conduct of commercial and economic relations with the developing countries.[51] It should be emphasized that the socialist countries base their co-operation with the developing countries on a 'new kind of economic relations' which 'from the outset have been founded on equality, respect for sovereignty, mutual advantage, non-interference in internal affairs, and support for the developing countries' efforts to overcome their backwardness'.[52]

It should not be left unmentioned that the developing countries are not the only victims of the established international order as the socialist countries are also subject to discriminations in many important fields, quite often due to political considerations. It is, therefore, completely unfounded for the developing countries to make the same demands in relation to both capitalist and socialist countries.

The basic philosophy behind the socialist countries' attitude towards a NIEO is that a new order, if global by nature, must be composed of principles and translated into practical actions which would serve the interest of all states irrespective of any differences in political, economic, and social systems.

Moreover, the UN decisions alone do not predetermine the feasibility of implementing a NIEO which depends largely on the measure of solidarity between the developing and socialist countries. The dispassionate analysis of the economic goals and policies pursued by these two groups of countries reveals unambiguously the convergence of their basic interests which, as may be added, has found an explicit reflection in the UN long-term voting patterns.

As rightly pointed out by J. Pajestka and J. Kulig, the socialist countries have no vested interests in the developing countries, they are ideologically inclined to support the objectives of greater quality and justice for all, they represent an alternative outlet for trade and co-operation of the developing countries, and they have no ties of solidarity with existing capitalist market arrangements, including the transnational corporations.[53]

Following this line of argument, a NIEO should be based on non-exploitative relationships and be conducive to the expansion of co-operation between all countries, whether in the North–South or East–West context, by an elimination of all vestiges of discrimination in trade and other fields.

4. The Socialist Countries as Partners in Co-operation[54]

Six years have elasped since the members of the UN solemnly proclaimed their determination to work urgently for the establishment of a NIEO. The main lesson of the implementation process is that further progress depends primarily on the pace of progressive change in the world as well as on the degree of political resolve both in the developed and developing countries to participate in global and regional actions leading to common solutions.

Now that we are on the threshhold of the Third UN Development Decade and about to adopt the International Development Strategy for the Eighties, the international community is faced with the necessity of formulating a new, much more effective system of international co-operation. This should not signify the departure from the already adopted principles, as the General Assembly has already decided that the New International Development Strategy 'should be formulated within the framework of the New International Economic Order'.[55] Conversely, the adoption of this strategy may become a step forward on the way towards real democratization of international economic relations, provided it confirms and strengthens, instead of diluting, the political content of earlier UN decisions.[56]

It is also important that the new strategy should include effective provisions for intensifying trade and economic co-operation among countries having different economic and social systems and particularly between the socialist countries and the developing countries.[57] As pointed out by the UNCTAD secretariat, the socialist countries can play a major part in the process of structural change in the international division of labour and make an important contribution to the restructuring of international economic relations.[58]

The socialist countries declared that their 'policy with regard to economic co-operation with the developing countries remains unchanged. Its main goal is to assist those countries in their efforts to solve their economic development problems and strengthen their economic independence.'[59] In line with this policy, the socialist countries have been undertaking measures to put into effect, both at home[60] and internationally, many UN recommendations connected with a NIEO.

It is often conveniently forgotten that the countries of the socialist community already provide a considerable amount of economic assistance to the developing countries, which utilizes mechanisms of co-operation corresponding to the social and economic structures of these countries and has proved their effectiveness.[61] In the planned economies of the socialist countries, sometimes called 'supply determined', the productive capacities are fully utilized which, in contrast to the market economies, makes it unnecessary to supplement the insufficient or dwindling domestic demand by external stimuli.

Seen in this context the pattern of economic relations between the socialist countries and the developing countries should not be based mainly on the concept of resource transfer which in the former group of countries is tantamount to a real sacrifice, be it in terms of investment or consumption.[62] Accordingly, the optimal model of these relations should lead to mutual long-term structural adjustments through trade and other forms of economic co-operation.

The socialist countries strongly advocate the concept of the all-round industrialization which constituted the main pillar of their own reconstruction and economic growth.[63] They are trying to become important 'partners in development' by assisting in the setting-up of new productive capacities and infrastructural facilities in the less-developed regions. The CMEA representative said during the Thirty-third Session of the General Assembly that the member countries of the Council provided assistance on mutually beneficial terms to 76 developing countries and had col loborated in some 4,000 co-operative projects in the developing countries, 2,800 of which have already been completed.

The assistance rendered by the CMEA countries to the developing countries is channelled primarily to the public sectors of these countries' economies. First of all to the branches of iron and steel, non-ferrous metallurgy, power industry, engineering and metal working, chemical industry, oil extraction and oil processing, transport and communication, light and food industry, production of constructional materials, and the like.[64] The co-operation of several socialist countries in rendering economic and technical assistance to developing countries has recently been gaining ground. For example, by the mid-seventies the organizations of several CMEA member-countries were jointly constructing 30 projects in Egypt, 12 in Iraq, 13 in India, 15 in Guinea, etc.

By doing so, the socialist countries enhance the ability of the developing countries to increase their productive capacity and introduce changes in productive structures, thus helping them to attain the projected growth rates as well as reduce their dependence on the capitalist countries, particularly on former colonial metropolies.

It is equally obvious that changes in productive structures are inseparably linked with the development of foreign trade, which is a critical constraint for many if not most of the developing countries.[65] The level of trade between the socialist countries and the developing countries is still rather low, mainly because of historical reasons. However, in quantitative terms, trade between the two groups of countries has increased substantially in recent years. Taken as a whole, this flow of trade has been constantly growing at high rates, exceeding the rates of expansion of both East–West trade and intra-CMEA trade. In the two-year period 1976–77, East–West trade increased by 14.9% and intra-CMEA trade by 24.9%, whereas trade between the developing countries and the socialist countries went up by 27.6%.[66]

A specific feature of trade between the socialist countries and the developing countries is its fairly high concentration on twenty to twenty-five developing countries which accounted for about 90% of the over-all turnover. There is also a certain imbalance in this trade as exports of the socialist countries to the developing countries registered an increase of 9% in 1978 while imports attained the rate of 3%.[67] This, however, is brought about mainly by large deliveries of capital goods on credit terms under various agreements on economic, technical, and scientific co-operation that to a large extent account for the high dynamics of this trade.[68]

By 1978 the network of such agreements, which included all the socialist countries and about eighty developing countries, had covered approximately 90% of the over-all turnover.[69] For example, Poland maintains trade relations with nearly all developing countries and it has signed trade agreements with fifty-one of them. Eighteen countries signed agreements on long-term economic co-operation with Poland, while agreements on scientific and technical co-operation have been signed with as many as forty-two developing countries.[70]

Further progress in socialist integration should create new stimuli for the expansion of co-operation with the developing countries.[71] In the process of co-ordinating the national economic plans of the CMEA member-countries, and especially in co-ordinating their national investment plans, due consideration is being given to the trade needs of the developing countries as envisaged by resolution 95/IV of UNCTAD.[72] The implementation of both the Concerted Plan for Multilateral Integration Measures and long-term joint co-operation programmes will require further intensification of the external relations of the CMEA member-countries including expansion and diversification of imports from the developing countries.

Referring again to Poland, the growth of its trade with the developing countries should result in an increase of their share in Poland's total trade to about 12–14% in 1990. Assuming that the volume of trade of the developing countries will increase at a rate of 6% annually, Poland's share in it should grow from 0.33% in 1977 to approximately 0.7% in 1990. The consequence of this growth will be an increase in the share of manufactures in Polish imports from developing countries from 17.4% in 1977 to some 30% in 1990.[73]

The more advanced stage of the socialist integration facilitated also new forms of multilateral co-operation between the CMEA countries and the developing countries, which included also tripartite industrial co-operation, i.e. projects in which an enterprise from the developing countries takes an active part together with enterprises from socialist and market-economy countries. By the middle of 1975 about 140 agreements on tripartite industrial co-operation were registered by the UNCTAD secretariat, involving 33 developing countries, 7 socialist countries, and 13 market-economy countries. Hungary and Poland have been the most active participants, accounting for more than half of the total involvement of the socialist countries.

Industrialization and trade are probably the most important, but certainly not the only, areas of broad economic co-operation between the socialist countries and developing countries in the forthcoming Third UN Development Decade.[74] There are good prospects for future co-operation between these countries due to:

— their mutual interest in developing economic relations on a stable and equitable basis, possibly with the elements of planning;
— similar perceptions of the role that foreign trade should play in their increasingly complementary economies;
— the jointly recognized need to restructure the existing international economic relations in the process of establishing a NIEO;
— fast rate of growth of the socialist countries[75] and their passing on to the intensive growth patterns;
— effects of industrialization in the developing countries;
— passing on to the more advanced forms of economic co-operation as both groups of countries engage themselves more actively in the international division of labour and gain experience in their mutual relations;
— positive impact of the socialist countries' integration on their co-operation with the developing countries.

Notes

1. See Chossudovsky, E. M. (1969). 'UNCTAD and Co-existence Part one — From Geneva to New Dehli.' *Co-existence* VI. 1: 97–118.
2. Formulated pursuant to GA Res. 2626 (XXV), 24 Oct. 1970.
3. UNCTAD. *Interdependence of Problems of Trade, Development Finance and the International Monetary System.* UN Doc. TD/B/756 (14 Sept. 1979), 9.

4. ECOSOC, Committee for Development Planning. *Report on the Fifteenth Session* (26 Mar. - 5 Apr. 1979). UN Doc. E/1979/37, 3.
5. ECOSOC *Development Trends since 1960 and their Implications for a New International Development Strategy*. UN Doc. E/AC. 54/L98 (13 Feb. 1978), 8.
6. ECOSOC. *World Economic Survey, 1978*. UN Doc, E/1979/63/Add. 1 (4 May 1979), 1
7. World Bank (1978). *World Bank Annual Report 1978*. (Washington, D.C.: World Bank), 9.
8. World Bank (1979). *World Development Report 1979*. (Washington, D.C.: World Bank), 3–4.
9. In his *Address to the Board of Governors* (Belgrade, 2 Oct. 1979; mimeo, 6) the President of the World Bank, Robert S. McNamara, stated that 'had the DD II strategy given more direct emphasis to reducing absolute poverty these and other quality of life factors could have improved substantially more than they did'. In this connection, the fundamental difference in the understanding and interpretation of the term 'quality' of development should be noted when used in capitalist and socialist countries, reflecting the basic differences in principles underlying their respective socio-economic systems.
10. UNCTAD. *The Evolution of a Viable International Development Strategy*. Report by the Secretary-General of UNCTAD. UN Doc. TD/B/642 (30 Mar. 1977), 2.
11. 'The Conceptual Framework for a New International Development Strategy.' *Trade and Development* 1 (Spring 1979): 83.
12. Joint Statement submitted by the Byelorussian SSR, Czechoslovakia, the German Democratic Republic, Hungary, Mongolia, Poland, the Ukrainian SSR, and the Union of Soviet Socialist Republics. UNCTAD, Trade and Development Board, OR, 8th Special Session (25 Apr. – 4 May 1977), Agreed Conclusions and Decisions.
13. See United Nations (1975). *The Seventh Special Session of the General Assembly. Issues and Background* (New York: UN).
14. During the last regular ECOSOC session in 1979, several Western countries expressed the view that there are too many international meetings devoted to economic and social questions. This 'boredom of the West' reflects the stiffening of the negotiating stance of the capitalist countries in their dialogue with the Group of 77, already visible during UNCTAD V.
15. *Declaration on the Establishment of a New International Economic Order* (GA Res. 3201 (S-VI), 1 May 1974) and *Programme of Action on the Establishment of a New International Economic Order* (GA Res. 3202 (S-VI), 1 May 1974).
16. *Charter of Economic Rights and Duties of States* (GA Res. 3281 (XXIX), 12 Dec. 1974).
17. The author attempts in this section to present the position of the socialist countries based on joint statements, communiqués, etc., both within and outside the UN. However, views expressed here are strictly personal and should not be attributed to any institution or government, unless otherwise indicated.
18. In this context, the principle of full and permanent sovereignty over natural resources, including the right of nationalization, is of particular importance.
19. *Pravda*, 10 July 1976; see also CMEA (1977). *Survey of CMEA Activities in 1976* (Moscow: CMEA Secretariat), 836.
20. See the declaration of the WTO member-states at the meeting of the Political Consultative Committee, Bucharest, 25–6 Nov. 1976, *New Times* (Moscow) 49 (Nov. 1976): 26.
21. For the official attitude of the socialist countries towards the UN recommendations on development see *Joint Statement* at the Twenty-fifth and Twenty-eighth Sessions of the GA (GAOR XXV, Annexes, agenda item 42). See also a

Statement on the restructuring of international economic relations circulated by the USSR during the Thirty-first Session and fully supported also by other socialist countries (UN Doc. A/C.2/31/2 and UN Doc. A/31/483). *Joint Statements* by socialist countries were also considered by UNCTAD's Trade and the Development Board at its Sixth and Eighth Special Sessions (OR S–VI, Agreed Conclusion 129, Annex C, UN Doc. TD/B/548 and OR S–VIII, Agreed Conclusions and Decisions, Supp. 1, UN Doc. TD/B/669). As an important policy document, see the *Joint Statement* by socialist countries at the Fourth UNCTAD Session (UN Doc. TD/211, 28 May 1976). A *Joint Statement* at the Fifth UNCTAD Session, 1979, *Evaluation of the World Trade and Economic Situation and Consideration of Issues, Policies and Appropriate Measures to Facilitate Structural Change in the International Economy* took into account 'the interrelationships of the problems in the areas of trade, development, money and finance with a view to attaining the establishment of a new international economic order and bearing in mind the further evolution that may be needed in the rules and principles governing international economic relations and UNCTAD's necessary contribution to a New International Development Strategy for the Third United Nations Development Decade' (UN Doc. TD/249, 19 Apr. 1979).

22. See the letter *Deepening and Consolidation of International Détente and Prevention of the Danger of Nuclear War* of the Minister of Foreign Affairs of the USSR to the Secretary-General (UN Doc. A/32/242).

23. Ibid.

24. *Joint Statement* (*n. 21*), UN Doc. TD/211, 1–2.

25. *Joint Statement* (*n. 21*), UN Doc. TD/241, 9.

26. The Group of 77 decided on a collective negotiating strategy for UNCTAD V (1979), see the *Arusha Programme for Collective Self-Reliance and Framework for Negotiations* (UN Doc. TD/236).

27. General Assembly, Preparatory Committee for the New International Development Strategy. *Report of the First Session*. UN Doc. A/34/44, 30 May 1979.

28. The UN Secretary-General in his Report on the Work of the Organization stated that the results of the Fifth Session of UNCTAD were 'limited and disappointing'. *United Nations Press Release*, 56/54/387, 14 Sept. 1979.

29. Especially GA Res. 33/193 on *Preparations for an International Development Strategy for the Third United Nations Development Decade* (UN Doc. A/33/527).

30. A recent study of the UNCTAD secretariat concludes 'Progress so far towards the establishment of the NIEO has been very limited'. UNCTAD. *Assessment of the Progress Made Towards the Establishment of the New International Economic Order*. UN Doc. TD/B/757, 25 Sept. 1979.

31. *Joint Statement* (*n. 21*), UN Doc. TD/249, 2.

32. See Perczynski, M. (1979). 'Ideas and Reality: New International Economic Order.' *New Perspectives 2* (1979).

33. According to the UNCTAD secretariat 'the essential difference between the two concepts arises in their treatment of the institutional framework governing international economic relations'. UN Doc. TD/B/757, 2.

34. Obminsky, E. (1978). *Co-operation on an Equitable Basis. The Soviet Viewpoint. Problems of Restructuring International Economic Relations*. (Moscow. Novosti Press Agency Publ. House), 3.

35. *Joint Statement*, (*n. 21*), UN Doc. TD/249, 9.

36. 'The Conceptual Framework . . .' (*n. 11*), 9.

37. Kosma, F. (1976). 'On the Possibilities of Creating a New World Economic Order.' *Acta Economica*, XVI. 3–4: 234.

38. That is why the developing countries '. . . are seriously concerned at the fact that the creation within the framework of the capitalist international division

of labour of new, export-oriented manufacturing capacity in developing countries is not only not helping to strengthen those countries' economic independence, but it is in fact binding them still more closely to capitalism's main industrial centres'. *Joint Statement* (*n. 21*), UN Doc. TD/249, 3–4.

39. *Joint Statement* (*n. 21*), UN Doc. TD/B/668 7.
40. In their *Joint Statement* (*n. 21*), UN Doc. TB/211, 9, the socialist countries expressed their view 'that acceleration of the economic development of the developing countries depends above all on the mobilization of their own internal resources, but that the inflow of foreign financial resources into the developing countries is an additional means to this end'.
41. The experience of the socialist countries is referred to in the *Joint Statement*, (*n. 21*) UN Doc. TD/211, 3, as evidence that 'the decisive factors in this process are: the full mobilization of domestic resources; the introduction of efficient planning of the national economy, industrialization, agrarian reform, progressive economic legislation; and the development of international co-operation on a basis of equality'.
42. Delegations of nine socialist countries emphasized during the Thirty-first GA Session that their assistance to developing countries is provided 'in conformity with the socialist system and the interests of the developing countries themselves. By this we mean genuine assistance and not economic activities . . . which are in fact related to the promotion of foreign private capital and are aimed at maintaining economic backwardness and intensifying the policy of the further exploitation of the natural and human resources of the developing countries.' See UN Doc. A/31/483/Annex, 2.
43. A valuable guideline is a resolution adopted during the Thirty-third GA Session (UN Doc. A/33/446/Add. 1, 9) stressing that the important role of the public sector should be taken into account in proposals for the New International Development Strategy.
44. See UNCTAD. *Economic Co-operation Among Developing Countries: Priority Areas for Action — Issues and Approaches*. UN Doc. TD/244.
45. *Joint Statement* (*n. 21*), UN Doc. TD/211, 26.
46. Ibid. 27.
47. Streeten, P. B. (1978). 'Basic Needs and the NIEO. Must there be a Conflict?' *Development Forum*, VI. 5 (June).
48. UN Doc. A/31/483/Annex, 1. The best-known initiative is the Soviet proposal concerning the reduction of military budgets of permanent member-states of the Security Council by 10% and a transfer of funds thus saved to development tasks.
49. Jegorov, J. (1979). 'Path to the NIEO.' *Development Forum* (Aug./Sept).
50. *Joint Statement* (*n. 42*), UN Doc. A/31/483/Annex, 2.
51. *Joint Statement* (*n. 21*), 5.
52. Ibid. 5.
53. Pajestka, J. and Kulig, J. (1979). 'The Socialist Countries of Eastern Europe and the New International Economic Order.' *Trade and Development* 1 (Spring): 72.
54. The socialist countries of Eastern Europe or, where indicated, CMEA member-states.
55. GA Res. 33/193.
56. In discussions on basic elements to be included in the preamble of the Strategy, socialist countries objected to the omission of the following elements: control over the activities of transnational corporations, promoting industrialization, strengthening public sector, training national personnel, mobilization of broad masses for the implementation of national development programmes. See UN Doc. A/34/44 (Part II), 13.

57. According to the Declaration on the NIEO, the NIEO should be based *inter alia* on 'common interest and co-operation among all states, irrespective of their economic and social systems'.

58. *Contribution of UNCTAD to the Preparation of the New International Development Strategy.* UN Doc. TD/B/758, 20 Sept. 1979, 11.

59. *Joint Statement (n. 21),* UN Doc. TD/211, 29.

60. Commenting upon the implementation of the Charter of Economic Rights and Duties, the Soviet Union pointed out the relevance of Articles 28 and 29 of its new Constitution, adopted in October 1977, ECOSOC. *Implementation of the Charter of Economic Rights and Duties of States.* UN Doc E/1979/74, 19 June 1979, 2.

61. As pointed out by the Ukrainian SSR, UN Doc. E/1979/74 *(n. 60),* 15.

62. For an elaboration see Pajestka and Kuhlig (1979) *(n. 53),* 72–3.

63. Poland's representative stated in the Preparatory Committee for the New International Development Strategy that 'industrialization was the main force in the creation of economic and social development in any state, at any stage of its growth'. UN Doc. A/34/44 (Part II)/Add. 1, 4.

64. See CMEA (1979). *Council for Mutual Economic Assistance. 30 Years.* (Moscow: CMEA Secretariat), 35.

65. The socialist countries consider the intensification of protectionism by the developed market-economies as a negative effect for the development of international trade as a whole, and in view of the interdependence of world-wide trade flows also as adversely affecting trade between the socialist countries and developing countries. See *Protectionism: Trends and Short-term and Long-term Policies and Actions Needed to Deal with the Problem.* Document submitted by the Byelorussian SSR, Bulgaria, Czechoslovakia, the GDR, Hungary, Mongolia, Poland, the Ukrainian SSR, and the USSR. UN Doc. TD/257 (14 May (1979), 257.

66. *Trade Relations Among Countries having Different Economic and Social Systems.* UN Doc. TD/243 (May 1979), 5.

67. UN Doc. TD/B/756, 17.

68. *Le mécanisme de co-operation entre pays avec des systèmes économiques et sociaux différentes.* UN Doc. TD/243/Supp. 3 May 1979.

69. UN Doc. TD/B/754, 15.

70. For further elaboration see Karas, A. (1979). 'The Third World — An Important Area for Co-operation.' *Polish Foreign Trade* (June).

71. A detailed description of CMEA activities in respective fields in CMEA (1979). *Collected Reports on Various Activities of Bodies of the CMEA in 1978* (Moscow: CMEA Secretariat).

72. Connections between investment decisions in socialist countries and foreign trade and other forms of international co-operation are analysed by Kotynski, J. (1977). 'Macro-Economic Decisions Concerning the Level and Financing of Investments' in *Factors of Growth and Investment Policies: An International Approach.* UN Doc. ECE/EC.AD, 15 July 1977.

73. *Prospects in Trade with the Socialist Countries of Eastern Europe: Poland, Policies, Developments and Institutional Framework.* Study prepared by B. Wojciechowski, UN Doc. TD/B/749, 27.

74. UNCTAD. 'Economic Co-operation between Socialist Countries of Eastern Europe and Development Countries.' *UNCTAD Report Series 3* (June 1978).

75. UN experts project growth rates for the socialist countries of Eastern Europe of 4.7–5.2% for the 1980s and 4.0–4.7% for the 1990s. A certain deceleration of growth rates is explained mainly by a tendency towards higher capital/output ratios (due largely to rising costs of developing mineral resources) and slower growth of labour force (mainly due to demographic factors).

6 NIEO: A STRATEGY WITHOUT AN ALTERNATIVE?

RAJENDRA CHANDISINGH
University of Hamburg/Georgetown, Guyana

*Es ist aber eben nicht so was Unerhörtes, dass nach langer Bear-
beitung einer Wissenschaft, wenn man wunder denkt, wie weit man
schon darin gekommen sei, endlich sich jemand die Frage einfallen
lässt: ob und wie überhaupt eine solche Wissenschaft möglich sei.
Denn die menschliche Vernunft ist so baulustig, dass sie mehrmalen
schon den Turm aufgeführt, hernach aber wieder abgetragen hat, um
zu sehen, wie das Fundament desselben wohl beschaffen sein möchte.
Es ist niemals zu spät, vernünftig und weise zu werden; es ist aber
jederzeit schwerer, wenn die Einsicht spät kommt, sie in Gang zu brigen.
(Kant, Prolegomena.)*

1. Introduction

Contrary to George Abbott's claim that 'very little is now heard of NIEO'[1]
a great deal continues to be talked about it and the so-called North–South
Dialogue, as the recent report by the Independent Commission on International Development Issues (the Brandt Commission) demonstrates.[2]
It is not talk of NIEO which is not heard today, but rather optimistic
talk, which is not, and the reasons are not hard to find. The great thrust
of the Group of 77 and the Non-Aligned Movement launched in 1974
has yielded precious little in concrete terms, and the problems of world
poverty remain just as acute. The 1980 UNIDO Conference in Delhi
showed the reluctance on the part of the Developed Market Economics
(DMEs) to provide the hefty transfer of resources demanded by the Group
of 77. On the resolution proposed by the Group of 77 calling for the
setting up of a US$3 million fund to help the Third World, there was a
majority in favour of 4:1 (83 votes for and 22 against). Unfortunately, those
voting against were those expected to make the funds available, i.e. the
members of OECD. Ahmed Gezal of Tunisia, Chairman of the Group of
77, is reported to have commented that the industrialized countries had
played a consistently negative role at the Conference.[3]

Of course, discussions about NIEO can be conducted in many different ways, but not all of them equally fruitful. In his review article John White suggests that NIEO is a specific set of propositions, serious discussion of which must meet 'at least three tests':[4] (1) discussion must begin from the basic texts containing the terms of reference; (2) discussion should be limited to the agenda 'trade and commodities; financial transfers and monetary reform; science and technology; industrialization and trans-national enterprises; and collective self-reliance'; and (3) 'since the NIEO is a programme of action, one looks for some discussion of strategy'.

Indeed, all of these and more are worthy objects of intellectual effort. There is nothing disreputable in tracing the history of the development of the ideas expressed in NIEO, the role played by the various inter-national organizations in establishing the legal and moral basis of the proposals, in examining the technical details in each of the concrete proposals, etc. This is not only useful but necessary. But when discussion has proceeded as intensively as that on NIEO has, and after we have had the concrete experience of some 6 years, and the slim achievements of these years, it may also be necessary to return to the basis of NIEO and ask again, what kind of NIEO is possible and how will it be achieved, for clearly the thrust of 1974/5 has not fulfilled its expectations. If this exercise is undertaken we are then not limited to accepting the terms of reference as pre-given and not forced to build an edifice on shifting sand. We may begin by questioning the terms of reference themselves and the assumptions which lay behind them. If we do that we may then want to question the items placed on the agenda, and indeed the proposed strategy, for if we were to follow the advice of John White, for example, we may expend much time and effort in what might be a vain search for a successful strategy on the assumption that for every given set of proposals there must exist a successful strategy, if only we can find it.

The purpose of this essay, therefore, is to examine the NIEO pro-gramme and strategy from this critical standpoint, and on the basis of those critical observations, and as a positive contribution, to suggest the outlines of another way of looking at the heart of the matter, which, after all, is world poverty.

2. The Objectives of NIEO and its Strategy

The objectives of NIEO and the North–South Dialogue may be sum-marized as the removal of inequalities internationally, the alleviation of world poverty, and achieving at least minimum living standards for all individuals. Coupled with this Third World nations want this to be a continuing, self-sustaining process over which they have control and this means stepping up the diversification and growth in their production bases, i.e. to increase their rates of industrialization. To do this they need capital goods from the wealthy industrialized nations, the imports of which have to be paid for. A number of measures are proposed whereby they will secure the means of paying. Since many Third World countries are largely dependent on the export of primary products, they will gain much needed extra foreign exchange, if the prices of these were to increase, therefore they must seek to increase commodity prices. In addition they would like to see some reform of the international monetary system and institutions, particularly the IMF and the World Bank, in so far as they affect international liquidity and the scheduling of debt-service payments. They call for an increase in official development assistance and, finally, they propose to rely increasingly on self-help through individual and collective self-reliance.

Apart from the strategy of individual and collective self-reliance, and, in so far as the programme involves a transfer of resources from the haves to the have-nots, the initiators of the demand for NIEO would rely on a combination of hard economic trading with the rich, mainly through producers' associations, through political pressure and bargaining, and through moral persuasion (a plea for justice: the rich have historically plundered the poor and have a moral obligation to make restitution for the loss and damage caused). The rich for their part, realizing that there was going to be no confrontation after all, seized the opportunity offered by NIEO's terms of reference, i.e. assumptions of 'interdependence' and 'co-operation', to initiate the so-called North–South Dialogue with the Conference on International Economic Co-operation, 1975, in Paris, followed in 1977 with the setting up of the Brandt Commission to investigate 'North–South' issues.

Of course, one could argue that it is still early days given the magnitude of the problems. The Brandt Commission, for instance, has only just completed its report after 2 years of work, and it will take time to get concrete results. And, as the Secretary-General of UNCTAD maintains, when one casts aside 'the glamour of broad resolutions and really tries, through a complex process of discussion and negotiation, to reach agreement with the developed world', the process calls for 'perseverance and a lot of effort'. According to Corea,'In the Common Fund, in international agreements on commodities and the code of conduct on transfer of technology, we can show to the world that UNCTAD has achieved something more than mere debate'.[5]

Nevertheless, we could remain sceptical for a number of reasons. Our fundamental questions here are the following:

(1) Given the objects of NIEO, to what extent is it necessary to achieve NIEO for their fulfilment?
(2) Conversely, assuming that the NIEO programme is achieved in full, to what extent would the objectives of NIEO be fulfilled?

Let us consider the greatest single object of NIEO, the alleviation of poverty, the goal of satisfying at least the individual's basic needs for housing, food, and clothing. To what extent is NIEO necessary for this to be achieved? For the poorest societies it is clearly necessary that resources from the rich be transferred to the poor, but there are the large number of not so absolutely poor societies, where much could be achieved through a redistribution of what already exists within the society, if the goal is to remove the worst aspects of poverty. In countries such as Venezuela, Brazil, Kenya and Nigeria, Trinidad and Tobago, and Singapore, to name a few, the decisive determinant is not the size of the cake — it is already large enough for that purpose — but the distribution of it. We know, for example, that in the case of Brazil, an economic strategy was pursued which, far from reducing poverty, actually created it by the marginalization and pauperization of North-East Brazil.

We may also compare the experiences of India and China. In 1949 both societies had rather similar economic structures and problems. Today, while millions in India live in the most abject poverty and, scores die nightly on the streets of Calcutta, in China at least the basic biological needs of individuals are largely catered for. And China has achieved this without relying on a transfer of resources from the rich. On the contrary, until the advent of 'ping-pong' diplomacy, China had almost completely isolated herself from the outside world. India, for its part, is wealthy enough to support the giant Tata empire and to be an exporter of small capital.

What has been said above is not intended to suggest that the Third World need necessarily limit its aspirations to securing the barest essentials for its population. To reduce the indecent levels of inequalities internationally will require resource transfers to developing countries. What we are suggesting is that a radical restructuring of the capitalist world economic order, while it is essential for securing the well-being of developing countries, is by itself not sufficient. It is suggested that even more essential than the radical restructuring of the international economic order, is the radical restructuring of domestic political orders. More specifically, that it is absolutely essential to achieve a revolution in the class content of the stateform. Cuba is only the most recent example of what can be achieved in this way.

The criticism about NIEO is that most Third World governments, although they have formulated their claims by recourse to universal principles and objectives, in fact speak for themselves and for those whose interests are not necessarily those of the masses they govern or reign over.[6] They cannot speak for the masses, since they are the political moment in the ensemble of groups which compose the bridgeheads through which imperialism has succeeded in maintaining neo-colonial control of their respective territories. For governments to express the concerns of peoples there would have to be a revolution in the stateform which would itself be the best guarantee that NIEO will mean something for the masses.

It is, however, not being argued that the domestic struggle must have priority in time. On the contrary, one has to combine the struggle and fight on many fronts. The point here is merely to dispel any illusion that until NIEO is achieved nothing can be done about world poverty.

We may now turn to the second question. What will have been achieved were all NIEO demands to be fulfilled? Here we find Sauvant, after examining each aspect of the NIEO programme,[7] contending that 'the structures of the international economic system would not be changed appreciably. On the contrary, they might even be solidified. For the underlying philosophy of the NIEO program is essentially reformist; it is aimed at improving the existing mechanisms, not at changing the existing structures. Its main objective is to put the developing countries (DCs) — within the framework of the present system — in a better position to pursue their goals, especially to engage in trade and to participate in a "rational" international division of labour.'[8] His correct conclusion is that while the NIEO Programme is necessary for the immediate alleviation of the worst DC-problems, its benefits are short term. For permanent relief, fundamental structural changes are necessary. 'Elaborate measures have been proposed to deal with the symptoms of the problems — but the strategies aimed at their causes are still vague.'[9]

The reason for their being vague and why the problems must persist is, as we have suggested above, to be found in the structures of the several domestic societies and specifically in the class specificity of their state-forms. Certainly, the bridgeheads of imperialism would like a larger slice of the cake, partly for reasons of nationalism, partly for appeasing their increasingly discontented populations, for heading off threats to their thrones, but most of all for themselves. It is hardly to be expected that these governments would demand a radical transformation of the international capitalist economic system, for if they were to make such a demand and succeed, they themselves, as cornerstones of the old order, would have to go with it.

3. The Bargaining Power of the Poor and its Basis

For some of its goals the NIEO itself is not necessary, and even if the whole NIEO programme is achieved, some of its goals will not have been fulfilled. But as was said at the very outset, even the NIEO programme as it stands has hardly begun to be fulfilled. Could the reason lie in its bargaining strategy? An important aspect of its economic strategy is the use of commodity power through producers' associations modelled after OPEC. But as George Abbott has argued, this strategy is not likely to be very successful, particularly when the DME's are in such deep economic recession, and he advances two reasons. First, developing countries cannot exercise monopoly power either because they do not control sufficient of the supply or because their products can be substituted for either easily in the short run, or, for some, less easily in the medium term.[10] There were only four minerals where developing countries accounted for more than 50% of the world's exports: bauxite, copper, manganese, and tin, and of these the prospects for cartelization — number of producers involved and substitutability — seemed reasonably good in the case of bauxite and possibly of tin. For commodities, the possibilities for strong bargaining to increase prices were practically non-existent. Secondly, because 'Differences in their cultural and historical backgrounds, as well as their diverse political and economic philosophies, deny them the necessary degree of cohesion and discipline'.[11]

Mahbub Ul Haq, on the other hand,[12] argues that the bargaining power of DCs is not only economic but political, and that the strategy, by implication, lies not just in cartel formation and commodity bargaining. Wherein then resides this power? On the economic front and taking a long-term view, developed countries need the natural resources of the Third World; synthetics, for example, have only made them more dependent on oil and all that that implies. In addition, although some commodities, such as tea, coffee, rubber, etc., may not be important in themselves, the spin-off effects through the processing of these through shipping, advertising, and distribution are important, and it is not easy to substitute for these. Haq estimated in 1976 that the added value of these activities was US $150 billion.[13] Further, developed capitalist economies needed the markets in the Third World for their output, and then there was always the danger of the spread of nuclear weapons to the Third World and the threat which that posed to the rich. As he summarized his argument, 'the real bargaining power of the poor lies in their ability and their willingness to disrupt the life styles of the rich. In any such confrontation, the rich have far more to lose.'[14] He proposes, therefore a 'trade union of the poor', and given the 'interdependence' of the parties to the conflict, it would be in the self-interest of both sides if there were to be a new 'New Deal' programme, this time on an international scale.

Abbott's position appears to be more persuasive than that of Haq. Eight years after OPEC, no second producers' association of anything approaching the effectiveness of OPEC has appeared, and world commodity prices lie in a trough. On the other hand, it is hard to see how the Third World has disrupted the life styles of the rich. OPEC has, but then OPEC has disrupted the life styles of the poor even more. Further, even where foreign assets have been nationalized in the developing countries, processing, marketing, shipping, etc. are still conducted by the West, and there is no evidence that the metropoles have suffered any great loss through nationalization. Given generous compensation they may even have benefited in that they have liquidized their assets, have no responsibility for heavy capital investments, but control the most profitable parts of industry. Nor is it clear what Haq's point is about the substantial, non-substitutable gains earned by the rich from processing, marketing, etc. How does this strengthen the bargaining power of commodity producers? The transfer of at least some of these activities to the developing countries is part of NIEO and it is difficult to see how a demand for the transfer of these, i.e. how the threatened loss to the developed countries of these non-substitutable and profitable enterprises, strengthens the hand of Third World negotiators. Unless they are not a serious part of the NIEO programme and will be traded off against something else!

Nor is the so-called 'interdependence' of rich and poor a reliable power source for the poor. We know that the mere fact of interaction does not create interdependence and we know, too, that there can indeed exist mutual dependence, but dependence which differs qualitatively among the interdependent parties. In this respect the distinction between *sensitivity interdependence* and *vulnerability interdependence* is particularly important. Keohane and Nye explain the distinction thus: 'In terms of the costs of dependence, sensitivity means liability to costly effects imposed from outside before policies [by the affected actor] are altered to try to change the situation. Vulnerability can be defined as an actor's liability to suffer costs imposed by external events even after policies have been altered.'[15] And sensitivity interdependence is 'less important than vulnerability interdependence in providing power resources to actors. If one actor can reduce its costs by altering its policy, either domestically or internationally, the sensitivity pattern will not be a good guide to power resources.'[16]

Now it seems that the dependence of the DMEs on developing countries is more in the nature of sensitivity interdependence while that of DCs is vulnerability interdependence. The DMEs are in an extremely strong position. Surely they benefit greatly by their continued relationship with DCs and will maintain those relationships so long as they remain so. But when one considers the size and continuing growth in intra-DME relationships — trade, investments, institutionalization, etc. — and their diminishing proportion of trade with, and investments in DCs, together with their capacity to fragment DCs and exploit divisions between them, on the one hand, and the absolute dependence of DCs as a whole on trade with DME's, on the other hand, together with the known disunity between DCs on practically all but general principles, one gets the impression that even the level of sensitivity interdependence of the industrialized capitalist nations on developing countries may be very low.

The fourth source of power, the power of moral appeal, is also not going to work and indeed has not worked, for it has been a part of the armoury for a long time now. At one level, when DC's talk of exploitation and inequalities, DMEs dilute the force of appeal by urging the appelants to put their own houses in order. 'Take the beam out of your own eye', etc. When they urge less military spending and more aid, they are reminded that 70% of all arms exports, DM 23,800 million (about US $13,225 million) in 1978,[17] twice the figure supposedly needed for setting up the Common Fund, goes to developing countries.

But at a more fundamental level moral appeal which, if heeded, will threaten the very substance of capitalism is unlikely to succeed. Briefly, DME's will not preside over their demise and will grant no concessions to DCs unless these are deemed to be in their own interests.

4. The Imperatives of the World Capitalist System

It is not that moral arguments may not form a useful part of a total package of measures, particularly political ones, in an attempt to establish new norms of accepted international behaviour, and a crucial role in the politics of confrontation. But in the politics of 'co-operation', we have to understand the logic of the system and deal with that. World capitalism seeks in the first place to reproduce itself; in the second place, it seeks its extended reproduction. When it makes concessions it does so on two bases: (1) when it has found new ways to maintain old relations or when the old relation is no longer needed, and might even be to the advantage of world capitalism to be dissolved. The dissolution of the British Empire illustrates this very well. Imperialism was able to maintain colonial relations without the responsibilities and costs of maintaining colonies. Many nationalizations of foreign assets by DCs also fall within this category of concessions. Multinational concerns have in many instances been relieved of the burden of heavy capital investments in primary producing industries in the Third World, have been generously compensated, and have been able to put their new liquid assets into more profitable ventures while at the same time continuing to control processing, shipping, advertising, and sales of primary products, i.e. the most profitable aspects of the various industries. In this way world capitalism has been able to make concessions in the form, without disturbing the content, of its relationships with developing countries. (2) Capitalism makes concessions when it finds it necessary to sacrifice a part of itself in order to preserve the whole, i.e. the maintenance of the system as a whole takes precedence over any of its parts.

These two bases of capitalist 'concessions' must be our starting-point in any 'dialogue' or appeal to DMEs. The dialogue, in other words, must be cast in terms of an appeal to the national interest of DMEs, i.e. it must be consistent with the dictates of capital in a market system.

Corea admits this. He says that, 'the US is now committed to a policy of stabilising commodity markets through international commodity agreements', and that, 'this new policy of theirs *is not simply a response to North–South issues*, but . . . it is something which they see as being in the interest of the US economy and as another instrument for combating inflation and recession. In other words, the US is making an effort to convince public opinion in that country about the validity of this approach, in terms of the interests of the US itself.'[18]

The economic interests of the industrialized capitalist economies are also the rationale for the main thrust of the Brandt Commission Report.

Edward Heath, former Prime Minister of Britain and one of the co-authors of the Report, claiming that the fate of the industrialized (capitalist) world was dependent on the fate of the Third World (they were 'clearly interdependent'), stressed that the main recommendation of the Report was that the industrialized countries and OPEC must help the under-developed countries. Why? Because by doing so, by stimulating the in-dustrialization process in the Third World, they would be stimulating Third World demand for capital goods produced in the metropoles and thereby reverse the process of world recession,[19] i.e. recession in the domestic economies of the metropoles. The Third World will become the motor to bring international capitalism out of its deep recession through what appears to be the transposition of Keynesian fiscal policies to the world arena. The implicit strategy seems to be that by stimulating Third World demand through a transfer of resources for the products of DMEs, each dollar then spent by the Third World in the capitalist metropoles would, through the multiplier effect, stimulate economic activity in those centres by an amount greater than the original expendi-ture, the exact size of the added production being conditioned by the marginal propensity to consume prevailing in the various DMEs.

Finally, we hear now from Lord Carrington, the British Foreign Sec-retary, that a higher proportion of Britain's aid will in future be specifically reserved for allocation in furtherance of Britain's economic interests and foreign policy.[20] This very likely means that more will be going to coun-tries like Turkey and Pakistan and less to the poorest of the poor.

5. Individual and Collective Self-reliance

The NIEO strategy does not only rely on external assistance. A major pillar of it is the idea of self-help through individual and collective self-reliance. This concept was introduced into the discussions of the Non-Aligned Movement by Julius Nyerere during the 1970 (preparatory) Conference of the Non-Aligned-Movement in Dar es Salaam,[21] formally incorporated into its programme at its 1970 Summit in Lusaka and further elaborated at the Georgetown Conference in 1972. The thinking was, 'whether one could not regard the mass of people as an asset whose creative potential, when released and combined with other local resources and with appropriate technology, could be the basis of autonomous development, aimed at the satisfaction of the minimum needs of the entire population', that is, 'the mobilization of indigenous resources for primarily indigenous needs'.[22] The idea has, unfortunately, sometimes been distorted and has come in for some rather unfair criticism and analysis.[23]

Self-reliance does not mean self-sufficiency and the idea that a society will attempt more self-help does not necessarily dispense with the need for external assistance. The idea of individual and collective self-reliance is really quite simple and of powerful appeal. Its point of departure is that, rather than sustaining the capitalist international division of labour grounded in the theory of comparative advantage which means concretely that DC's produce primary products for export to industralized countries and rely on imports from those countries to satisfy practically all of their own domestic needs, developing countries will resolve this contradiction by embarking, in so far as this is possible, on the development of domestic production for domestic consumption, i.e. for the satisfaction of local needs.[24] In doing this they would seek first of all to use domestically available resources and when this is not possible to co-operate regionally among themselves, etc., to meet the need. Only when all of these sources are exhausted, and the need has still not been satisfied, will they deal with DME's. One thing is abundantly clear. Neither for individual nor collective self-reliance as they are understood here, is it necessary to enter into a dialogue with the industrialized capitalist metropoles. And in so far as any discussion is necessary, it is among the participants to the strategy itself, i.e. those who wish to co-operate in the effort of collective self-reliance. A programme of individual self-reliance could be undertaken quite unilaterally.

Collective self-reliance can only find its basis in individual self-reliance. To achieve this at least two prerequisites are essential. First, there has to be the will at governmental level to pursue this path. But it is unthinkable that such a will exists in those cases where the state represents the interests of a political bloc whose interests are deeply interwoven with the fortunes of the DMEs and antagonistic to those of subordinate groups within their own societies. Secondly, individual self-reliance means utilizing domestic resources to the full. In the Third World the most important single resource are the people. This means, therefore, releasing their tremendous energies and imagination and mobilizing them for the great task of economic construction – mobilizing here meaning galvanizing these into a great co-operative effort.

How will this be achieved? Surely not on the basis of the levels of domestic inequalities and exploitation prevalent in most developing countries. If such a programme is to stand any chance of success the masses will have to participate authentically in the political life of the society and share more equitably in the distribution of the social product. In other words, the socio-economic basis of capitalist and quasi-capitalist societies will have to be revolutionized. There will have to be a form of state which more accurately reflects the needs and interests of the masses.

6. An Approach to NIEO

Our considerations have led us to the following two positions: (1) that for some important aspects of NIEO, a dialogue with industrialized capitalist countries is not needed; and (2) that the objectives of NIEO will not be fully realized without radical changes in the stateform of the over-whelming majority of developing countries.

One other matter which influences us in what is said about NIEO is how we see the structure of world society. There are many different ways in which we may carve up the world to get an insight into its char-acter. None is perhaps less useful, either as a description or as an analytical tool than that of North and South. A division reflecting the fundamental importance of stateforms and socio-economic structures would, for us, be much more useful. Instead of the undifferentiated 'north–south' dicho-tomy, our world would look like this:

	Capitalist	*Non-capitalist*	*Socialist*
Industrialized	OECD countries	–	e.g. Soviet Union, GDR, Czechoslovakia, etc.
Non-industrialized/ industrializing	Most DC's e.g. India, Nigeria, Singapore, Trinidad & Tobago	e.g. Guinea, Tanzania, Somalia, per-haps Algeria, perhaps Jamaica	e.g. China, Cuba, North Korea, perhaps Mozambique

What distinguishes non-capitalist from socialist industrializing societies is not their goals, but the process for reaching those goals. Primarily, the difference lies in the class composition of the state. Non-capitalist stateforms can be hybrid in character, i.e. they need not reflect unam-biguously working-class power but can represent a power bloc including 'progressive' petty-bourgeoisie, small capitalists, and so on. Further it should be borne in mind that because the dividing line itself between capitalist and non-capitalist cannot always be rigidly drawn, it is sometimes difficult to characterize some states which are a mixture of fish and fowl.

Both societies on a non-capitalist path of development and industrial-izing socialist societies share, however, one very important common feature: the antagonism between the low level in the development of the economic base and the more progressive state form. So long as the level of development of the productive forces and the structure of the economic base generally lag behind the character of the state form, they will act as a constant brake on the political initiatives of the state, even to the extent of threatening its continued existence.

One final point about stateform, and this involves the question of movement over time and the distinction between qualitative and non-qualitative changes. In characterising a stateform, the direction of change and the quality of the movement are equally important.

Regarding the direction of change, it is obviously important to know whether the stateform is moving in a 'progressive' direction, i.e. whether the working classes and their allies are becoming increasingly influential in the decision-making process or not. A stateform moving from a position where the dominant bourgeoisie and/or petty-bourgeoisie are strongly entrenched to a position where their dominance is seriously weakened and threatened may be judged more hopeful, even where the stateform remains within the ambit of capitalism, than one moving, say, from a non-capitalist stateform (where the working classes are firmly entrenched in the dominant power bloc) to a position still within a non-capitalist stateform (where they have had to yield ground to an increasingly powerful non-socialist/pro-capitalist power bloc). In these two illustrations the latter stateform remains objectively more advanced than the former; it continues to be non-capitalist, whereas the latter is still capitalist. But viewed dynamically the *potential* of the two cases looks very different. The potential for progressive change appears greater in the case where the stateform is still capitalist than in that where it is non-capitalist. This question of potential was crucial to the thinking of the Cuban government in its relations with the Manley government of Jamaica. When the Manley government showed signs of moving leftward, the Cubans attempted, in co-operation with the more radical sections of Manley's PNP, to influence the government towards a further leftward shift and succeeded in moving it well along this path. In the case of Algeria the movement has been different, from a position on the borders of a non-capitalist/socialist stateform to the present one along the non-capitalist/capitalist border. With Egypt the regressive movement has been even more dramatic, from a position of what was also a non-capitalist/socialist stateform right back to a position within the ambit of a capitalist mode of production.

On the other hand, progressive change *within* a stateform, while not without importance, is still limited by the constraints of the stateform. A progressive capitalist stateform, for all its progressive qualities, remains capitalist. This means that we can hardly expect it to initiate fundamental changes in the economic base. For a revolution in the economic base we need a *qualitative* change, i.e. a revolution in the stateform.

With these considerations in mind, our world, *for purposes of NIEO*, will have the typical relationships shown in Fig. 1.

NIEO and the Process of Change

It is very often the case that designers, when they construct new models of development and make their recommendations, very often forget the concrete reality which consitutes the point of departure of the proposed programme. The result is they develop abstract models which say 'if x and y are done, then z will follow' without addressing themselves at all to the conditions under which x and y will be fulfilled. On the question

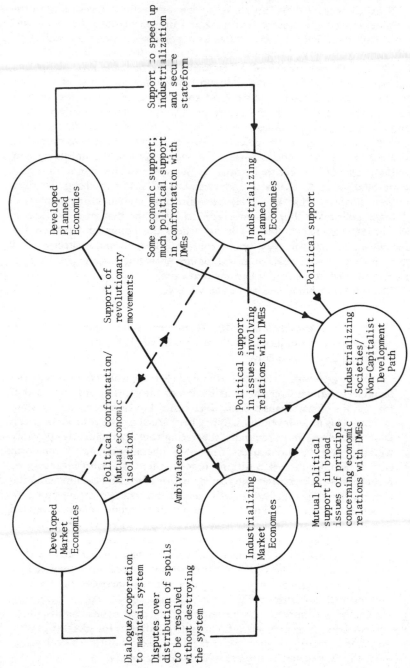

Fig. 1 Relations between states with different political and economic development in the NIEO-context

of NIEO, it is wholly inadequate to design abstractly a new order or programme of action without considering and integrating into the model the
most important concrete structures and processes actually prevailing in
international society. Even less useful is to ask whether there will be a
new order. That there will be a new order is certain, the process for this
has been going on for a long time now, an important stage of it being
the break-up of colonial empires and the emergence of the host of new
nation-states on the international stage. The new international economic
order is an unfolding process whose further development will represent
a lengthy unfolding of the dialectical processes in international economic
and political transactions. In short, it will represent the unfolding and
working out of the contradictions in the system. This is not to imply
some fatalism or mechanistic understanding of systemic change. It does
suggest, however, that in so far as conscious, human effort expressed
through political will is to intervene to influence that process, then it
will be of inestimable value to know where the points of weakness lay
and where human will may be exerted with some hope of success. And
these points of weakness, or nodal points providing leverage for change,
are to be found in the contradictions that exist.

There are *four broad levels of antagonisms*:

(1) *Antagonisms within DMEs themselves*; inter-imperialist rivalries
provide some possibilities for pressing limited claims which will affect
individual DMEs unequally.

(2) *Antagonisms between DMEs and their bridgeheads in developing
market economies* over the distribution of the gains of production and,
for reasons of nationalism, etc., over control of resources and decision-
making. This provides the possibility of sharpening the conflict between
DME and client and eventually separating them permanently, possibly
winning over in the process the more liberal sections of the local
élite to a more radical position. Indeed, there is a whole strategy of
revolution which justifies supporting nationalist claims against imperialism on the basis that the socialist revolution must go through an anti-
imperialist phase.[25] Even if the nationalist regime remains wedded
to a capitalist path, it would have weakened the ties with imperialism,
thus performing an essential task which any subsequent socialist regime
would have had to accomplish, and perhaps with greater success than
would have been allowed a socialist state. Secondly, it may reduce
the level and chances of success of any external intervention against a
subsequently socialist government. Thirdly, in so far as bourgeois
nationalist governments in the periphery succeed against metropolitan
governments, it creates more favourable conditions for socialist governments and particularly governments on a non-capitalist path of development to share in similar successes, if not in identical ones.

(3) *Antagonisms domestically between élite and exploited, dispossessed masses*; the purpose of intervention here is clear: to bring about a change in the class content of the stateform.

(4) *Antagonisms between developing countries*. It is important here to know the limits of possible intra-Third World co-operation. Of course, knowing the limits helps us to know what the areas of successful alliance or co-operation are likely to be. Awareness of the antagonisms will also raise awareness of where external opposition is likely to operate and will make it possible to take some precautionary measures, perhaps the most important being the organization of developing countries.

If one were to construct a strategy on the basis of these antagonisms it would be: support socialist states against all others; support governments on a non-capitalist path rather than those on a pro-capitalist path; support revolutionary movements against bourgeois states, but liberal bourgeois governments against reactionary ones; and support any Third World state in conflict with imperialism over the distribution of world resources.

On Economic and Trade Relations with DMEs

In the context outlined above, it is now possible to situate economic and trade relations with DMEs and the whole question of the current struggle over NIEO, which revolves around the question of winning autonomy from DMEs. As a long-term strategy, societies which set as their goal the imitation of the industrialized societies are doomed to failure, for they must remain within the game played by the industrialized countries and play by their rules. A successful long-term effort resides in the strategy of individual self-reliance, of the utilization of domestically available materials — particularly the capacities of the masses — for the domestic production for domestic consumption, above all, producing to satisfy the basic needs of the masses for food, clothing, housing, medical care, and schooling. But that is for the long term. What does the short term hold, especially for societies attempting a non-capitalist transformation to socialism?

The pattern of international economic relations influences, either positively or negatively, the internal socio-economic structure. The continuing process of unequal exchange between commodities and manufactures, the role of foreign capital in the commodity-producing sectors of the economies of underdeveloped countries, the uncertainties regarding price and markets of commodities are all of crucial importance. Particularly so for a society on a non-capitalist development path, for its place in the international capitalist division of labour means that not only is it, in its position of dependence and weakness, the victim of the exploitation which characterizes the capitalist international division of labour, but through this very weakness it remains (potentially) constantly threatened by those who dominate and determine the system and who are prepared to use their economic power to destroy any attempt at radical change in the periphery which they judge will weaken the world capitalist system and their influence.

Furthermore, a society attempting non-capitalist development pays a heavier price than those which do not, since its goals are different and more vitally and negatively affected by its participation in the international capitalist division of labour. The goal they share with all underdeveloped societies of raising the level of development in the economic base means that they share the common problem of capital accumulation and concentration. But whereas the capitalist society may achieve this through increasing levels of domestic exploitation within the society, a society on the non-capitalist path to socialism has as its goal the progressive reduction of inequalities within the society. This means that from the very beginning, if it is to successfully increase the level of capital accumulation, another of its core aims, it needs to command a higher level of resources than if it had embarked on a process of capitalist capital accumulation.

At the same time it is no easy matter either to change the system of international capitalist division of labour or unilaterally to decline to participate in it, despite the disadvantages and attendant dangers. First, as we have observed before, it is a long process to change the structure of a deformed commodity-producing economy. Even when one begins the process of producing domestically for domestic consumption, and especially in the initial stages of an industrialization programme, the society in transition will continue to be heavily dependent on imports, the paying for which must remain dependent on the earnings of commodity exports. Secondly, the socialist bloc does not have the capacity to absorb all, or even a great part, of the output of underdeveloped economies and is far from recommending or encouraging that societies attempting non-capitalist development should sharply reduce their trading links with capitalist metropolitan centres and emphasize their trade with it.

Finally, in so far as a peripheral society finds that it must in the foreseeable future continue to participate in the world capitalist economic system, but nevertheless wishes to influence changes in the international economic order, to improve its position in it, it is unable to undertake this process unilaterally and must attempt this in association with like-minded states. In this case it will share in an improved position, only to the extent that the movement or group as a whole has been able to win improvements, and must await these improvements. This means that the more radical society attempting non-capitalist transformation, while it can play a vanguard role in setting the targets of the demands for change, must in the end settle for what the group as a whole is prepared to struggle for. In the present world system, where most periphery states are not opposed in principle to the capitalist world economic order, but only how, in certain limited respects, it functions, it is to be expected that the demands for change will more or less gravitate towards the minimum demands of the capitalist-orientated periphery states. And our experience (especially since 1974 when agitation was intensified) of the struggle for a NIEO tells us that even in this case, with its limited programme of demands, that too much is not to be expected in the short run and perhaps not even in the longer run.

On the Organization of DCs

Not expecting much does not mean expecting nothing, that the struggle must be abandoned altogether. But if anything concrete is to be achieved through negotiation, a lot will depend on the organization of developing countries. S. Ramphal, Secretary General of the Commonwealth, has pointed out the urgency for more organization among developing countries.[26] He points out that, 'OECD has a staff of 1,750; it is serviced by 548 professionals — 305 more than all the professionals working for UNCTAD. It has a budget of over £59 million. The DAC Secretariat alone, within OECD itself, comprises 70 staff members.'[27] In 1977 'only 56 of the 117 Group 77 countries had resident missions in Geneva, the great majority of them with single digit total staff complements. The US staff in Geneva for the Multinational Trade Negotiations . . . alone was in excess of 150.'[28] He recommends 'a modicum of organization' to hold developing countries together, organization for co-ordinating the interests of developing countries in the negotiating process, and organization for working out concrete steps for tackling 'the still untrodden paths of collective self-reliance'.[29] This need for more expertise and more organization in support of DC's in negotiation is echoed by Corea,[30] and there should hardly be a need to add anything to the views of these two very experienced men! Except perhaps that if developing countries are so divided or lack the will to establish a permanent organization to service *their* efforts in negotiation in furtherance of *their* call for NIEO, can we expect their sustained co-operation on anything else of substance?

Notes

1. Abbott, George (1978). 'The New International Economic Order — What Went Wrong?' *Co-Existence*, XV. 1:5.
2. *North–South: A Programme for Survival* (1980). Report of the Independent Commission on International Development Issues (London: Pan Books).

3. BBC World Service, 9 Feb. 1980.
4. White, John (1978). 'The New International Economic Order: What is it?' *International Affairs*, LIV. 4: 627–8.
5. Corea, Gamani (1979). 'North–South Dialogue. An Interview.' *Third World Quarterly*, I. 3: 10.
6. White (1978) (*n. 4*), 627, seems to imply that governments are not obliged to speak for their peoples.
7. Sauvant, Karl P. (1978). 'The Poor Countries and the Rich — A Few Steps Forward.' *Dissent* (Winter), 47–9.
8. Ibid. (*n. 7*), 47.
9. Ibid. (*n. 7*), 49.
10. Abbott (1978) (*n. 1*), 14–22.
11. Ibid. (*n. 1*), 20.
12. Haq, Mahbub Ul (1976). 'The Bargaining Power of the Poor Nations.' *Marga*, III. 3: 7–15.
13. Ibid. (*n. 12*), 13.
14. Ibid. (*n. 12*), 14.
15. Keohane, Robert O. & Nye, Joseph S. (1977). *Power and Interdependence: World Politics in Transition* (Boston: Little, Brown), 13.
16. Ibid. (*n. 15*), 15.
17. From *Die Zeit* (Hamburg), 15 Feb. 1980.
18. Corea (1979) (*n. 5*), 2 ; emphasis added.
19. Interview on BBC Radio 4, 12 Feb. 1980.
20. Statement in the House of Lords, 21 Feb. 1980.
21. Sauvant, Karl P. & Jankowitsch, Odette (1978). 'The Origins of the New International Economic Order: The Role of the Non-Aligned Countries' in Sauvant, Karl P., ed. (1978). *The New International Economic Order: Changing Priorities on the International Agenda* (Oxford: Pergamon Press), note 38.
22. Sauvant (1978) (*n. 7*), 51.
23. Cf. Abbott, (1978) (*n. 1*), 6–8, where he counterposes co-operation on the one hand, and freedom and independence on the other as mutually exclusive alternatives. See also Bauer, Peter T. (1977). 'Collective Self-Reliance as Development Strategy.' *Intereconomics*, XII. 5/6: 120–5, where he argues (1) that imperialism played no part in the underdevelopment of the Third World, and (2) that collective self-reliance equals more government intervention, which implies less individual initiative. If the LDCs want to enjoy prosperity, they will achieve this in two ways: (1) they will have to earn it, and (2) they will stand a much better chance of doing so by trading freely with the West.
24. For a comprehensive analysis of the necessity for socialism of a development model based on this thesis, see Thomas, Clive (1974). *Development and Transformation. The Economics of the Transition to Socialism* (New York: Monthly Review Press).
25. For a full statement on the rationale of this tactic see 'Declaration of the Meeting of Communist Parties of Latin America and the Carribbean'. *Granma*, 22 June 1975, 2–5.
26. Ramphal, Shridath (1979). 'Not by Unity alone: The Case for Third World Organization.' *Third World Quarterly*, I. 3: 43–52.
27. Ibid. (n. 26), 46.
28. Ibid. 1979 (*n. 26*), 47.
29. Ibid. (*n. 26*), 48–51.
30. Corea (1979) (*n. 5*), 12–13.

7 FROM HIERARCHICAL TO EGALITARIAN INTERNATIONAL DECISION STRUCTURES: NON-ALIGNED POLICIES IN THE UNITED NATIONS SYSTEM

ANNEMARIE GROSSE-JÜTTE
Institute of Peace Research and Security Policy at the University of Hamburg

1 Introduction

'The United Nations has a vital role to play in safeguarding the independence and sovereignty of the non-aligned nations. It also provides the most suitable forum for cooperative actions by the non-aligned countries to facilitate the democratization of international relations.' This assessment of the UN, set forth in a special 'Resolution on the United Nations' adopted by the non-aligned summit conference in Lusaka, 1970,[1] reflects representatively the importance which non-aligned countries attribute to the institution for the advancement of non-aligned objectives. The demand for a democratization of international relations is a continuing theme in the non-aligned critique of structural conditions in the system of international relations which preclude their countries participation in international affairs on a basis of genuine sovereignty and equality. The international constellation that gave rise to the evolution of the non-aligned movement was in fact characterized by the domination of major parts of the ensemble of international relations by the two superpowers, which represented the poles from where power was exercised and translated into persistent patterns of bloc structures and bloc politics. The non-aligned critique initially focused on the subordination of the political development of smaller, and especially newly independent, countries to the conflict between the superpowers over their antagonistic political designs. It was later broadened into a criticism of practices by developed states using established positions and privileges in their relations to developing countries to undermine the latter's formal political independence.[2] In either case, such positions rested on a capacity to provide a variety of 'services' to other countries, and it remained unchallenged as long as these countries were dependent on and ready to accept them. The notion of services should be understood very broadly, comprising not only forms of material assistance (initially in particular by economic co-operation and/or aid), but also less tangible transactions of political (providing political status, external security if it could not be guaranteed independently) as well as normative character (providing 'models' of social, economic, and political development, ideological schemes, and cultural orientations). If the flow of such services is sufficiently large and asymmetrical, actors providing them acquire power in that they may influence or control the recipient's preferences and goals, especially and the more so if services extend to the normative level.[3] The positive acceptance of services establishes power relations with an essentially consensual foundation ('normative power'). This often neglected type is more stable and can be maintained usually with less political costs than 'political power' — pressures, the temporary withholding of services on which a country is dependent without being able to substitute them or provide them from other sources, finally, the threat or even use of armed force. Also, normative power relations tend to become institutionalized and thereby gradually acquire a legitimacy of their own, which is particularly resistant to change if it comes to questioning the underlying distribution of power. Given the *de facto* dependence of most non-aligned countries — in material, political, or normative-cultural terms — their aspirations to change established structures supporting and perpetuating their dependent positions implied complicated problems for the conduct of their policies.

In this analysis we will review how non-aligned countries have used the framework of the UN to advance their goals, the procedures and techniques that were employed, and the extent to which they were able to influence and/or modify decision processes in international relations. The non-aligned programmatics stresses in particular three fields requiring change, whereby the emphasis varied in the course of time. The first part will address non-aligned attempts to adjust principles and rules governing the general political relations of states and their international behaviour; the second part will focus on issues of economic relations and development; the third part will discuss — though much less extensively — questions of disarmament. The concluding fourth part will then compare the activities and their results with a view to arrive at certain generalizations. Throughout the analysis we will concentrate on the task to identify and characterize the specific actions taken. No attempt will be made to discuss in detail the controversial implications of substantive issues.

2. General Principles of International Behaviour

Non-aligned countries had placed themselves with their programmatics in opposition to the prevailing actual international power structure and to the more formal normative conceptions. In order to define their position they faced two problems: (1) the development of a critique of this power structure in the light of their specific interests and, simultaneously, the development of a viable counter-image that would provide the group with a sense of identity. The focus on 'ensuring national independence and full sovereignty of all nations on a basis of equality'[4] provided the link for the critique of the dominance of the superpowers and the restrictive effects of bloc structures and bloc politics on the genuine national development of states on the one hand as well as, on the other hand, the advocacy of principles and rules for international behaviour to promote these goals. The criteria set out at the first conference of non-aligned countries (Belgrade, 1961) to qualify the non-aligned character of a state served a twofold function. While ensuring the internal homogeneity and solidarity of the movement, they defined in addition, and more important, a new type of international actor by differentiating the non-aligned status from that of classical neutrality. The neutralist principle of equidistance in relation to superpowers and bloc structures applied only to the then prominent East–West conflict dimension, but not to political initiatives towards overcoming these structures and their effects.[5] (2) The internal consolidation of the group was facilitated by the basic identity of orientations, which helped to overcome certain divergencies after the Cairo Meeting in 1964 under Yugoslav leadership.[6] The more difficult task was to actually exercise such influence in the international domain that could contribute to initiate changes in accordance with the stated goals of the movement without disposing over any significant material power resources to further these goals. It was also complicated by the fact that the complex task of national development, in both social and economic terms, seemed to be unmanageable without a comprehensive co-operation of these very states whose dominant influence was challenged by the non-aligned as violating or restricting the 'freedom, independence, sovereignty and territorial integrity'[7] of their countries with a view to developing their national identities.

In this situation, the only means to engage in and carry out the conflict was to reflect on and eventually question the normative bases from which the legitimacy of the continued existence and preservation of these structures was derived. The political language of the non-aligned declarations with its confrontative accent was not likely to establish a basis on which the differences in opinion could be meaningfully discussed. The political intentions and claims were therefore formulated as competing claims in the language of international law in order to introduce them into an established and generally accepted framework of co-ordination of inter-state relations. While the non-aligned countries had from the beginning stressed the importance of the UN as a political forum for articulating their interests due to its universal character, it also proved a suitable framework in this context in that the Charter entrusted to the General Assembly the task of 'encouraging the progressive development of international law and its codification' (Art. 13 (1a) UNCh).

Thus, the political argumentation was continued and further elaborated into greater detail as regards the analysis of the international situation,[8] but it was accompanied from the beginning by an active role to adjust basic rules of international law to their needs in a process of co-operation with the established members of the international community.

In the initial phase of the non-aligned movement, its member's main concern was the danger of becoming instrumentalized as objects in the contest between East and West.[9] Therefore, the efforts to adjust legal norms focused on the traditional rules of inter-state relations with a view to modify them so as to restrict the influence of dominant powers on smaller and weaker countries. In legal terms, then, problems of the substance and extent of state sovereignty, foreign intervention, and state responsibility *vis-à-vis* obligations still existing from times prior to independence, came into the centre of attention. Western scholars frequently observed a non-observance of legal rules by the newly independent states and asserted the existence of a general attitude of disregard of the traditional international law. Such observations were most probably premature if one takes into account that these states entered the established legal community essentially unprepared, facing the problem of having simultaneously to identify their interests and define their needs in a normative system not only unfamiliar as to its specific procedures and functioning, but which in its 'actual body . . . is not only the product of the conscious activity of the European mind, but has also drawn its vital essence from a common source of European beliefs, and in both of these aspects it is mainly of Western origin'.[10] Anand considers it 'therefore (not) surprising to find that states that were the victims of such an unequal position, and were passive objects of these rules of international law, often give the impression that they rebel against their application'.[11] Similarly, Bedjaoui summarized the character by stating that '. . . formé à partir de "faits de puissance" régionaux, il ne pouvait être un "droit international de *participation*", mais un "droit international *octroyé* à la planète tout entière par un ou deux group d'états dominants',[12] an observation that had already been made in 1957 by the International Law Commission when it admitted that '. . . the countries on which international law had formally been imposed in order to facilitate their exploitation were now called upon to partake in its formulation'.[13] The irritation and insecurity on the side of these states to act in this domain became clearly visible during the Conference on the Law of the Seas in 1958.[14] This phase of necessary socialization, rather than denial, had passed by the early sixties when the newly independent states began to participate actively and constructively in international legal bodies. In the present context it is sufficient to point out some representative examples.

Among the first attempts of the non-aligned countries to transform their political goals, usually summarized under the formula of (active) peaceful co-existence, into specific and operational rules of international conduct is their participation in the Special Committee on Principles of

International Law Concerning Friendly Relations and Co-operation Among States of the UN General Assembly.[15] The decisions establishing the committee and defining its tasks were already influenced between 1960 and 1962. During the subsequent work of the committee, until the adoption of the results of the work in 1970 by the General Assembly as a resolution under the same title (GA Res. 2625 (XXIV)), it became clear that the non-aligned members of the committee stressed the element of progressive development of international law (rather than codification of its status quo, as did Western states) in order to emphasize its function as 'correctrice des inégalités de développement entre les nations et créatrice de bien-être pour l'ensemble de la communauté internationale'.[16] The non-aligned conception of (active) peaceful co-existence not only objects to Western attempts to preserve traditional privileges, it is also more general than the Soviet variant in three respects. The thesis of the inevitability of wars is repudiated, and this also includes the 'cold war'.[17] Co-existence is, furthermore, not limited to relations between the blocs. Rather, a more comprehensive 'multilateral' orientation extends it to relations among *all* states irrespective of their political and social systems so as to transcend the status quo partition. Finally, it does not relate exclusively to the ideological division but takes into account the difference in North–South relations, in the words of Bedjaoui, '. . . lutter contre tous les phénomènes d'oppression, économique ou politique, direct ou indirect, pour parvenir à une égalité véritable dans les relations internationales. C'est à cela que tend en définitive la coexistence pacifique lorsqu'elle est appliquée réellement entre tous les États'.[18] Accordingly, non-aligned proposals for elaborating formulations of both the principle of prohibition of force and the principle of non-intervention favoured extensive interpretations which comprised all forms of pressures, in particular of an economic and political character, that might threaten the integrity or political independence of a state. On the other hand, the principle of self-determination of peoples was interpreted to extend to the legitimate use of force as a means of self-defence against colonial rule. The final formulations were the results of numerous compromises. As far as the non-aligned countries were concerned, they had a clear understanding of the necessity to remain within a consensual domain in order to maintain the possibility of general acceptability. Although certain claims originally put forward could therefore not be incorporated into the final text, it is noteworthy that some of the aims and intentions referred to above are reflected, though somewhat imprecise in form, in the principle of non-intervention. It states the prohibition of any intervention, indirect or direct, into the internal or external affairs of a state in such a way that, aside from traditional armed intervention, all forms of interference or threats affecting the 'personality' of a state or its political, economic, and cultural elements are contrary to international law.

Another forum of activity serving the needs of the non-aligned countries, though less spectacular by its more technical orientation towards codification of existing law, is the International Law Commission. One of the results of particular relevance, obtained only more recently, is the codification work pertaining to state succession where, with respect to countries formerly under colonial rule, a so-called *tabula rasa* principle was established.[19] It provides a legal remedy for a situation which Anand described and complained of in the early sixties, viz. that 'these states which have recently achieved independence have generally begun their existence in the position of a debtor under the traditional legal order. It means their authority or territory or both are burdened with debts, concessions, commercial engagements of various kinds or other obligations continuing from earlier colonial regimes.'[20]

The activities of the non-aligned countries in these two institutions represent a particular phase in their on-going involvement of adjusting the normative basis of international structures and behaviour to perceived needs as a consequence of the development of international relations. Its *main characteristics* are, first, that this engagement coincided with the formative phase in the development of the movement and the entrance of a growing number of newly independent states into the international legal community. Secondly, these activities emphasized and were concentrated on the development of international rules on the basis of existing international law as points of departure. Thirdly, this fact provided for certain limitations in the results that were eventually achieved. While the need to observe strictly consensual decision principles restricted the extent to which existing law could be given future-orientated, progressive interpretations, the results have the advantage of general acceptance. Although they by no means touch basic legal issues, the significance of particular results cannot be overseen. Fourthly, under a structural aspect, the initiatives of the non-aligned countries have decisively contributed to activate the development of international law as a continuing task of the UN and to gradually provide an outstanding role for the group of non-aligned countries in the international law-making process. Fifth, and finally, the examples briefly introduced have shown that in some way or another socio-economic problems were, directly or indirectly, much in the background of most issues under discussion. Their importance steadily increased for the members of the non-aligned group as developing societies — although not restricted to them alone. The procedures and techniques within these institutions on the basis of the *existing* international law proved no longer sufficient to deal with the broader implications of these questions such that their discussion gradually shifted to the political forum of the General Assembly. The uncertain legal validity of its decisions notwithstanding, the adoption of resolutions such as the Charter of Economic Rights and Duties of States (GA Res. 328 (XXIX)) as well as decisions by various UN conferences in the context of framing a NIEO have legal implications by far transcending the traditional understanding of central legal concepts, e.g. the content of sovereignty, by systematically subjecting the whole field of social and economic relations to a 'legalization'. While the process is still in a phase of exploring and defining issues, determining specific positions, and bargaining, it can be anticipated with some certainty that the eventual outcome will significantly change some of the basic assumptions as well as central notions of the international legal order, which in turn only reflects a change in the perception from a system of independent states to a global society with a net of mutual responsibilities among its various elements.[21]

In addition to the broadening of the concept of sovereignty (nationalizations, permanent sovereignty over natural resources, and related economic activities), the political notion of solidarity as a principle advocated to guide the restructuring of social and economic relations touches, at the legal level, the fundamental assumption of the formal equality of states and suggests a tendency towards a system of privileges and its principle legal recognition. The development from elaborating the principle of 'co-operation among states' in the Friendly Relations Declaration to the notion of 'solidarity' as a guideline for a NIEO suggests the revival of a tradition in legal thinking essentially absent in the present order of positive international law. It becomes obvious by comparing Art. 14 of the Charter of Economic Rights and Duties of States, which states that it is the obligation of each state to participate in the efforts to improve the welfare and standard of living of all peoples, in particular the developing countries, with an observation by Vattel, one of the fathers of international law, suggesting — as early as 1758 — that what today is referred to as solidarity constitutes an obligatory element of state sovereignty: '...chaque Nation doit contribuer au bonheur et à la perfection des autres tout ce qui est en son pouvoir.'[22]

That these considerations today dominate the agenda of international discussion is not the least a result of the growing influence of the nonaligned countries. How this influence was developed from normative conceptions into effective political influence is the focus of the following section.

3. International Economic Relations and Development

In its first phase, until the end of the sixties, the UN General Assembly devoted its primary attention and political concern to the broad themes of the East–West conflict, decolonization and self-determination, and general pleas for disarmament efforts. Nevertheless, problems of economic development received attention from the beginning although they appeared to be comparatively less problematic. At that time, the process of decolonization was still gaining momentum, and development problems were still largely viewed in terms of primarily Western models of political and economic development. The attention paid to these issues at the initial conference of the non-aligned countries in 1961 was only rather general and — compared to the attention devoted to other issues — marginal.[23]

However, in the following year a conference was convened, sponsored by non-aligned countries, which was exclusively devoted to Problems of Economic Development (Cairo, 1962).[24] It considered — now under a structural perspective — a comprehensive catalogue of problems which probably inspired the quest for a resolution, adopted by the General Assembly in the following year, expressing the need for a new international division of labour. Also, the Declaration suggested the holding of an international economic conference under the auspices of the UN to deal with the whole range of questions relevant for development. At that time the comprehensive catalogue of issues in conjunction with the procedural recommendation seemed more important than the new analytic approach of focusing on distortions in international economic relations. This becomes apparent against the background of essentially negative, or ineffective, results of prior attempts towards a comprehensive approach. Within the structure of economic institutions, the scene was dominated by GATT, the only institutional element that had survived the much more comprehensive approach of the Havana Charter. Its eventual failure under the influence of the growing East–West conflict meant a 'disintegration' of development problems. Initially, non-aligned countries therefore conceived them primarily in the East–West context, i.e. shortcomings were not attributed in the first place to the substance of approaches so far pursued, but rather to the rudimentary institutional machinery available.

Development problems were thus essentially neglected within GATT, which concentrated on a liberal reconstruction of the world economic system in the post-war period. The same spirit also prevailed in the ECOSOC with its domination of decision procedures by the Western industrialized countries. This, as well as the extreme fractionalization in the dealings with development problems within the UN system, had seriously affected meaningful approaches to the negative. The attempt by developing countries to establish a Special United Nations Fund for Economic Development as a counterpart to the World Bank and its repeated failure in the General Assembly highlights this constellation. Further attempts, especially the project of a United Nations Capital Development Fund (UNCDF), in 1958, proved similarly unsuccessful.

The unresponsiveness and lack of political will within the centralized part of the UN thus generated a series of deceptions and caused a shift of activities on the part of the developing countries to their respective regional levels.[25] This decentralization of the work within the frameworks of the UN Regional Economic Commissions was tolerated by the Western countries since there arose no direct initiatives that might have probed their reluctant attitudes.[26] An important development initiated in the

Economic Commission of Latin America (ECLA), then directed by R. Prebisch, consequently took place largely unnoticed. The analysis of distortions in international economic relations, in particular trade relations already referred to, advanced a comprehensive criticism of the disadvantageous position imposed on the developing countries by a variety of discriminatory practices on the markets of industrialized countries along with increasingly unfavourable terms-of-trade relations on the raw material markets (*gap-theory*). In addition, it was pointed out that so far no comprehensive approach had been developed that would have taken into account adequately the functional relations between trade and development. This led to the general conclusion, in Prebisch's own words, that '. . . problems of international trade are dealt with in a fragmentary fashion and not as a part of a general problem of development which must be tackled on various fronts and with clearly defined objectives'. Instead it was postulated that '. . . a broad policy of international co-operation in trade, in financial resources and in the propagation of technology is unavoidable'.[28] Irrespective of certain questionable aspects of the analysis, it provided, in 1962, a comprehensive and well-elaborated conception to which the Cairo Conference could refer, containing both a critique of prevailing approaches and a detailed positive programme for action. In adopting the essentials of this approach in the Cairo Declaration of Developing Countries, the Conference followed a proposal made by the Egyptian and Yugoslav Heads of State, on the occasion of a prior meeting, that the Conference should take into account the necessity of comprehensive rather than only partial measures in order to achieve decisive improvements for the situation in the developing countries.[29]

The importance of the Cairo Conference derived from the fact that it provided a common ground for all developing countries after the concentration of activities in various regional contexts during previous years. The operational problem, then, was to bring the programme into a more comprehensive framework of discussion. The proposed international conference on trade problems appeared a suitable forum. Although this project had already been introduced in a vague fashion into the UN Declaration of the (First) Development Decade (1961),[30] the further pursuance of the project in concrete terms on the substantive basis of the Cairo Declaration met the decisive resistance of the Western countries in ECOSOC. It was then shifted to the General Assembly, where this resistance of the Western countries could be overridden by a voting coalition of developing and socialist countries. As a result, in late 1962, ECOSOC was instructed by the General Assembly to convene a Conference on Trade and Development of the UN, which subsequently took place in 1964.[31]

The proceedings of the Conference were strongly influenced by the preparatory work of the developing countries. Its substance closely reflected the work of Prebisch as adopted by the Cairo Conference and thus established this programme as a framework for all future considerations of the development issue. This was further underlined by the subsequent designation of the Conference as a permanent organ of the General Assembly (UN Conference on Trade and Development — UNCTAD), in accordance with a recommendation of the Conference (December 1964). The definition of the institutional character of the body and its procedural provisions implied a number of complications.[32] It suffices here to mention some of the main results of importance for the present context.

By institutionalizing the Conference as a permanent organ, the developing countries created a forum which allowed them a close control via the General Assembly as its parent body. This applies to both procedural and substantive aspects. Procedurally, it was possible to prohibit any special status for the permanent members of the UN Security Council, as was the case in ECOSOC as an established practice. The negotiating process follows a carefully balanced system of group representation in combination with decision procedures, for which it was also possible to prevent any qualified voting arrangements. These practices, in effect, strongly support bargaining orientations which eventually produce consensual decisions. The more substantive aspects are related to the fact that the developing countries, with their majority in the General Assembly, are in a position not only to influence the work of UNCTAD but also to assign to it new tasks, as well as normative standards to guide the direction of its work. The first Conference, by its final decisions, established an agenda which subsequently inspired a series of decisions by the General Assembly, which operationalized the field of socio-economic relations and development issues in terms of fundamental normative principles to be observed, specifications of specific problem areas, as well as detailed action programmes. The institutionalization of UNCTAD also provided a precedent for the creation of additional bodies under the auspices of the General Assembly. The decisions of the General Assembly have created a substantive framework that is now referred to as the programme for a New International Economic Order. The variety of elements contained therein and related with respective specialized tasks have in turn initiated a significant growth of subsidiary bodies within the UNCTAD framework ranging from permanent working bodies to specific conferences. Similarly to the UNCTAD pattern, though at a still less elaborate level, a practice has been developed to assign other problems not directly within the competence of UNCTAD to *ad hoc* conferences or to conferences meeting with some periodicity.

As is well known, definite and generally accepted results have been achieved only in a very limited extent. Indeed, some of the UNCTAD meetings are considered as clear failures in achieving further progress.[33] The reasons and explanations are manifold. The most often cited circumstance is also put forward as a criticism, viz. the tendency of the developing countries to initiate proposals and subsequently force related decisions in the General Assembly forum which are dependent as regards their implementation on the – from that point on no longer enforceable – willingness of the richer countries to allocate, or at least reallocate, necessary resources. Irrespective of this basic problem which, as a matter of fact, constitutes the core of the conflict itself, there are a number of substantive and procedural reasons. The nature of the bargaining and decision process tends to favour comprehensive package deals which exclude intermediate final results that are ready for implementation. This constellation is further aggravated and complicated by the fact that the agenda of problems introduced is more or less steadily expanding.

Thus, the extreme slowness of the process as well as the reluctance of implementing partial results is a critical issue also for the developing countries. On the other hand, they faced a choice: 'Modest' partial solutions were likely to be implemented but, as regards their substance, equally likely to remain far behind existing expectations, given the often experienced reluctant attitude to engage in long-term problem resolutions on the side of the industrialized countries. Even at the expense of delays in obtaining quick, concrete results, they seem to favour longer decision periods that ultimately lead to at least principle political decisions closer to their actual aims. The reluctance on the part of the advanced countries to discuss more long-term solutions in principle and in a comprehensive manner has often placed them in unfavourable negotiating positions, forcing them to accept more far-reaching solutions and leaving flexibility only in technical details.

Given this particular balance of costs (i.e. the lack of immediate and directly visible results) and (expected long-term) benefits, the developing countries seemed to favour the advantages of the over-all decision mechanism which allows them to introduce their claims in terms of normative conceptions and have these increasingly legitimized in a gradual and step-wise process, hoping that the implemental follow-up will eventually become unavoidable.[34] Thus, while its actual results were all but satisfactory, the UNCTAD process mobilized the group spirit and strengthened the development of the so-called Group of 77, which by now has reached a numerical size much larger than the circle of its original members.[35] There is a high degree of overlap between membership in this group and membership in the non-aligned movement, and on this basis a specific form of 'division of labour' in advancing development goals. The Group of 77 primarily functions as a trade-union-type pressure group in specific negotiations, while the programmatic development takes place in the framework of non-aligned gatherings. These elements form a closed circle allowing for a smooth process of defining and formulating particular goals or conceptions, legitimizing them within the forum of the General Assembly as resolutions of general character or as specific task assignments to some negotiating body, and finally introducing them into such bodies for action. The President of Yugoslavia stated on the occasion of UNCTAD of this mechanism can be demonstrated in a variety of cases, here we mention only some representative examples from which further generalizations may be drawn.

Aside from the unsatisfactory results of the two UNCTADs in 1964 and 1968, they had noticeable constructive effects on the non-aligned unity for action. The President of Yugoslavia stated on the occasion of UCTAD II: 'A particular problem faced by the developing countries is the question of activating their own forces by adequate forms of international cooperation, and if possible, also by creating common economic, financial and other institutions to serve, among others, to further a position of equality in the relations between less developed countries.'[36] The importance of mutual co-operation was subsequently further stressed and also given a new dimension by President Nyerere's address to the Preparatory Meeting of Non-Aligned Countries for the Third Conference of Non-Aligned Countries (1970) in which he introduced the concept of self-reliance.[37] The development strategy thereby implied is an important – though not uncontroversial and unproblematic – element in an over-all strategy of development. Here, the internal consequences of an organizational character are of primary relevance as far as they promoted the institutional consolidation of the movement. The period between the Third Conference and the Georgetown Meeting of Foreign Ministers (1972) marks the beginning of an expansion and stricter periodization of non-aligned gatherings and a systematic timing and co-ordination with the work of the UN and international conferences.

Thus, the non-aligned summit meeting takes place at three-year intervals shortly before the General Assembly Session. In addition to a mid-term Foreign Minister Conference there are frequent ministerial meetings on specific questions, and the continuity of activities is taken care of by a permanent co-ordinating bureau and frequent consultations during the General Assembly sessions. A further type of policy definition and co-ordination is a variety of seminars, working and expert groups, and the co-ordination of specific policy sectors or activities by 'co-ordinating countries'.[38]

These organizational provisions have clearly strengthened the group's capacity to prepare and advance policy initiatives well beyond general political declarations, but rather in the form of detailed proposals and action programmes.

The shift from the earlier concentration on general issues towards non-military, in particular economic, influences of the great powers as threats to political independence is also marked by the Third and Fourth Non-aligned Conferences 1970/3. The relation between political independence and economic constellations was particularly stressed at the Fourth (Algiers) Conference: 'It is also essential to ensure a genuine independence

by eliminating foreign monoplies and taking over control of national resources and utilizing them for the benefit of the people.' This was further
extended to comprise also cultural dimensions: 'The peoples of the Third
World must maintain their identity, revive and enrich their cultural heritage
and in all domains, promote their authenticity . . . they must consolidate
their independence through the effective exercise of their national sovereignty against any type of hegemony, in other words, the rejection of any
form of subjugation or dependence and interference or pressure, be it
political, economic or military.'[39] A separate economic declaration of the
conference elaborated these ideas in the context of a critique of the prevailing mechanisms of economic international exchanges, distribution and
utilization of resources, whereby the chances for a reformative change were
seriously questioned: 'The unanimously acknowledged failure of the international strategy of development is explained both by the lack of political
motivation . . . to carry out urgent measures and by the fact that the development targets do not accord with the preoccupations of the developing countries.'[40] In positive terms, their aspirations were formulated in an
Action Programme of Economic Co-operation.[41] It became an essential
success of the non-aligned programmatics when the content of this programme was adopted at the Sixth Special Session of the General Assembly
in a Declaration on the Establishment of a New International Economic
Order (GA Res. 3201/S–VI) and a Programme of Action (1974). Similarly,
the Charter of Economic Rights and Duties of States was adopted in the
General Assembly of the same year (GA Res. 3281 (XXIX)). Many implications contained therein were then gradually introduced into the international process of discussion and negotiation in the conferences under the
auspices of the UN, and more specifically the General Assembly.

This sequence illustrates the closed-circle mechanism described above in
general terms. Here is not the place to extend this analysis to the manifold
differentiations in substantive sub-sectors which show quite similar patterns
of problem definitions, formulations of strategies, and subsequent decision
processes under the influence of the non-aligned and developing countries
such that the activities of the UN system in the social and economic field
have in important respects become a function of their initiatives. More
important still, the advanced countries have no serious opportunity to
isolate themselves or even step out of this continuing process. On the basis
of the conceptions brought into the international discussion via the UN
by the non-aligned and developing countries on the one hand, and the
reluctant or even resistant attitudes of the advanced countries on the other
hand, the conflict over development goals has reached a higher degree of
polarization, characterized by increasing polemics as well as more radical
critique and claims. The initial elements of co-operation have thus given
way to a confrontative climate, such that efforts to establish a new economic order increasingly show traits of a struggle for the redistribution
of global resources with zero-sum characteristics.

4. Disarmament

The question of disarmament belongs to the tasks of the UN directly referred to in the Charter, where specific competences are given to both the General Assembly (Art. 11 UNCh) and Security Council (Art. 26 UNCh). For the non-aligned states, disarmament has been a central concern since the movement's foundation. It is, however, hardly possible to observe any achievements of the non-aligned comparable to those discussed in the preceding sections.

The general preconditions for any activities on the part of the non-aligned countries in this field differ significantly from the two other areas so far considered. Obviously, the non-aligned countries play a definitively secondary role as regards their immediate involvement in the substance of the *problématique*. Though this constellation has not unsignificantly changed as a result of a process of militarization spreading also into the Third World, the dominant issues and their material development in the form of expansion of resources devoted to armaments and their transformation into arms races are elements of the relations between the two superpowers and their bloc systems. Accordingly, the discussion of questions in this area has essentially remained a matter dealt with directly by the superpowers and characterized by a significant degree of exclusivity. This is constantly supported by a concern for as much secrecy as possible whenever actual dealings enter a stage of concrete consideration. These specifics of the substance matter explain to a considerable degree that actors not immediately involved with some necessity cannot play but marginal roles, restricted to political appeals and statements of a mainly declaratory character.[42] The only organ where non-aligned countries directly participated in the generation of actual measures was and is the Eighteen Nations Disarmament Committee (ENDC), after changes in membership and procedures later designated as the Conference of the Committee on Disarmament (CCD). The work of this body also reflects the general pattern already referred to in that any agreement requires a prior understanding between the great powers, which is typically obtained in separate and mostly bilateral interactions and then submitted for a legitimizing acceptance *in toto*.

It is not necessarily the exclusive merit of non-aligned countries to have pointed out the increasingly heavy burden on pressing development tasks that results from allocating resources to armament efforts. Thus, it is generally acknowledged that efforts towards disarmament or (materially relevant) arms control, constitute an urgent necessity, and that efforts should go beyond repetitive pleas and declarations to this effect which remain without visible consequences. An assessment of the series of proposals and pleas that have so far been put forward, in particular within the UN as well as declarations by the non-aligned group, have not led to any appreciable success beyond this state, marginal effects notwithstanding.

The growing discrepancy between the increasing urgency of the problem and the lack of results was probably an important incentive to revive the consideration of disarmament issues. The non-aligned proposal for a special session of the General Assembly (Colombo Summit Conference, 1976) played an instrumental role for the convening of the Tenth Special Session in 1978.[43]

It is by no means surprising that there are no immediate effects. The final document of the Special Session[44] reaffirms all those items in relation to questions of disarmament that can be found in the more than 200 resolutions that have been adopted by the General Assembly in the past. The Programme of Action lists the main fields of concern and specific problems to be dealt with, suggesting possible steps in more or less general terms. More importance than to such reaffirmations must perhaps be attributed to certain organizational innovations which are likely to be developed into instruments bringing about more definite actions in accordance with the Programme of Action. Such expectation finds some support in the fact that the institutional innovations suggest the possibility of a pattern of action similar to that observed in the general political and economic fields. This will be discussed on a comparative basis, and in more general terms, in the concluding part.

The first of these innovations trying to improve the organizational machinery pertains to the Conference Committee on Disarmament (CCD), which was renamed the Committee on Disarmament (CD). Apart from an expansion of its membership, the non-aligned countries succeeded in having changed the presidency of the conference from an exclusive co-presidency of the superpowers to a system of equal rotation among all its members. A second measure is the reactivation of the Disarmament Commission of the General Assembly. As a subsidiary body, it is to perform advisory functions and to promote new initiatives, while the CD body functions as an actual negotiating forum towards the formulation of conventions in the field of disarmament.[45] Finally, in the future the General Assembly will regularly re-examine the implementation of decisions of the Tenth Special Session, including the convening of further special sessions of the General Assembly on disarmament.

5. Conclusions

The concluding generalizations will address both major institutional consequences and what appear to be prerequisites for their achievement.

Apparently, the degree of success or progress, in the realization of the non-aligned aspirations as reflected in the non-aligned conception varies. There is one common characteristic to be observed in each of the three fields considered, viz. that the restriction to declaratory — and that is essentially: moral — appeals generated only extremely limited results. Despite the visible differences in progress in the field of general principles of international behaviour and in the area of economic relations and development, attempts in both fields showed definitely more favourable results than in the disarmament sector. A common trait of the approaches in the former two areas is that the development was carried forward when two conditions were fulfilled: (1) the transformation of the political goals into an operational code of rules to govern the definition and evaluation of the behaviour of the members of the international community,· (2) the access to an international forum where they can be introduced as claims competing with traditional and established rules.

A further qualification that seems to be a determinant factor is the comprehensiveness of these competing claims, i.e. the chances of success seem to be greater the more it is possible to speak of alternative normative conceptions rather than challenges to individual rules. This differentiation may explain the lesser degree of progress in the field of general relations as compared with the field of economic relations and development. Thus, before introducing the claims in the latter field, an extremely far-reaching conception was developed to which recourse could be made. It combined a differentiated analysis with conclusions of clearly normative character that challenged the existing types of 'services' that developing countries could expect from those powers on which they were dependent.

Further, a prerequisite for the ability to develop conceptions of this type seems to be that alternative needs and, respectively, alternative 'services' have already become clearly visible in order to formulate alternative conceptions in sufficient detail and breadth.

The second condition of introducing them into an international forum also requires some qualification. To the extent that existing institutions are dominated by powers against which the competing claims are directed, it seems unlikely that these institutions can be transformed so as to develop a sufficient responsiveness. Rather, it became obvious, in both cases, that progress was dependent on achieving the control of such institutions. In the first case, it is not fully appropriate to speak of a full control. However, in the Friendly Relations Committee the developing countries had achieved an influence that was still extended by strengthening their membership in the course of the Committee's work. The progress in the economic field demonstrates the next step, i.e. counteracting the lack of responsiveness of established institutions by the creation of new 'parallel' institutions. In this process the General Assembly plays a crucial role by its universal character and numerical strength of the developing countries. But its significance is still essentially on the level of introducing alternative conceptions and to provide them with a sense of legitimacy. The type of parallel institutions required is of a character on the border-line between a general political orientation (clearly visible in the role of the UNCTAD Secretariat under the direction of Prebisch) and functional specialization. The creation of such parallel institutions under the supervision of the General Assembly combined with their (quasi-) permanent character and specific egalitarian decision procedures provides for a *de-hierarchization* of the *decision structures* and thereby a *democratization* of the over-all *international decision process*. This formal aspect does not in itself guarantee immediate substantive results.

The mechanism of the 'closed circle', described in part 3, is, however, a means by which alternative conceptions, including their adjustment and expansion as may become necessary in the course of time, may be introduced such that it is hardly possible to prevent their consideration on practical working levels. The institutionalization of these working bodies, their supervision by the General Assembly, and the typical bargaining patterns exercise pressures to the effect that the substance of such conceptions are no longer subject to simple rejection/acceptance alternatives, but rather a matter of the type of compromise to be achieved. In so far as the *formal democratization* of the decision process is further extended to a *substantial democratization* in terms of sizable opportunities to influence the contents of decisions.

This process is time consuming. But it reflects on the one hand the material relations of power and dependencies, on the other hand, the mechanism available to (more or less) dependent actors in the international system to break up, and eventually to overcome, structures of dominance by changing the institutional pattern underlying the exercise of dominance.

Confronting this pattern with developments in the disarmament field suggests certain similarities to the possible use of the recent organizational arrangement to expand the machinery in this area, described in part 4. Parallels are visible in terms of participation and decision mechanisms, closer supervision by the General Assembly, and a greater permanency. What is lacking, however, is sufficiently detailed programmatics, although the work of the Special Session may signify a beginning in this regard.[46]

Nevertheless, this aspect leads to considerations suggesting caution in assessing potential progress. This caution is, in addition, not restricted to the disarmament field but may potentially also apply to the progressive momentum that the non-aligned movement has been able to generate so far.

Characteristically, the needs felt by the non-aligned and developing countries *vis-à-vis* the 'services' provided for by the dominant powers (and becoming increasingly less functional), could be formulated initially with a considerable degree of consistency. However, the more they had to be transformed from general claims to operationally detailed levels, the more it became obvious that initial homogeneity decreased. In the context of UNCTAD, this tendency was compensated by simply adding claims even if they were not relevant to the group of non-aligned or developing countries as a whole. The growing specialization of demands limits the potential use of such practices, and the more so, the more they become contradictory. Certain divisions within the Group of 77 relative to economic issues, but also within the non-aligned movement relative to general political orientations, may be traced back to developments of this kind. Thus conflicts within the groups ranging from alternative courses of trade relations with industrialized countries to conflict behaviour with the open use of armed force in violation of principles of international behaviour otherwise fervently advocated may threaten the credibility of the movement and seriously diminish its effectiveness, which ultimately derives its momentum from the *'force de frappe morale'* (Bedjaoui), which is based on the legitimacy flowing from congruency between normative claim and actual behaviour.

Notes

1. Text in *Documents of the Gatherings of Non-Aligned Countries 1961–78* (1978). (Belgrade: Jugoslavenska Stvarnost/Medjunarodna Politika), 53.
2. For general presentations of the non-aligned movement and non-aligned policy cf. Mates, Leo (1972). *Non-Alignment. Theory and Current Policy* (Belgrade: Institute of International Politics and Economics/New York: Oceana Publ.); Korany, Baghat (1976). *Social Change, Charisma and International Behavior: Toward a Theory of Foreign Policy Making in the Third World* (Leiden: Sijthoff); Tadic, Bojana (1976). *Nesvrstanost u Teoriji i Praksi Medjunarodnih Odnosa* (Belgrade: Izdenje Instituta za Mdejunarodnu Politiku i Privredu); Willets, Peter (1978). *The Non-aligned Movement: The Origins of a Third World Alliance* (London: Frances Pinter); Declarations of non-aligned states' important meetings are collected in Documents, 1978 (*n. 1*). The most comprehensive documentation of non-aligned activities is now Jankowitsch, Odette and Sauvant, Karl P., eds. (1978). *The Third World without Super-Powers: The Collected Documents of the Non-Aligned Countries* (Dobbs Ferry, New York: Oceana Publ.).
   For the initial statement of this critique by the non-aligned countries cf. the 'Declaration of the Heads of State or Government of Non-Aligned Countries' at the conclusion of the First Conference of Heads of State or Government of Non-Aligned Countries, Belgrade, 1–6 Sept. 1961, in Documents (1978) (*n. 1*), 3 ff.
3. For an elaboration of the power concept along these lines cf. Hondrich, Karl Otto (1973). *Theorie der Herrschaft* (Frankfurt/M.: Suhrkamp).
4. 'Declaration on Peace, Independence, Development, Cooperation and Democratization of International Relations', Third Conference of Heads of State or Government of Non-Aligned Countries, Lusaka, 8–10 Sept. 1970, in Documents (1978) (*n. 1*), 43.
5. For the differentiations between non-aligned conceptions and neutrality cf. Petkovic, Ranko (1974). *Teorijski pojmovi Nesvrstanosti* (Belgrade: RAD), 65–71.
6. For a brief description of the background events causing this temporary setback cf. Willets (1978) (*n. 1*), 31 ff.
7. 'Declaration on Peace . . .' (*n. 4*), para. 12.
8. See the Documents of the non-aligned gatherings (Documents (1978) (*n. 1*)), in particular those of the Head of State meetings, which in their initial part regularly contain an assessment of the international situation in general, followed by opinions on specific international events and developments.
9. Cf. the 'Declaration . . .', First Conference of Heads of States (*n. 1*), sect. I, p. 5.
10. Verzijl, J. H. W. (1955). 'Western European Influence on the Foundations of International Law.' *International Relations*, 1: 137.

11. Anand, R. P (1962). 'Role of the "New" Asian Countries in the Present International Order.' *AJIL*, LVI: 384–5.

12. Bedjaoui, Mohammed (1977). 'Non-alignment et droit international.' *Recueil des Cours*, 382.

13. *Yearbook of the International Law Commission I* (1957), 165.

14. For the behaviour of newly independent states on the Conference cf. Friedheim, Robert L. (1965). 'The "Satisfied" and "Dissatisfied" States Negotiate International Law', in Quester, George H., ed. (1971). *Power, Action and Interaction: Readings on International Politics* (Boston: Little Brown).

15. For a detailed description of the work of the Committee see Neuhold, H. P. (1977). *Internationale Konflikte — verbotene und erlaubte Mittel ihrer Austragung* (Wien–New York: Springer) in general and the specific sections on the prohibition of force and intervention for the following. The contributions in Sahovic, Milan, ed. (1972). *Principles in International Law Concerning Friendly Relations and Cooperation* (New York: Oceana Publ.) for assessments by Yugoslav international lawyers.

16. Bedjaoui (1977) (*n. 12*), 389.

17. 'Declaration . . .', First Conference of Heads of State (*n. 3*), sect. I.

18. Bedjaoui (1977) (*n. 12*), 419.

19. Work of the ILC began in 1962, in pursuance of GA Res. 1686 (XVI), under the title 'Succession of States and Governments' (*ILC Yearbook 1962*, II/1, p. 101). The draft of a treaty proposed by the Commission is presented in the Commissions Report of the Twenty-sixth session (1974), cf. *ILC Yearbook 1974*, II/1, p. 157. For the further development cf. the following Yearbooks.

20. Anand (1962) (*n. 11*), 400.

21. For a problem analysis cf. Weber, Hermann (1978). 'Der Anspruch auf Entwicklungshilfe und die Veränderungen des Internationalen Wirtschaftsrechts.' *Verfassung und Recht in Übersee*, 1: 5–25.

22. Vattel, E. (1758). *Droit des Gens*, Preliminaries § 13.

23. Cf. the 'Declaration . . .', First Conference of Heads of State (*n. 1*), 8, paras. 21–4.

24. Cf. the 'Cairo Declaration of Developing Countries' in Documents (1978) (*n. 1*), 13 ff.

25. Cf. Gosovic, Branislav (1972). *UNCTAD — Conflict and Compromise. The Third World's Quest for an Equitable World Economic Order through the United Nations* (Leiden: Sijthoff).

26. For problems of regionalism see Gregg, R. W. (1966). 'Programme Decentralization through the Regional Economic Commissions', in Mangone, G. J., ed. (1966). *UN Administration of Economic and Social Programmes* (New York–London: Columbia Univ. Press), 242 f.

27. See Gregg (1966) (*n. 26*), 237: 'ECLA has been . . . rewriting development theory under the stimulating leadership of . . . Raúl Prebisch.'

28. See the report by Prebisch *Towards a New Trade Policy for Development* (1964). Report by the Secretary-General of the UN Conference on Trade and Development, 12 Feb. 1964. UN Doc. E/CONF. 46/3. Citations from this report, pp. 52, 64.

29. Cf. *Yugoslav Survey*, III. 10 (1962): 1499.

30. For the declaration of the first development decade see GA Res. 1710 (XVI). The Conference project is mentioned in GA Res. 1708 (XVI) 'International Trade as a Primary Instrument for Economic Development'. It took up earlier proposals by the Soviet Union, against which the developing countries had, however, a number of reservations as long as it should mainly deal with trade problems in the East–West context. Cf. also Gosovic (1972) (*n. 25*), 15.

31. GA Res. 1785 (XVIII). Cf. Cordovez, Diego (1967). 'The Making of UNCTAD, Institutional Background and Legislative History.' *J. of World Trade Law*, 3: 243–328 for an analysis of the decision process in ECOSOC and the GA.

32. Cf. Cordovez (1967) (*n. 31*).
33. Aside from more technical analysis, cf. the political evaluation by Myrdal, Gunnar (1970). *The Challenge of World Poverty* (New York: Pantheon Books/ Random House), ch. 9, Trade Flows and Capital Movements, in particular sect. VI referring to UNCTAD.
34. For more recent considerations in this regard see Nyerere, Julius (1979). 'Third World Negotiating Strategies.' *Third World Quarterly*, I. 2: 20–3.
35. The formation of the group, and the group system of the Conference in general, is described in Cordovez (1967) (*n. 31*), 277 *et passim*.
36. 'Yugoslavia at the Second Session of the United Nations Conference on Trade and Development' (1968). *Yugoslav Survey*, IX. 3:124.
37. Nyerere, Julius (1977). Opening Address to the Preparatory Meeting of the Conference of Non–Aligned Countries in Lusaka: 'Future Tasks of Non-Alignment.' Text (in German) in Khan/Matthies, eds. (1977). *Collective Self-Reliance: Programme and Perspektiven der Dritten Welt* (Müchen–London: Weltforum Verlag), 57–75.
38. For the development of the organizational fabric of the movement cf. the Introduction by Janković and Sauvant in Jankovic and Sauvant (1978) (*n. 1*).
39. 'Political Declaration', Fourth Conference of Heads of State, Algiers, 5–9 Sept. 1973 in Documents (1978) (*n. 1*), 89, para. 18.
40. 'Economic Declaration', Fourth Conference of Heads of State, sect. III, in Documents (1978) (*n. 1*), 93.
41. Text in ibid., 98.
42. For a critical evaluation of disarmament efforts see Myrdal, Alva (1976). *The Game of Disarmament. How the United States and Russia Run the Arms Race* (New York: Pantheon).
43. The proposal for a special session of the General Assembly and/or a World Disarmament Conference can be traced back to the first non-aligned meeting in 1961, and it was subsequently frequently repeated. A recommendation by the General Assembly in 1965 (Res. 2030 (XX)) took up this proposal, but actions taken were not carried beyond some preparatory work.
44. GA Res. S–X/2, 30 June 1978.
45. The formal relations are not fully clear and may become subject to different interpretations. By its origin the CD (then ENDC) was no UN body; the re-structuring in connection with the Special Session was accordingly based on an agreement reached between the USA, USSR, UK, and France. In substantive terms, however, the present institutional arrangement is probably connected with expectations by a majority of countries that the CD will function in response to General Assembly initiatives.

8 AUTONOMY AND DEPENDENCE IN RELATIONS BETWEEN NON-ALIGNED COUNTRIES AND THE SUPERPOWERS — A COMPARISON OF VOTING AGREEMENTS IN THE GENERAL ASSEMBLY AND BILATERAL FOREIGN RELATIONS

KLAUS BURRI
University of Zürich

1. Introduction

The structure and functioning of an international organization such as the UN only becomes fully apparent if the analysis is placed into the context of the structure of the international system, i.e. the types and modes of relations among states as its constituent elements. For the UN was founded as a global, universal institution, performed its tasks, and developed in constant interaction with, and as a reflection of, the network of international relations. Inter-state relations in terms of existing dependencies, rivalries, and changing international issues are thus major factors which influence the organization's institutional and functional growth.

Since the foundation of the UN at the end of the Second World War, issues of the cold war and problems of the emerging Third World — in other words, the East–West and the North–South conflicts — have been dominating as conflict configurations within the international system and, as a consequence, also within the UN. In both conflicts the USSR and the USA have been, and still are, playing central roles. As the strongest industrial and military power of the Eastern and Western bloc system, respectively, they are not only the protagonists of antagonistic political and economic orders. For less developed countries (LDCs), they are actually or potentially (possibly alternative) donors of development aid and/or military assistance, international or domestic protection and security, and trade partners. The demarcation, maintenance, and expansion of spheres of interests by the two great powers is indeed reflecting the existence or evolution of such patterns in their relations with the Third World. Accordingly, whenever the establishment of a particularly close bilateral relationship between some LDC and one of the superpowers becomes visible on the international scene, it is usually perceived (notably in the mirror of the international press) as a partial victory for one of these powers and a partial defeat for the other.

Such views are not restricted to international affairs in general, but we find them likewise on the more narrow stage of the UN. Despite the different roles of ideology in the conduct of Soviet and American foreign policy (in the former case a close interaction between ideology and international practice, in the latter an almost complete separation between international behaviour and its ideological legitimization), the attitude of the superpowers towards the UN and the LDCs is strikingly similar. Both attribute only a rather limited role to the organization by opposing any significant supranational competences which are likely to restrict their own freedom of action. In their relations with LDCs, both superpowers demonstrate almost identically (1) a constant awareness of the rivalry with the other side in gaining influence over, and establishing stable, advantageous relations with, LDCs; (2) the expectation that the LDCs honour development aid and military assistance received by supporting policy positions of the donor; and (3) the attempt to contain the influence of the adversary by extending such aid and assistance, the development of trade relations, and supporting other countries in their foreign policies, and thereby to consolidate and possibly broaden their own influence.

This is the point of departure for the present analysis. The central question can be formulated in a twofold manner, depending on the perspective adopted. What is the impact of these expectations held by the two major powers on the voting behaviour of the LDCs in the UN? Do their respective expectations to receive in return for development aid, military assistance, and other forms of co-operation the political support of the recipient countries indeed materialize? In other words, does the dependency of a developing country in its external relations on one of the superpowers extend into the UN, more specifically into its General Assembly as the main organ of policy formulation?

Conversely, from the point of view of the developing countries, one may ask whether and to what extent it is possible to receive substantial economic and military assistance from the superpowers while simultaneously pursuing a foreign policy and, in particular, a UN policy in accordance with their specific interests (which at least in the economic sphere are very likely to differ considerably from those of the superpowers). Developing countries were confronted with this basic and most irritating dilemma when they entered the international system and became members of the UN. How deeply it was felt is shown by the growth of the *movement of non-aligned states*; its programmatics and activities were supposed to provide a constructive answer to, and a way out of, the dilemma. Since its foundation in 1961, most of the LDCs have become members of the non-aligned movement, and with one exception[1] all members of the movement are LDCs. Though they vary in their domestic social and political structures as well as in specific foreign policy orientations, the common fate of development problems has given a notable degree of unity to the movement.[2]

The general objectives of the movement have been summarized by Bojana Tadić as

> . . . safeguarding the national independence and the necessity to assure the economic development in a peaceful way, which has to be accompanied by a modification of the present forms of international relations in the political and economic sphere as well as the creation of a new type of relations in the international community, based on the principles of peaceful coexistence and active cooperation.[3]

More specifically, there are in particular two objectives in the non-aligned strategy, i.e. (1) the avoidance of any involvement in the power struggle of the two superpowers as the pacemakers of the East–West conflict so as to escape from and diminish dependence on either of them or any of the members of their respective blocs, and (2) common action in the international system in general, and international organizations in particular, as a group joined as closely as possible to promote their demands as developing countries.

The UN has been an important forum for the non-aligned countries, since the movement's foundation, to advance their objectives. We will thus examine how and to what extent the non-aligned countries were able to transform their stated goals into an effective foreign policy *vis-à-vis* both the USSR and the USA at the level of their direct 'material' relations with these powers and within the UN. We will pay special attention to the question of whether or not there is any characteristic behaviour of non-aligned countries in their attempt to escape from the demands placed upon them by the superpowers, between non-aligned countries themselves as well as in comparison to 'non-nonaligned' LDCs. The data to be analysed for this purpose and the scope and method of the analysis will be discussed in more detail in the following section to make explicit the approach and design of our exploration.

2. Scope and Method of Analysis

Fig. 1 shows the two levels of relations with which we will be concerned. The upper part (International System) lists some types of relations which are generally considered as especially salient for the character of the bilateral relationship between two countries. At this *level of bilateral foreign relations*, roughly grouped into economic, military, and general political, a developing country will be the more dependent on a developed country in general, and on one of the superpowers in particular, the greater the strength, in terms of scope and intensity, of its interaction with such countries. A dependence will be the more significant, the more exclusive the relationship, i.e. the greater the proportion of relations directed only to one specific country. Furthermore, it may be assumed that in general the autonomy in the conduct of foreign policy becomes the more restricted, the stronger the dependence in foreign relations.

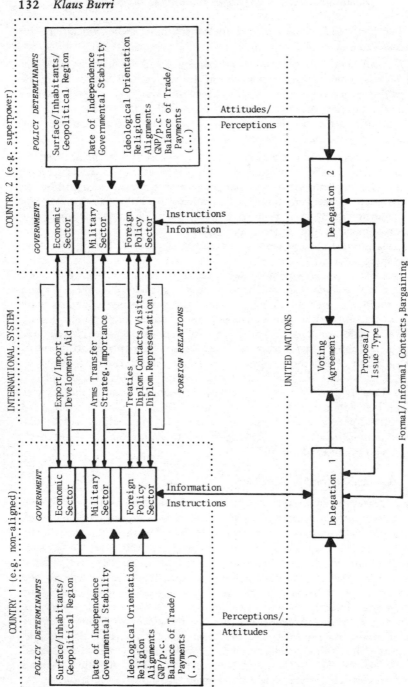

Fig. 1. Bilateral foreign relations and voting behaviour in the United Nations: major determinants and interactions

The lower part of Fig. 1 represents relations within the UN. At this level constraints on the autonomy are, at least partially, suspended. Since the UN practically has no direct executive, let alone coercive power to enforce its decisions, decisions by the majority of the LDCs in the General Assembly do not directly endanger the interests of the major powers. Within the UN the LDCs thus have a greater margin, more or less unaffected by dependencies that may arise from certain patterns of their foreign relations, to articulate their specific interests. They may even be in a position to exploit the superpowers' competing attempts to win the support of the LDCs for their respective antagonistic objectives. On the other hand, it is likely that the superpowers' continuous efforts to transform the dependence of some LDC in its foreign relations into loyalty within the UN will be the more successful, the more an LDC finds itself in an extremely dependent position and/or if its domestic political constellation is highly unstable. The interaction between the level of foreign relations and the decision process in the UN is indicated in the scheme by the links 'attitudes/perceptions' and 'information/ instructions'.

The media and public opinion in the developed industrialized countries have more or less accepted the 'hypothesis' advanced by the major powers that voting alignments as visible in the UN conform to and reflect the pattern of bi- and multilateral relations in the international system as well as their relative strength. This perspective has been 'returned' as a demand to the UN (more precisely to its members), i.e. that the voting behaviour within the organization *should* indeed be guided by due regard for the existing international power relations. In a very similar way, such parallelity of voting behaviour and national foreign policy orientations is also assumed, explicitly or implicitly, in most of the research on the UN voting behaviour. In the majority of studies, then, this assumption in turn leads to the tacit conclusion that results derived from analyses of the voting behaviour not only explain relations of states within the UN, but also allow for assessment of their foreign policy behaviour in the broader context of international relations outside the organization.

If one confronts these claims and demands as to the foreign policy behaviour of developing countries with the programmatics of the non-aligned movement, the apparent question is whether, and to what extent, the goal of maintaining an independent position with respect to the superpowers and, simultaneously, the consequent pursuance of specific development interests can be realized. The development of the non-aligned movements suggests that the intensity of a country's commitment to the activities of the movement is an important prerequisite for achieving non-aligned objectives.

At the level of (bilateral) foreign relations, the non-aligned 'quality' should express itself in a certain similarity of its relations to the USSR and the USA in both qualitative and quantitative terms. One would not only expect to see 'equidistance', but in addition possibly even a gradually decreasing strength of relations developing over time. An analogous picture should characterize its position within the UN and become apparent in its voting. The voting of a country (delegation) in the General Assembly is the expression of, among other aspects, two considerations. It indicates, first, the compatibility of the content of a given proposal with the perceived national interest and, secondly, the relation of that country (delegation) to other countries (delegations) voting in the same manner. Both are, though in varying degrees, the result of influences emanating from a comprehensive process of bargaining which usually precedes the actual taking of votes. In fact a delegation may *accept* a proposal despite certain reservations about its content if it considers it important to demonstrate its *agreement* with other countries (delegations) — especially if this is the case regarding the sponsor(s) of a proposal — or to join a respective voting coalition. Fig. 1 indicates the rather complex picture of influences that combine in determining the voting behaviour of a country's delegation. In the late sixties the majority in the UN General Assembly gradually changed in favour of the developing countries, and the majority of issues voted on became increasingly linked in one way or another to North–South issues. Non-aligned policy goals could thus be transformed into a specific UN policy either by, again, an 'equidistance' of the non-aligned countries to the USSR and USA, or, even more strongly, into a particularly articulated 'southern' position. In sum, we would expect that the *bilateral foreign relations* of a developing country with the superpowers are the more balanced (and possibly tending to a lower level) *and* that its *voting behaviour* in the UN shows a more balanced position between the superpowers (or even a strong southern orientation), the greater the *non-aligned tradition* of the country and its *participation in the movement's activities*.

Empirical data to test these relations cover the period 1961–72 (non-alignment) and 1968–72 (foreign relations and voting). The limitation on the time period places certain restrictions on the eventual interpretation of the results. Since then non-alignment has further developed both in terms of an expansion of its membership and priorities in its policy concerns. However, the purpose of the analysis is not to examine non-alignment *per se*, nor to explain aspects of non-aligned foreign policy behaviour. Our central question whether non-aligned policy orientation has an impact on the autonomy of foreign policy in relation to the superpowers gained a renewed critical assessment during the period under examination here. At the end of the sixties non-alignment developed new initiatives after a certain passivity after 1964. In addition, development issues moved increasingly into the foreground of the non-aligned policy concerns, and gave new momentum to the movement. Our examination thus focuses on how these new approaches were transformed at the two policy levels so far discussed.[4]

To ascertain the intensity of a country's *commitment to non-alignment* we will refer to the frequency with which it participated in major non-aligned conferences.[5] This appears as a valid indicator considering that the decision to participate in non-aligned conferences implies a decisive declaration of a country's intentions and foreign policy orientation. It should be noted that membership in the movement requires an 'application' in order to be admitted to participate fully and formally in the movement's activities. The decision to join the movement in turn shapes, or even modifies, expectations held by other states as to the international behaviour of such country in general, and more particularly the country is confronted with expectations of the non-aligned states that it conducts in conformity with the goals of the movement, especially in its international relations.

Table 1 (Column Participation) gives a grouping of the developing countries according to the frequency of their participation in major conferences of the non-aligned countries from 1961 to 1972. The first group includes those which participated in all six conferences during this period. The second group includes countries with a participation rate between 66 and 99% (four to five conferences). The third group consists of states which participated in 1–66% (three conferences, or less). Finally, the fourth group comprises those developing countries which are not members of the movement, and accordingly never participated in any of the conferences.

The *voting agreement* as an indicator of closeness, or, conversely, distance to policy positions of either the USSR or the USA is measured by Lijphart's Index of Agreement, for the period from 1962 to 1972. The index measures how often country A agrees with country B in a given number of votes.[6] To interpret the index, a value of 80 or more (with a maximum value of 100) indicates a 'high' agreement, values between 61 and 79 show a 'moderate', and values of 60 or less a 'low' level of agreement. The maximum value of 100 implies that two delegations voted identically in all votes taken and accordingly adopted similar views on the voting issues.

Table 1 (Column Voting Agreement) gives the agreement index with both the USSR and the USA for all the developing countries and each of the years 1968 to 1972. Table 2 aggregates these data into two averages, first the agreement index with the USSR and the USA for each of the country groups for each of the years (mean) and, secondly, for the whole period (mean and median).

The *strength of foreign relations* is measured by a composite Index of Foreign Relations (FRI) which takes into account a variety of indicators (see Fig. 1) reflecting general political relations (treaties concluded; size of diplomatic staff; visits of heads of state and other delegations); economic relations (export, import, development aid); and military relations (military presence of the USSR/USA, supply of armaments).[7] The FRI

Table 1 (1) Participation in non-aligned conferences, 1960–72; (2) GA voting agreement with Soviet Union and United States, 1968–72; (3) Strength of foreign relations with Soviet Union and United States, 1968–72

Country	Partici- pation (%)	Voting Agreement										Foreign Relations									
		With SU					With USA					With SU					With USA				
		68	69	70	71	72	68	69	70	71	72	68	69	70	71	72	68	69	70	71	72
Group 1																					
Afghanistan	100	70	78	72	84	83	40	39	47	38	51	417	417	493	379	434	86	64	62	85	60
Algeria	100	78	85	82	85	85	29	33	39	35	46	354	325	236	384	240	19	53	55	24	34
Burundi	100	76	83	77	83	82	32	31	40	39	48	–	3	3	0	–	–	123	84	130	–
Centr. Afr. Rep.	100	56	70	70	66	79	55	50	49	59	51	8	64	72	44	–	48	23	15	16	–
Ceylon – Sri Lanka	100	74	85	79	87	80	40	32	40	35	48	89	59	68	196	25	116	233	64	146	202
Cyprus	100	68	77	72	81	81	46	46	49	43	48	24	49	21	25	49	94	97	33	155	110
Ethiopia	100	66	79	71	80	80	45	43	50	43	50	42	43	42	57	62	318	357	319	370	365
Ghana	100	69	80	74	67	74	41	41	47	56	51	36	10	79	11	68	170	197	163	245	238
Guinea	100	85	89	84	85	89	26	26	34	35	34	307	320	253	301	282	157	131	111	83	75
India	100	74	82	74	87	82	36	40	45	35	46	345	356	363	393	394	261	236	200	190	151
Indonesia	100	70	85	75	78	79	42	36	45	44	46	6	11	48	81	39	338	226	214	297	218
Iraq	100	85	89	83	92	87	28	30	35	32	44	219	236	356	408	453	3	7	8	44	16
Kenya	100	77	86	74	73	80	33	32	45	48	46	9	3	18	13	49	68	69	72	76	73
Kuwait	100	63	86	79	88	85	35	29	40	35	47	10	5	6	13	1	69	33	80	33	35
Lebanon	100	63	83	72	75	83	53	38	47	49	47	22	14	52	162	73	136	131	171	228	166
Mali	100	76	86	80	83	84	34	30	39	35	43	109	191	71	65	–	55	92	46	50	–
Morocco	100	72	83	76	82	80	40	32	43	40	43	118	82	87	88	72	160	267	206	316	106
Nepal	100	74	76	67	78	78	37	43	54	44	56	0	42	53	–	–	128	130	134	–	–
Sierra Leone	100	65	66	70	79	83	46	48	49	43	45	27	12	9	78	16	106	125	98	94	142
Somalia	100	75	79	84	87	80	28	37	34	36	49	231	210	129	309	376	72	95	90	54	53
Southern Yemen	100	78	88	85	90	84	26	29	34	34	45	256	358	279	354	–	8	2	0	0	–
Sudan	100	82	87	87	87	82	28	31	32	37	48	245	352	346	329	90	15	45	11	14	49
Syria	100	83	90	84	87	83	29	28	34	34	44	390	411	380	363	518	12	7	5	12	8
Tunisia	100	71	79	74	77	81	42	40	45	45	48	89	51	5	81	51	164	180	108	105	157

Uganda	100	76	82	82	79	83	34	30	37	43	47	135	84	40	36	55	124	74	175	81	79
Un. Arab. Rep.	100	72	90	80	84	80	28	27	39	37	45	474	510	513	615	504	17	21	18	52	61
Un. Rep. Tanzania	100	78	87	82	87	81	30	29	37	38	44	74	46	48	121	42	107	93	70	112	61
Yemen Arab Rep.	100	78	88	76	87	86	26	27	43	35	44	246	193	204	181	153	0	0	68	3	5
Zaïre	100	63	71	83	58	77	45	48	38	66	50	0	12	0	–	–	132	120	86	–	–
Zambia	100	73	85	83	83	85	32	27	33	40	46	8	13	7	54	65	21	55	55	27	22
Group 2																					
Burma	67	76	85	66	83	81	40	43	51	40	47	51	15	71	28	78	161	161	63	58	64
Cambodia	67	85	93	57	60	76	24	27	64	64	53	104	75	0	0	0	–	–	246	272	253
Cameroon	83	71	73	66	82	79	38	47	53	38	46	16	19	47	49	43	60	61	68	67	126
Congo P. R.	83	75	82	60	86	83	35	33	56	34	43	45	65	149	69	–	11	46	13	16	–
Cuba	83	78	87	95	89	90	32	31	26	32	38	–	–	–	–	–	0	33	0	0	–
Guyana	75	65	69	68	82	84	41	52	52	43	46	1	1	1	4	17	253	170	146	184	151
Jamaica	80	56	56	56	68	75	51	60	63	56	51	0	2	1	0	–	186	322	218	209	309
Jordan	83	74	82	75	75	80	41	37	44	47	51	27	144	89	40	39	249	265	237	358	245
Laos	83	59	69	68	61	70	57	54	53	60	64	0	3	0	0	0	247	358	375	360	352
Liberia	83	49	63	53	56	71	58	59	66	62	56	0	0	3	1	4	423	423	421	321	326
Libya	83	73	87	81	87	83	34	31	38	36	41	16	105	116	7	41	233	170	42	37	35
Malawi	80	28	48	41	32	60	82	69	78	83	71	0	0	0	0	0	51	52	51	53	50
Malaysia	67	52	73	72	81	80	60	50	47	40	47	68	49	14	29	50	132	127	158	131	186
Mauritania	83	83	88	84	83	85	27	29	34	38	43	108	106	12	5	15	22	23	25	59	54
Nigeria	67	64	82	88	83	82	40	37	31	40	44	138	171	148	107	65	120	131	140	150	151
Senegal	83	65	73	71	75	81	48	53	50	46	46	8	9	43	45	20	51	52	53	53	54
Singapore	75	66	73	65	73	76	46	54	56	52	56	31	42	7	23	9	85	121	100	105	157
Group 3																					
Chad	50	67	69	62	72	79	42	43	59	51	51	15	4	33	111	48	20	46	10	42	45
Chile	17	55	63	73	86	80	59	55	46	38	47	0	3	53	171	211	211	298	308	168	211
Dahomey/Benin	17	65	67	52	63	79	45	54	69	60	47	10	2	3	26	–	36	58	20	54	–
Madagascar	17	58	63	53	55	80	58	52	66	63	45	0	0	1	1	8	41	80	79	79	42
Mauritius	50	55	71	63	42	82	55	46	56	63	47	0	78	89	55	63	27	44	77	55	85

(–) No data available.

Table 1 continued

Country	Partici-pation (%)	Voting Agreement With SU					Voting Agreement With USA					Foreign Relations With SU					Foreign Relations With USA				
		68	69	70	71	72	68	69	70	71	72	68	69	70	71	72	68	69	70	71	72
Rwanda	60	66	63	47	72	80	46	47	74	49	55	0	1	4	7	2	15	48	50	51	61
Saudi Arabia	33	65	77	77	77	81	42	38	42	42	49	1	1	2	1	0	128	104	50	151	211
Togo	33	59	72	60	80	77	48	54	58	45	50	10	69	25	73	30	12	47	46	49	48
Trinidad & Tob.	40	58	67	66	73	77	53	56	53	51	48	0	0	0	0	0	82	122	144	97	106
Group 4																					
Argentina	0	56	63	52	56	72	59	55	69	69	57	4	4	3	42	3	131	264	264	287	283
Barbados	0	57	67	55	58	66	50	50	61	57	56	0	0	0	0	0	106	66	64	53	58
Bolivia	0	50	57	50	45	64	65	58	71	78	59	0	0	143	134	67	361	274	210	210	302
Brazil	0	40	57	47	57	64	67	66	72	71	61	4	9	4	37	63	403	344	301	304	298
Colombia	0	60	48	55	62	64	55	68	66	58	60	–	9	24	7	1	430	243	294	301	249
Costa Rica	0	50	45	48	44	61	62	74	71	66	58	0	11	125	108	70	247	262	248	226	228
Dominican R.	0	49	61	51	50	56	63	57	70	65	62	0	0	0	0	–	473	384	464	310	–
Ecuador	0	73	57	63	73	77	41	59	58	49	49	20	35	4	9	1	352	265	298	289	283
El Salvador	0	56	44	37	52	64	59	77	84	66	62	4	0	0	0	4	282	286	188	194	187

(–) No data available.

Table 2. Voting agreement and strength of foreign relations of non-aligned/developing countries with Soviet Union and United States by country groups: (1) Group means for individual years; (2) Group mean/median 1968–72

| | *Voting agreement* | | | | | | | | | | | | | | *Foreign relations* | | | | | | | | | | | | | |
| | *With SU* | | | | | | | *With USA* | | | | | | | *With SU* | | | | | | | *With USA* | | | | | | |
	68	69	70	71	72	Mean	Median	68	69	70	71	72	Mean	Median	68	69	70	71	72	Mean	Median	68	69	70	71	72	Mean	Median
Group 1	73	82	78	81	82	79	80	36	35	41	41	47	40	38	148	149	143	184	171	159	75	104	110	94	109	104	104	83
Group 2	66	76	69	74	79	73	74	44	45	51	48	49	47	46	38	50	44	25	25	37	15	143	157	139	143	168	150	121
Group 3	61	68	61	69	79	68	68	50	49	58	51	49	51	51	4	18	23	49	45	28	8	64	94	87	82	101	86	52
Group 4	54	58	55	62	71	60	59	59	61	64	59	55	60	60	36	26	34	36	29	32	3	250	245	258	245	245	249	261

varies numerically between 0 and 700. It measures only the intensity of bilateral relations of a country with (in this case) the USSR and the USA rather than their respective relative share in the totality of foreign relations of a country. The construction of the index provides a measure of the average intensity of relations, without allowing further conclusions as to the contribution to the over-all value of any of the fields mentioned above in comparison to the other fields. However, since the individual indicators are highly correlated (e.g. a substantial supply of armaments is usually connected with a high level of development aid as well as close diplomatic ties) the index, despite its simplicity, conveys a fairly realistic picture of the over-all intensity of bilateral relations of a particular LDC with each of the superpowers. Table 1 (Column Foreign Relations) gives the FRI for all developing countries with both superpowers and for each year. Table 2 gives the averages corresponding to those given for the Voting Agreement.

3. Results: Degree of Non-alignment, Voting Agreement, and Foreign Relations

The various aspects of the non-aligned policy goals discussed in the introductory part and their transformation into actual foreign policy may be reformulated for purposes of analysis in terms of three criteria. These express those characteristics of relations which non-aligned policy should transcend, i.e. we would expect them to be absent or decrease in order to speak of a successful transformation of non-aligned policy goals in terms of a (growing) autonomy and 'equidistance'. The 'negative conditions' are:

(1) *Exclusivity of strong foreign relations.* If there are strong foreign relations to one superpower, then relations to the other one are low.

(2) *Exclusivity of high voting agreement.* If there is a high voting agreement with one of the superpowers, then the agreement with the other one is low.

(3) *Correlation of foreign relations with voting agreement.* A high strength of foreign relations with one of the superpowers correlates positively with high voting agreement with the same power.

We first consider the characteristics of the individual groups of countries. The first group of countries has the longest non-aligned tradition (its members participated in all conferences) and comprises mostly North African and Middle East states as well as a few Asian and African states. The group has the highest average voting agreement with the USSR and the lowest with the USA in comparison to all other groups. The group also has the highest strength of foreign relations with the USSR in comparison to the other groups, and ranks second lowest in foreign relations with the USA. Some individual members of the group deviate from this pattern: African states such as Burundi, Kenya, Zaïre, and Zambia, and North African/Middle East states such as Ethiopia and Cyprus, maintain close relations to either the USA or their former colonial centres. One notes, however, that even countries without any or only a low strength of foreign relations with the USSR have a high degree of voting agreement with this power.

The second group of countries is — according to our criteria — less intensively involved in the history of the movement's evolution. It comprises most African countries and a smaller number of North African and Middle East countries. The voting agreement is higher with the USSR than with the USA, and the agreement is higher (lower) than for the following groups. Only Cuba maintains strong foreign relations with the USSR; Cambodia, Guyana, Jamaica, Jordan, Laos, and Liberia have strong relations with the USA while the remaining members still have close ties with their former colonial powers.

The third group participated to a lesser degree in non-aligned activities/conferences than groups 1 and 2 and is thus composed of the least 'socialized' non-aligned countries. Apart from a small number of North African and Middle East states there is a majority of African states. The voting agreement is again highest with the USSR, but the absolute level is lower than for each of the two former groups and the difference to the USA has further narrowed (the exception is Southern Yemen). The foreign relations within the group are strongest with the USA, though only at a moderate absolute level. The exceptions are Chile and Saudi Arabia, which both stand out with high levels in foreign relations with the USA.

The countries of the fourth group never took part in any of the non-aligned conferences during the period. Relative to the three groups of non-aligned countries, this group of 'non-nonaligned' states can be considered, in statistical terms, as a 'control group' since only a few of its members are seriously aligned formally with either of the major powers (though the traditional ties of the Latin American states, which are strongly represented, with the USA should be taken into account). In comparison with the non-aligned groups, the 'non-nonaligned' group shows the lowest degree of voting agreement with the USSR (without any country departing from this pattern), and correspondingly the highest agreement level with the USA. The absolute figures, however, are almost identical, i.e. there is practically no difference in voting agreement with the USSR and the USA. The foreign relations are strongest with the USA, at a level more than twice as high as the highest level of foreign relations with the USA among the non-aligned groups, and almost non-existent with the USSR. The exceptions within the group in this regard are Iran, Pakistan, and Turkey with rather balanced relations, and Gambia, Gabon, Niger, and Upper Volta with strong ties to former colonial powers.

Comparing the four groups according to the three criteria introduced, we find (see Table 2 and Fig. 2): in the field of *foreign relations*, the average strength (median) is highest with the USA for all groups. This general condition can be qualified in two respects. The average level of foreign relations of the 'non-nonaligned' country group with the USA is standing out by rising between more than two to five times above the non-aligned groups. Comparing the strength of foreign relations with the USA and the USSR, we note, with the exception for the first group, an

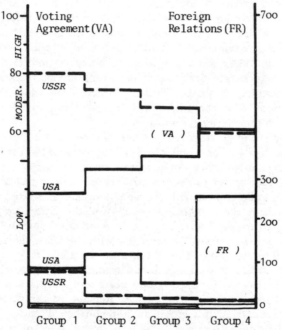

Fig. 2.   Average strength of foreign relations and voting agreement with USSR and USA, 1968–72 (median)

inverse relationship, i.e. the higher the level of relations with the USA, the lower the level with the USSR. For group 1, the countries with the longest non-aligned tradition, the strength of relations is at roughly the same level with both superpowers. Within the non-aligned group there is a slight inconsistency. With respect to the USSR, the strength of foreign relations is highest for group 1, and it decreases in accordance with the decreasing non-aligned tradition of the groups. This clear-cut pattern cannot be seen in the relations with the USA, where group 3 deviates. The explanation must probably be sought in the presence of African countries in this group, with relations to former colonial powers rather than to the USA. This possible 'substitute effect' cannot be investigated in this analysis, though it might again establish the consistency of the pattern at the 'bloc level' so as to find a decreasing strength of relations with increasing non-aligned tradition. The differences in the level of foreign relations for each of the groups also reflects this order: it is greatest for group 4 'in favour' of the USA and then decreases, reaching the lowest level for the first group.

In the field of *voting agreement*, we find the highest agreement level between group 1 and the USSR, which decreases in accordance with the non-aligned tradition. In comparison with the USA there is a consistent inverse relationship, i.e. the higher the agreement with the USSR, the lower the agreement level with the USA. It should be noted, however, that the agreement level reaches a certain base line in the case of group 4, for which the values are practically identical with respect to both powers. Taking this 'balanced' situation as a starting-point, we can observe increasing differences in favour of the USSR with the growing non-aligned tradition of a group.

The consequences of the degree of non-alignment of a country and both its foreign relations and voting agreement with the superpowers so far discussed are summarized and further specified by the correlation (Pearson's r) between non-alignment and both types of relations:

Table 3. Correlation between degree of non-alignment and foreign relations/voting agreement

	Voting Agreement		Foreign Relations	
	With USSR	With USA	With USSR	With USA
Degree of Non-alignment	0.72	−0.72	0.35	−0.27

The coefficients express what is already visible in Fig. 2. There is a strong positive correlation between the degree of non-alignment and the voting agreement with the USSR, while the relation with the USA is equally negative. The relation between non-alignment and strength of foreign relations is less intensive, and again positive for the USSR while moderately negative for the USA.

4. Conclusions

Relating these findings to the goals of the non-aligned policy, the following conclusions emerge. In the field of foreign relations the condition of exclusivity is strongly present, only group 1 tends towards a certain balance with respect to both the USA and the USSR. A look at the development over time shows that the relation to the USA has been rather stable, such that the balance is the result of a strengthening of relations with the USSR. However, all non-aligned groups differ strikingly from the 'non-nonaligned' group. Regarding the voting agreement there is a similar trend towards exclusivity with the other superpower, the USSR. It becomes the greater, the greater the non-aligned tradition. Looking again at the development over time, we note that the voting agreement of the USSR with all groups markedly increased from 1968 to 1972. To a much lesser degree this also applies to the agreement with the USA for groups 1 and 2, while it slightly decreased with respect to groups 3 and 4. The strength of the correlation between non-alignment and voting agreement in the case of the USSR must be seen in conjunction with the much weaker correlation between non-alignment and foreign relations. With this small 'material' basis, the USSR strongly supports for tactical and ideological reasons the positions of LDCs, while the USA opposes these positions during this period in favour of 'northern-industrial' interests. Within this context, then, LDCs have a greater flexibility to follow a southern course while maintaining comparatively strong relations with the USSR. On the other hand, strong ties to the USA, at a higher level in absolute terms, restrict freedom to act and transform into a tendency towards greater voting agreement with the USA, or, less flexibility for 'southern' positions. The conditions in the foreign relations field reflect a fact which is of fatal significance for Soviet foreign policy, viz. that the USSR as a consequence of its mode of production, quality, and quantity of its products is in a weaker position to absorb exports from LDCs and to offer exports itself as compared with the USA. Thus, despite its general international position, it does not yet appear as a satisfactory alternative to the USA in the field of foreign economic relations. The changes in voting agreement between the USA and groups 3 and 4 signal however, that the countries with strong ties to the USA begin to emancipate from 'north-western' points of view in their UN voting attitudes.

Notes

1. The exception is Yugoslavia. Since data used in the present analysis were derived from data collected for an analysis of relations between developing countries and the USSR/USA in the UN, Yugoslavia is not included in this analysis since it does not qualify according to available indicators as a developing country. This is unfortunate with a view to the outstanding role of Yugoslavia as a non-aligned country. However, the results of the analysis will not be affected significantly by its non-inclusion.

2. The formal criterion of non-alignment introduced at the First Summit Conference in 1961 defines the non-aligned character in terms of non-membership in one of the blocs. The official formulation refers to various forms of alliance and treaty ties as well as to military bases as incompatible with a non-aligned status if they are related with the East–West conflict. In some instances these conditions were relaxed; the development problem has gradually become the 'second dimension' of non-aligned policy goals.

3. Tadić, Bojana (1969). 'Le non-alignement – Aperçu conceptuel et historique' in *Le Non-Alignement dans le Monde Contemporain* (Beograd, 1969), 123–42 (140). A more recent summary by the same author is 'preservation of peace (disarmament, peaceful settlement), consolidation of national independence (. . .), economic and overall social development (. . .), and democratization of international relations', cf. Tadić, Bojana (1976), *Nesvrstanost u teorij i praksi*

medunarodnih odnosa (Non-alignment in the theory and practice of foreign relations) (Beograd: Instituta za Medunarodnu Politiku i Privredu), 387 ff., translations by the author.

4. For a more broadly based analysis of voting behaviour and bilateral relations between developing countries and the superpowers, from which data for this analysis were derived, see Burri, Klaus (1977). *UNO- Abstimmungsverhalten und Bilaterale Beziehungen* (UN Voting Behaviour and Bilateral Relations). Kleine Studien zur Politischen Wissenschaft 114–16 (Zürich: Forschungsstelle für Politische Wissenschaft der Universität Zürich).

5. Conferences included for the period 1961–72 are the non-aligned summit conferences in Belgrade (1961), Cairo (1964), Lusaka (1970), the consultative meeting in Belgrade (1969), the preparatory meeting in Dar es Salaam (1970), and the meeting of foreign ministers in Georgetown (1972). Despite the different levels of the meetings, the two consultative/preparatory conferences are significant since they precede the first summit and the Lusaka summit, respectively. The latter took place after a period of disintegration in the movement, such that they are not only 'technical' but also of political significance in terms of participation. The Georgetown Conference is important as elaborating various 'Action Programmes', notably for the strategy of 'self-reliance', following respective decisions by the Lusaka Conference.

6. The calculation of the Index of Agreement (IA) is as follows:

$$IA = \frac{f + 0.5g}{t} \times 100, \text{ with } t: \text{ total number of votes under consideration;}$$

f: number of votes with full agreement;

g: number of votes with partial agreement (abstention).

For a detailed discussion see Lijphart, Arend (1963). 'The Analysis of Bloc Voting in the General Assembly: A Critique and a Proposal.' *American Political Science Review*, LVII. 902–17.

7. The Index of Foreign Relations is based on the following indicators: Imports from USA/USSR; exports to USA/USSR; Formal treaties with USA/USSR; development aid from USA/USSR; state visits from/to the USSR and size of diplomatic representation of the USA in LDC's (different indicator due to availability of data); armament transfer from USA/USSR; share of development aid (in %) by USA/USSR from total aid received by a country; military presence of USA/USSR in a country. The raw indicators were standardized as follows:

$$I_{st} = \frac{I_r \times 100}{I_r \text{ (max)}}, \text{ with } I_{st}: \text{ standardized indicator;}$$

I_r: raw indicator;

I_r(max) maximum value of raw indicator.

The resulting value of each individual indicator for each LDC is a percentage of the possible maximum value. Apart from the comparability of individual values, standardization has a further desirable effect. The bilateral relationship of a particular LDC with the USA or the USSR is 'filtered out' from the totality of its bilateral relations in that a particular value (e.g. of its imports, development aid, etc.) is compared with the respective maximum value that occurs in the relations of *all other* LDCs with that superpower. The Index is then calculated by simple addition of all standardized indicator values. For a further discussion of details, cf. Burri, 1977 (*n. 4*), 69 ff.

PART III

ADJUSTING NORMATIVE STANDARDS FOR INTERNATIONAL BEHAVIOUR

9 THE NEW INTERNATIONAL ECONOMIC ORDER AND INTERNATIONAL LAW: PROGRESSIVE DEVELOPMENT OR DECLINE?

KATARINA TOMAŠEVSKI
Institute of Social Studies, University of Zagreb

1. Introduction

According to Stanley Hoffmann there are only three possible attitudes towards the state of international law today: cynicism, hypocrisy, and consternation.[1] The apparent (non-) regulation of international economic relations seems to a cynic to support what is expressed in the old saying about the weather: everybody talks about it, but nobody does anything. While, on the one hand, we have principles and rules striving towards the creation of a just and equitable world economic order, we are facing, on the other hand, a worsening economic crisis in the whole world, affecting the majority of mankind.

There is room for consternation too. In any attempt to evaluate the role that international law plays in the endeavours for the establishment of the New International Economic Order (NIEO) we cannot escape the conclusion that there exists a discrepancy between (a) the state of that part of international law which is supposed to regulate international economic relations, and (b) the goals, principles, and rules for the NIEO. The body of legally binding rules applicable to the regulation of international economic relations has been created according to the traditional doctrine of the sources of international law,[2] but the documents embodying the principles of the NIEO have doubtful legal value. Being adopted by plenary bodies of UN organs, various forms of international organizations or groupings of states (e.g. the 'Group of 77', the 'non-aligned'), intergovernmental or international conferences, they do not fit into the enumeration of the sources of international law. The decision-making process that developed in the course of formulating the principles of the NIEO is based partially on the majority principle, and partially on 'consensus'. The conditions under which international norms are created and achieve *legal* validity are founded on quite different principles, as expressed in the notions of custom (following research of state practice), *opinio juris*, and ratification of conventions. The striking differences which characterize the processes generating these two bodies of rules as well as their actual contents pose a dilemma: is the *New* International Economic Order going to be based on *positive* international law, or are we going towards the establishment of some new kind of regulation? The answer to this question is dependent upon the possibilities and constraints in the development of international law ('progressive development'[3]) in the economic field, or, conversely, on the prospects that the establishment of the NIEO can be furthered within the legal framework as it presently exists.

If the establishment of the NIEO is to be considered as a part of international public policy (which, by all means, holds true for the UN), international law could be the best tool to govern the process of its implementation and subsequent operation. It is by now generally accepted that the mere interplay of market forces is by itself neither a sufficient, nor always a suitable, basis for the whole set of reforms that should transform the 'old' International Economic Order into the 'new' one. When it was realized that '. . . the development objective would not be served by the spontaneous operation of market forces, that conscious action was needed, that conscious policies had to be formulated and implemented, and that conscious changes were to be introduced in the prevailing network of systems and institutions',[4] rules were increasingly introduced to suppress or control market forces and developed gradually into an (though all but consistent) 'international economic law'.[5]

Any attempt to examine what is being done about the NIEO has to take as a point of departure an analysis of UN activities. Although national governments are still the primary international actors regulating and limiting the capacities of international organizations (which they form and attempt to reform according to their, often selfish, interests), every international organization obtains and develops a life of its own. The UN system of today is certainly a 'world of its own', much different from what was originally designed at the end of the Second World War.

2. The UN Challenged

'The institutions of today are the result of power relationships of yesterday . . . One central feature of the institutions is that they are devised to give stability to existing power and property relationships. When circumstances change, this means that institutions protect inherited privileges.'[6] Drastic changes in the membership of the UN[7] hardly effected any changes in the decision-making processes within the world organization. It should be stated that the UN, when founded, was burdened with the primary task of preserving the world order ('peace and security'). This is still one of the supreme values mankind is committed to, yet it is no longer *the* primary goal of the UN system as a whole. Furthermore, it has been stated more than once that '. . . the present international economic order is *in direct conflict* with current developments in international political and economic relations . . . The gap between the developed and the developing countries continues to widen in a system which was established when most of the developing countries did not even exist as independent states and which *perpetuates inequality.*'[8]

It is natural that in a world which had just undergone a world war, peace at any cost was the value that united mankind. The gradual transformation of the international community by the process of decolonization created more than a hundred newly independent states. Gaining independence and obtaining a formally equal status with the existing states was — as it became obvious in the 1960s — only the first step on the road to freedom and well-being. As Ashish Nandy correctly states, '. . . human civilization is continuously trying to alter or expand its awareness of exploitation and oppression. Oppressions which were once outside the span of awareness are no longer so . . ..'[9] Economic disparities, for ages outside the realm of activities of international organizations and beyond the concerns of international law, came to be pointed at as *the* sphere that should be tackled by them. Conscious of the fact that nobody is sufficiently motivated by goodness or altruism alone to give up inherited privileges, the 'Third World', organized in the 'Group of 77', set forth a demand for restructuring the world order which was eventually formalized in the NIEO Programme.

Most of the countries being non-European, they demanded changes affecting basic postulates of the international community. Without trying to list all the causes of the demands set forth, some should be mentioned: (1) the 'euro-centric' model of the world community cannot be applied to an international community in which Europe constitutes just a small part; (2) the emergence of socialist states proved that there are many different types of socio-economic systems that can co-exist in the world; and (3) the newly independent states were forced to model their foreign relations according to international legal norms (customary law) in the formation of which they did not participate.

3. Demanding A New Order: From Economic Growth to Development Needs

Demands of the underdeveloped countries for changing the 'rules of the game' in the international economic system started in the 1960s, advanced from the stage of bitter confrontations over conflicting proposals to the formulation of basic principles of the NIEO in the 1970s, and are developing into an elaboration of mechanisms for their implementation in the 1980s.

Through the process of fashioning the NIEO, the Third World countries have gradually redefined their demands. The reliance on GNP as the sole indicator of development resulted in an assumption that *the* way to development was economic growth. Accordingly, striving towards an increase of the GNP the Third World countries relied on loans and grants of capital and technical assistance, all needed to speed up the race in industrialization, which, ultimately, resulted in imitating the models that had proved successful. They realized later, it should be added, that these development models had been successful only for others. During that stage traditional mechanisms that foster inequality were preserved, both internally and internationally. The need for structural changes in the world economic system gradually became the major requirement for the establishment of the NIEO, followed subsequently by two important new issues. First, the development needs of the developing countries were emphasized, and the notion of *the* way of development was abolished. Autonomous development models and processes came to be emphasized instead, and the satisfaction of human needs and self-reliance were set forth, thus substituting the GNP race without considering the social consequences of growth without development. Secondly, 'as the shortage of resources is beginning to be recognized as a key global issue, however, another line of distinction will increase in importance – distinction between "resource-rich" and "resource-poor" defined in terms of the degree of self-sufficiency in the supply of those key-resources necessary for a nation to attain the desired rate of socio-economic growth'.[10] Conscious of the increase in their bargaining power, the developing countries changed their demands accordingly; now they demanded an economic system that would give them the ability to earn their living through stable commodity prices, control over their natural wealth and resources, access to new technology, and improved mechanisms for collaboration among themselves and global co-operation.

In such a context, the core goals and principles of the NIEO were formulated in the Declaration on the Establishment of the NIEO and in the Charter of Economic Rights and Duties of States as:

- sovereign equality of all states, non-aggression and non-intervention,
- equal rights and self-determination of all peoples.
- the broadest international co-operation to accelerate the development of all developing countries,
- the right of every country to follow its own way of development,
- full permanent sovereignty of every state over its natural wealth and resources and over all economic activities.[11]

The Preamble of the Charter of Economic Rights and Duties of States states, *inter alia*, '. . . the urgent need to establish or improve norms of universal application for the development of international economic relations on a *just* and *equitable* basis . . .'. The notion of both *justice and equality* is interwoven into most of the basic NIEO documents, and it poses the question of sufficiency of international law as an adequate tool for implementing NIEO policies. If we consider *justice* as adherence to standards set forth by fundamental international legal principles and

norms,[12] that part of the basis for the NIEO could be found by interpretation and further development of positive international law. But
the very notion of *equity* suggests that principles of the NIEO are going
further and seek supplementary sources, which can possibly be derived
only from 'the general principles of law recognized by civilized nations'.
There are thus clear limits to positive law as a means for the implementation of the principles and goals of the NIEO.

However, there are numerous ways and means for international lawyers
to take a part in the struggle for the establishment of the NIEO, besides
trying either to interpret international law to suit the demands for the
NIEO or to interpret the principles of the NIEO to fit into the existing
international legal framework. 'Lawyers perform a normative task (goal
clarification) that includes specification, elaboration and justification of
goals and the suggestion of priorities.'[13] Understanding international law
as a *means of communication*, not only as a *regulatory mechanism* for
relations among states, will increase its role in this particular stage of the
establishment of the NIEO, when the shared perceptions of common
goals and objectives of mankind concerning the international economic
order have to be converted from aspirations into rules of behaviour in
the international community.

4. International Law in Transition: Towards New Values and Principles Proclaimed in the Context of NIEO

As Professor Louis Henkin rightfully states, 'In the society we have,
international law sustains what order we have and promises better'.[14]
Most of the promises for a better world are found in documents concerning the NIEO. According to the Declaration on the Establishment
of a New International Economic Order, it is to be based 'on equity,
sovereign equality, interdependence, common interest and cooperation
among all states' and it 'shall correct inequalities and redress existing
injustices, make it possible to eliminate the widening gap between the
developed and the developing countries, and ensure steadily accelerating
economic and social development and peace and justice for present and
future generations'. Experience has always demonstrated that proclaiming
objectives is the easier part of the task as compared with their implementation through mechanisms of the existing order. However, if there exists
a basic consensus on the fundamental values, objectives, and principles
of the NIEO in the international community, it is an achievement that
should not be underestimated: it means that we know which way to go.
Naturally, it is not possible to list all the values and goals of mankind
in a couple of UN declarations and resolutions, but if those documents
are taken to represent the minimum common denominator of the international community, they can and should be the basis for the world
of tomorrow. What are the ways and means for building the new world

embodying the NIEO? And, what is the proper role of international law, especially of legal science and international lawyers in its creation? The answer to these two questions will demonstrate the role of law in the world of today and anticipate the role of international law in the future.

Basic principles and goals proclaimed in the NIEO documents are consistent with the UN law. The Preamble to the UN Charter, besides expressing the determination to maintain international peace and security, declares that international machinery is to be employed 'for the promotion of the economic and social advancement of all peoples'. Such notions as peace, economic welfare, social justice, non-discrimination, are vague enough to enable, probably, every human being to give them a different understanding. Peace, being the supreme value, is easy to define at first sight. However, it seems doubtful that it is susceptible of an internationally acceptable definition.[15] What then of terms such as: 'All States . . . as equal members of the international community, have the right *to participate fully and effectively* in the international decision-making process in the solution of world economic, financial and monetary problems.'?[16] What are the criteria for determining whether the participation of a state in deliberations of an international economic organization is effective? If there is no 'one state — one vote' principle in making a decision, does it mean that it jeopardizes equality of states? And, do we have sufficient grounds to believe that even state representatives, who drafted the provision quoted above, had a common understanding of what it means?

There is still another point of view to be taken into account. The emerging commitment to basic principles of the NIEO, even in an abstract form, is 'an indication of the unity on values and consensus on principles.'[17] Those principles represent a sense of shared values, aims, and goals that mankind will strive to promote and, possibly, develop into rules for behaviour based on such values and principles. There are hints of changes which reflect this aspect of international law as a policy-instrument: 'international law of co-operation', 'international law of development', 'international law of economic welfare', are doctrinal suggestions of innovations designed to accommodate alternations in international public policy.[18] Consequently, there is a trend to alter international law by activities and decisions of international organizations, which do not have binding power, and a parallel effort by international lawyers to find room — within the system of contemporary international law — for building the NIEO on the foundations of the present legal system. But, although claiming to act in pursuit of common values and interests of mankind, neither international organizations nor the doctrine have binding power to convert demands and aspirations into rules for behaviour.

5. 'Is-Orientation' v. 'Ought-Orientation'

'It is not the primary function of international law in the second half of
the twentieth century to protect vested interests arising out of an international distribution of political power which has irrevocably changed,
but to adjust conflicting interests on a basis which contemporary opinion
regards as sufficiently reasonable to be entitled to the organized support
of a universal community.'[19] That is also a doctrinal assessment, but it
is an inspiring beginning into a search for major discrepancies between
positive international law and the principles of the NIEO.

The principles of sovereign equality and non-discrimination of states
are undoubtedly among the basic principles of international law applicable
to the field of economic relations. The General Agreement on Tariffs and
Trade, for example, proclaims the general application of the most-favoured-
nation clause to contracting parties (Arts. XIII and XIV).[20] The postulated
rule states that, according to the principle of sovereign equality of states,
all states should accord to one another equal treatment. If any privileges
are granted, they are given out of free will and consent of the state grant-
ing them. So *reciprocity* came to be recognized as one of the corner-stones
of the international legal system. However, the NIEO proclaimed the
principle of discrimination in favour of the developing countries. The
Charter of Economic Rights and Duties of States proclaims it in the
following ways: 'Developed countries should extend, improve and enlarge
the system of generalized *non-reciprocal* and non-discriminatory tariff
preferences to the developing countries consistent with the relevant
agreed conclusions and relevant decisions as adopted on this subject, in
the framework of the competent international organizations' (Art. 18),
and, furthermore, '. . . International trade should be conducted without
prejudice to generalized non-discriminatory and *non-reciprocal* preferences
in favor of developing countries, on the basis of mutual advantage, equitable benefits and the exchange of most-favored-nation treatment' (Art. 26;
emphasis added). There is another provision empowering the developing
countries to establish a system of preferences among themselves: 'Developing countries should endeavour to promote the expansion of their
mutual trade and to this end may, in accordance with the existing and
evolving provisions and procedures of international agreements where
applicable, *grant trade preferences to other developing countries without
being obliged to extend such preferences to developed countries . . .*'
(Art. 21; *emphasis added*). The principle of discrimination in favour of the
developing countries thus became one of the postulates of the NIEO. Its
elaboration in the UNCTAD documents, within the non-aligned movement,
and by permanent efforts of the growing 'Group of 77' is gradually expanding into a guiding precept even for the 'rich men's club'.

One of the stumbling-blocks of the establishment of the NIEO is
contrariety between the international law principle *pacta sunt servanda,*

which emanated into the doctrine of vested rights, and the principle of permanent sovereignty over natural wealth and resources, proclaimed in the context of the NIEO. The Charter of Economic Rights and Duties of States, while paying lip-service to the principle that states have to fulfil in good faith their international obligations, gives in Art. 2(c) every state the right to nationalize, expropriate, or transfer ownership of foreign property, paying appropriate compensation. The core of the stumbling-block is in the subsequent rule, i.e. the question of compensation is governed by the internal laws of the nationalizing state. No wonder such a proposition resulted in an uproar of the developed countries, but it found no backing in judicial practice,[21] and there are no traces of its general acceptance in state practice.

So far we have pointed at two principles of the NIEO which are contrary to positive international law (discrimination in favour of the developing countries, and full permanent sovereignty over natural wealth and resources). Now we have to point out one that is so far non-existent in international law. There are numerous pronouncements proclaiming the *duty of international co-operation for development*, all stating that it is a duty of all states to co-operate in the economic, social, cultural, and technological fields. The use of imperative terms is striking: 'It is the duty of States to contribute to the development of international trade of goods . . .', 'States should co-operate in facilitating more rational and equitable international economic relations . . .', 'All States have the duty to co-operate in achieving adjustments in the prices of exports of developing countries in relation to prices of their imports . . .' — all these examples are contained in the Charter of Economic Rights and Duties of States. It is difficult, if not impossible, to base the duty of co-operation for development on positive international law. It only sustains the principle that no state may prevent co-operation or communication of other states. There is not even a duty to recognize another state, let alone to establish any kind of relations with it. It is natural that the principle of co-operation is proclaimed in the NIEO, as its establishment is impossible without co-operation and concerted action of all (or most of) the states. Yet an 'international law of co-operation' still has a long way to go to become law *stricto sensu*. Being proclaimed as a *duty* of states, it raises questions on its nature. Is it a legal rule, or a moral obligation, or possibly a moral obligation which is being transformed into a legal principle?[22]

6. How De We Get There?

The decision-making process that is being developed in the process of formulating the goals and principles of the NIEO introduced democratic procedural devices: the majority principle and — if and whenever possible — the consensus principle. They are based on the idea that the interests of the majority in the international community should ultimately prevail.

Nevertheless, developed countries overwhelmingly stick to the principle of voluntarism which is, in the domain of international law, expressed in the principle that no obligation can be created for a state without its consent. In its most extreme form, that attitude turned into calling the novel decision-making formulas 'the tyranny of the majority'. Otherwise, although conceding to the new modes of decision-making, the developed states retained their adherence to traditional norm-creating procedures which could shortly be described by defining international law as the 'crystallization of state practice'. That leaves us with the question: Is it possible for an overwhelming majority of the international.community to change the way in which rules of state behaviour are made?

This, again, brings the legal nature of the NIEO documents into the focus of our attention. The process of the establishment of the NIEO could briefly be described as consisting of three stages: stage one, in which shared perceptions of common goals and objectives were transformed into guidelines for restructuring the present world order; stage two, where common goals and principles were converted into international public policy by concerted efforts of the whole network of international organizations, mainly the UN; and, stage three, when international public policy has to be implemented by changing the behaviour of a variety of actors on international and domestic levels: states, international organizations (both governmental and non-governmental), multinational corporations, and political parties, to name only a few which take part in or influence international co-operation for development.

International organizations made the best of their task in the first two stages: they provided the opportunity for the world (although in most cases represented through states) to negotiate the foundations of the future international economic order. When it came to implementing the goals and principles solemnly agreed upon in the realm of day-to-day inter-state economic relations, things came to a stalemate. International organizations lack both the political power and the resources to directly effect any significant changes. Therefore, Ervin Laszlo was forced to conclude that 'changes tend to be confined to verbal behaviour'.[23] The principles that states committed themselves to by voting in favour of NIEO documents remained in the sphere of futuristic, if not Utopian, visions of the world in a distant future. In the actual performance, 'the free market argument calls into question the feasibility of reforming the world economic order through international negotiations'.[24] Assessing ten years and four conferences of UNCTAD, which had as principle terms of reference the formulation of principles and policies of global economic development and making proposals for putting those principles and policies into effect,[25] Raul Prebisch stated that '. . . we have lost the way and taken the wrong path'.[26] Evaluating UNCTAD V, A. M. B. Rahman wrote: 'These conferences will go on indefinitely because they are attempting the impossible: they seek solutions to the *status quo* from within the *status quo*.[27] Such criticism emphasizes the proper role and limits of international organizations as torch-bearers of the NIEO. The process of converting the demands for the *new* economic order into workable and applicable rules for its gradual materialization requires a slow and progressive elaboration of a *new* international economic law. Legal rules, as opposed to changes in market forces and bargaining power, offer predictability and authority to principles and rules which have been designed in the context of the NIEO. However, although it has been recognized that 'the restructuring of international economic relations presents a challenge to legal creativity',[28] and the item entitled 'Consolidation and Progressive Evolution of the Norms and Principles of International Economic Development Law' has been on the agenda of the General Assembly for the last four years, we cannot escape the conclusion that this aspect of the NIEO has been neglected so far. The *option of progressive development*, as contrasted to *possible decline*, should lead to more comprehensive and effective legal mechanisms and instruments adapted or designed to make the NIEO gradually existent.

Notes

1. Hoffmann, Stanley (1968). Introduction to Scheinman, L., Wilkinson, D., eds. (1968). *International Law and Political Crisis. An Analytical Casebook* (Boston: Little, Brown), xi.
2. Art. 38 of the International Court of Justice says that the Court, 'whose function is to decide in accordance with international law' shall apply:

   (a) international conventions, whether general or particular, establishing rules expressly recognized by the contrasting states;
   (b) international custom, as evidence of a general practice accepted as law;
   (c) the general principles of law recognized by civilized nations;
   (d) . . . judicial decisions and the teachings of the most qualified publicists of the various nations, as subsidiary means for the determination of rules of law.

3. The expression 'progressive development of international law' means, according to the Statute of the International Law Commission of the UN, '. . . the preparation of draft conventions on subjects which have not yet been regulated by international law or in regard to which the law has not yet been sufficiently developed in the practice of States'. Statute of the International Law Commission, GA Res. 174 (II), 21 Nov. 1947.
4. Corea, G. (1971). 'A Look to the Future.' *UNCTAD Tenth Anniversary Journal* (New York: UN) 15.
5. Cf. Schmitthoff, C. M. and Page, A. C. (1976). 'Economic Aims and Economic Law' in Kapteyn, P. J. G., ed. (1976). *The Economic Law of the Member States in an Economic and Monetary Union* (Leyden: Sijthoff), 107–8.
6. Adler-Karlsson, G. (1973). 'Some Roads to Humanicide.' *Instant Research on Peace and Violence*, III. 4: 204.
7. Out of 50 founding nations, present at the UN Conference on International Organization in San Francisco in 1945, there were only 7 Asian and African States, and only 5 of them were former colonies.
8. *Declaration on the Establishment of a New International Economic Order*, GA Res. 3201 (S–VI), 1 May 1974, paras. 1 and 2 (*emphasis added*).

9. Nandy, A. (1976). 'Oppression and Human Liberation: Towards a Third World Utopia.' *Alternatives — Journal of World Policy*, IV. 2: 166.
10. Sakamoto, Y. (1976). 'The Future of the United Nations: A Political Overview' in *The United Nations and the Future*. Proceedings, UNITAR Conference on the Future, Moscow, June 1974 (Moscow: UNITAR), 204.
11. Cf. the Declaration on the Establishment of a New International Economic Order, GA Res. 3201 (S–VI), 1 May 1974; Charter of Economic Rights and Duties of States, GA Res. 3281 (XXIX), 15 Jan. 1975. and the resolution on Development and International Economic Co-operation, GA Res. 3362 (S–VII), 19 Sept. 1975.
12. Richard Falk has a different attitude: 'The line drawn between "is" and "ought" in conventional legal reasoning provides a first approximation of the distinction between law and justice. The domain of law is concerned with existing legal mandates, whereas the domain of justice is concerned with law as it ought to be.' Falk, R. A. (1975). 'The Domains of Law and Justice.' *International Journal*, XXXI: 1.
13. Tipson, F. S. (1977). 'From International Law to World Public Order: Who Studies What, How, Why.' *Yale Studies in World Public Order*, IV. 1: 84.
14. Henkin, L. (1977). 'Does International Law Work?' *Dialogue*, IV. 2: 74.
15. Adda Bozeman asserts that even the notion of peace as the supreme value is questionable: '. . . peace is scarcely a shared value in this century, whereas war is a morally accepted way of life in most cultural traditions as they are now encompassed in representative political systems', cf. Bozeman, A. B. (1971). *The Future of Law in a Multicultural World* (Princeton: Princeton Univ. Press), 182. See also Ishida, T. (1969). 'Beyond the Traditional Concepts of Peace in Different Cultures.' *Journal of Peace Research*, VI: 133–45, and McDougal, M. S., and Lasswell, H. D. (1969). 'The Identification and Appraisal of Diverse Systems of Public Order', in The American Society of International Law, *International Law in the Twentieth Century* (New York), 169–97.
16. Charter of Economic Rights and Duties of States (*n. 11*), Art. 10 (*emphasis added*).
17. Levi, W. (1976). *Law and Politics in the International Society*, Sage Library of Social Research 32 (London: Sage), 142.
18. Friedman, W. (1972). 'Human Welfare and International Law — A Reordering of Priorities' in Friedman, W., Henkin, L. and Lissitzyn, O., eds. (1972). *Transnational Law in a Changing Society*. Essays in Honour of Philip C. Jessup (New York and London: Columbia Univ. Press), 113–34.
19. Institut de Droit International, 24. Commission (1958). *Competence Obligatoires des Instances Judiciaries et Arbitrales Internationales, Rapport Definitif*; Rapporteur: C. W. Jenks (Genève), 110.
20. The text of both the General Agreement on Tariffs and Trade and Charter of Economic Rights and Duties of States is given in Jackson, J. H. (1977). *Legal Problems of International Economic Relations, Documents Supplement*. American Casebook Series (St. Paul, Minn.: West Publishing Co.).
21. International Arbitral Tribunal (1977). 'Award on the merits in dispute between Texaco Overseas Petroleum Company/California Asiatic Oil Company and the Government of the Libyan Arab Republic', Geneva, 19 Jan. 1977, reprinted in *International Legal Materials*, 1 (1978): 1–38.
22. Babović, B. (1972). 'The Duty of States to Cooperate with One Another in Accordance with the Charter' in Sahović, M., ed. (1972). *Principles of International Law Concerning Friendly Relations and Cooperation* (Belgrade: Institute of International Politics and Economics), 277–321.
23. Laszlo, E. (1977). 'Global Goals and the Crisis of Political Will.' *Journal of International Affairs*, XXXI. 2: 200.
24. Hurtado, M. E. (1979). 'Can These Talks Ever Reform the World System?' *International Development Review*, XXI. 3: 48.

25. GA Res. 1955 (XIX), 30 Dec. 1964.
26. Address by Raul Prebisch at UNCTAD V, Manila, 7 May 1979.
27. Rahman, A. M. B. (1979). 'Second Thoughts on UNCTAD V.' *New African* (Aug. 1979), 72.
28. International Law Association, *Bulletin of the 58th Conference*, Manila 27 Aug.–2 Sept. 1978, 22.

10 NEW STANDARDS FOR INTERNATIONAL BEHAVIOUR AND INTEGRATION

HERMANN WEBER
Institute for International Affairs, University of Hamburg

I

Present international relations show clear signs of shifts in the substance of conflicts. The relations among states are no longer primarily determined by those concerns which traditionally defined the realms of foreign policy and alliance politics. They have been replaced by basic problems of economic and social 'co-existence', and these become increasingly visible in new patterns of international conflict. This phenomenon affects the structure and type of conflicts, their dynamics, the commitment of parties as regards their conflict behaviour as well as the alignments of the actors involved.

These observations apply most directly to all those conflicts which already display at their surface signs of strong economic inequalities, i.e. in particular to conflicts of interest between less-developed Third World countries (LDCs) and developed industrialized countries (DCs) in the East and West. But they are equally valid, though to a lesser degree, for conflicts in the East–West setting as well as in the relations among members of associative structures with a comparatively homogenous character, such as EC, CMEA, 'Club of Ten', or the 'Group of 77'. They all have in common that the traditional concerns of international politics (security policy, strategies, alliances) have given way to problems of securing economic growth, fluctuations in monetary stability, imbalances in foreign trade, inequitable distribution of resources, securing of energy supply, maintaining export shares, lacking participation in technological and industrial progress, and threats to elementary social needs.

The numerous regional or local armed conflicts are not evidence to the contrary: War-like conflicts over border security, questions of self-determination, human rights, and sudden changes of international constellations which appear as consolidated and of a long-term stability often only conceal the fact that governments — mostly only with a temporary, limited, political mandate — conceive their legitimacy in terms of their capacity to adequately respond to sociopolitical demands and basic economic needs of large sectors of the population which they represent.

Still in the more recent past, i.e. during the years following the Second World War, it was possible for both interest groups (usually without any specifically representative character but possessing disproportionate, often dominant, economic influence) and individual personalities (with more or less charismatic traits) to realize their particular goals in the context of national policies, and in doing so they could avail themselves, too, of the variety of means and channels that exist for the conduct of inter-state relations. This constellation was, in fact, supported by the importance attributed by the general public and governments to the reconstruction of the European economies as well as by the perceived threats — actual or imaginary — in East–West relations. It was quite anachronistic already at that time, for it almost totally neglected to give due attention to the needs of the emerging Third World. It was only with the emancipation of the colonial areas, beginning in 1947 with India and Pakistan becoming independent states, that the Euro-centric orientation of international politics reached a certain limit, and that problems of the Third World became matters of public concern throughout the world. Today, inter-national politics is confronted with the necessity to accommodate the economic and social inequalities between the rich and the poor nations, which result from a long-standing process of exploitation, without chal-lenging the status quo of the industrialized countries, which are supposed to make such accommodations possible. This is why the industrialized countries are so much concerned about maintaining a stable development of their economic capacities, countries dependent on the export of raw materials try to establish equitable prices for their products, and the 'have-nots' demand a greater share in the resources, products, and tech-nologies of the developed countries.

The most fundamental problems are seen to exist in the field of social and economic redistribution, or even in establishing a new structure of the distribution pattern. Consequently, the real conflicts arise over these issues. In fact, ideological confrontations are of relatively minor import-ance, and whenever they become an issue they function to legitimize and support the realization of social and economic conceptions and related policies adopted by a particular government, whether by con-stitutional procedures or as part of a revolutionary political change.

The shifts in the substance of international conflicts, therefore, do not necessarily indicate the existence of a broad consensus, transcending ideological or national partitions that otherwise exist, as to the rank-order of tasks to be solved. It seems more appropriate to consider them as an expression of a growing recognition that there are, within more or less broadly defined limits of state sovereignty, standards of international behaviour suitable to generate guidelines for a structural order beyond the possibilities of legally binding treaties under international law.

The United Nations are the most important example in this regard. Their organs, organizations, and special bodies — as well as a number of regional institutions outside the UN framework — have established a network of norms which, by its explicit economic and social orientation, deviates significantly in terms of both programme definition and execution from the classical examples and procedures of bi- and multilateral co-operation. This development is based on a re-orientation centring around the assumption that the former colonial areas have a legitimate claim that the more developed members of the community of states mobilize, in a spirit of solidarity, assistance and unconventional methods in coping with future tasks and problems. Still more generally, this implies the conviction that traditional considerations motivated primarily by self-interest and opportunistic attitudes are in fact no longer sufficient and suitable to guarantee the functioning of the international system. The organization of the UN has replaced such considerations by the notion of co-operation based on genuine partnership. In doing so, it has made use of changed boundary conditions and procedures as a lever to raise the awareness of the importance of problems. Interstate behaviour has thereby undergone a change, the implications of which will only become fully visible if one's attention is not restricted to the traditional processes of norm generation or the classical institutions of international law.

II

The changes in orientations, modes of behaviour, and the structure of conflicts towards the creation of norms and standards designed to take into account more thoroughly the economic and social needs of peoples have taken place as a result of *fundamental changes in the composition of the international community of states*.

The number of recognized subjects of international law, i.e. sovereign states, has almost tripled within the 30 years since 1945 as a consequence of the then emerging process of decolonization. For the first time the community of states has thereby assumed a truly universal character instead of the prior 'closed club' of a few privileged states (Art. 38 ICJ Statute: 'civilized states') which largely determined the fate of the nonmembers. This expansion of the number of subjects of international law is, first of all, a consequence of a consistent practice of the UN, but it may also be understood as an expression of a continuing trend of democratic emancipation, beginning with the American, French, and Latin American revolutions, and later followed by the self-determination movements in Europe after 1918. It rationalizes the experience that participation in processes aimed at forming the environment and developing economic growth and social progress can only be granted by a decentralized community.

The political and legal operationalization of the principle of self-determination in the practice of the UN since 1945 has also modified the forms of inter-state behaviour. Classical diplomacy was conceived primarily as an instrument in the hands of a few 'autocrats' – without any responsibilities whatsoever towards others – to maximize a calculus of interests determined exclusively by individual preferences in power-political terms against competing external boundary conditions and objectives. It was only consistent that these objectives were pursued by 'secret diplomacy' with actual intentions well hidden. Quite to the contrary, UN diplomacy diverts from this practice. It can be described as a type of conference diplomacy, even where traditional forms have been preserved. One of the major reasons for this is the necessity, much stronger than in classical diplomacy, to generate a type of consensus which makes manifest the relativity of the importance of specific particular interests so as to become ultimately acceptable to states, despite contradictory ambitions and interests. However, classical diplomacy also aimed at compromise, but it applied, in general, only to bilateral agreements which only occasionally gave due regard to the over-all interests of the international community.

On the institutional level the changes in orientations, modes of behaviour, and conflict structures become visible most significantly in the strong expansion, qualitatively and quantitatively, of international organizations as well as in the increasing division of labour among them in carrying out their tasks. The transfer of powers and competences, which originally belonged to the core of state sovereignty, to international decision organs and institutions with independent, though often limited, legal subjectivity demonstrates that what formally appears to be the result of free and consensual decisions is in fact often a consequence of self-restraint of states which have realized the constraints imposed on autonomy by economic interdependencies and a variety of other factual interrelations among a multitude of policy problems. New forms of organizational and institutional associative ties have in important respects substituted formerly well-established types of bilateral relations which emphasized the negotiation and conclusion of treaties under international law with well-defined rights and duties on the basis of reciprocity as well as – and particularly important – expectations for long-term viability. This technique has been complemented by new types and procedures of law-making which have (as a function of specific subject-matters) a varying, but in general a lesser degree of obligatory force, but at the same time a higher degree of effectivity. The rapid change of material conditions to be regulated is often more adequately met by recommendations, guidelines, catalogues of principles, and codes of behaviour than by explicit treaties, for the former allow fulfilment of obligations in quite flexible forms without preventing a party from reminding its partners of their specific obligations. This type of norm structure facilitates continued attempts towards consensus formation since it creates initial conditions to prepare the ground for the resolution of conflicts that, at first sight, often seem insoluble.

Changes of the kind just described may not be found with equal intensity in all fields of inter-nation relations, and they are probably less likely in areas pertaining to military security where the prevention of direct and immediate threats against the existence of a political unit supports more conservative attitudes in maintaining the traditional instruments of war prevention. However, in the fields of trade and general economic relations, which much more directly affect the functioning of states and prospects for their future development, the restriction of individual state autonomy by the transfer of competences to international organs has already become a well-established fact. The autonomy of individual states as to the creation of norms has been subject to change in substantial terms in all those cases where

- international organs introduce – with quasi-binding force – customs and trade preferences (GATT-rounds, UNCTAD);
- prices and sales contingents for raw-materials are fixed at global or regional levels (OPEC, Lomé Agreement);
- the distribution of development aid/credits is organized in centralized forms (World Bank, IDA);
- currency parities affecting the trade balances of third states are fixed periodically by a small group of countries;
- obligations for developed countries are established to channel a fixed share of their respective gross national product into development programmes for less-developed areas (UNCTAD, II. UN Development Decade);
- debts are cancelled while new credits are offered at the same time (as did Sweden and the Federal Republic of Germany, among others);
- international security regulations in shipbuilding are established that affect the competitive capacity of shipbuilding industries and shipping companies in specific countries.

The list of examples could be easily enlarged. It demonstrates that states engaged in some form, as donors or recipients, in organizational or institutional arrangements of international co-operation have an ever-decreasing chance to determine or even influence international decisions in terms strictly guided by their individual interest constellation. They become subject to pressures to accept compromise formulas, and the accumulated results of such processes increasingly contribute to the evolution of a specific type of international legislation. Its major characteristic is that the willingness to accept the standards formulated by such types of 'legislation' as obligatory tends to increase as an inverse function of the disadvantages that have to be expected from a withdrawal from the community (*ad hoc* or institutional).

III

The most far-reaching consequence of changes in orientations, modes of behaviour, and structures of conflict with which states are confronted on formal and institutionalized levels is the *dynamics by which the process of norm creation leads to integration.*

This applies specifically to all those areas where the majority principle has been substituted, partially or completely, by the consensus principle, as in the practice of UN organs and special organizations in the adoption of resolutions. This action is a direct consequence of the expansion of the community of states and of its quality as a (for the first time also *de facto*) decentralized legal community: the greater the number of independent and equal legal subjects participating in the process of norm creation, the less are the chances for any single member to exercise an impact on decisions in accordance with its specific interests – and likewise to refuse its consent. Both the duration and the outcome of a process of norm creation are variables dependent on the number of parties participating in the process. An increase in the number of participants will also prolong the duration of the negotiation processes, and this effect in turn diminishes the probability that eventual decisions will still focus on the original problem definition that brought the parties together to seek a joint problem solution. Multilateralization of decision-making causes the formation of coalitions; this condition diminishes the possibilities of any single participant in the process to define its position in any other way than in co-ordination with others and in a stepwise process. Seemingly constant interests thereby become 'variables' and assume a quality of mutual exchangeability. Alternate problem solutions emerge in the course of debates and consultations, and their adjustment often takes place under the influence of external factors or developments by which individual decision-makers are only indirectly affected. On the other hand, pressure-group tactics and collective-bargaining techniques as components of a group-orientated decision-making style strongly support a pronounced presentation of specific group interests. These factors contribute to the formation of a dialogue-type structure which facilitates the accommodation of interests both within and between groups.

Once the process of decision-making has been initiated the imperative to arrive at a consensus becomes the overriding interest and exercises a variety of effects on the content of norms to be formulated. Under these conditions, a 'retreat' from the scene of negotiations remains but a pure theoretical possibility since it would definitely imply, for all practical purposes, much greater disadvantages as compared to the acceptance of (some) undesirable results of the negotiations. The two big codification conferences that took place during recent years, the Third UN Conference on the Law of the Seas and the UN Conference on Humanitarian International Law, confirm this hypothesis, and it is further supported by the results of two other big conferences, UNCTAD and CSCE. Each of these turned out as ideal factors of integration for such groups as the 'Group of 77' of the nine EC countries.

However, the momentum inherent in international group-decision processes and their underlying 'laws' also produced integrative effects in those cases where the majority principle still prevails over the consensus principle. Whenever criticism or reservations are advanced, it becomes important to influence the result of a vote by making the potential majority aware of diverging positions in the course of the decision process. However, group-dynamic processes, be they positive or negative, neutralize subjective elements in the decision process. In particular, any challenge of fundamental structural norms that were previously unquestioned demands reassessments of individual positions and compel specific groups to clearly articulate their interests. Minority votes may thus produce integration effects quite similar to those related with majority attitudes.

These considerations suggest that such behavioural patterns generate, positively or negatively, effects which by far transcend the immediate act of norm creation. They contribute to changes in the structure of the international community of states from a legal community exclusively based on free co-ordination and equality towards a community integrated by a sense of solidarity *vis-à-vis* specific functional tasks to be performed. This becomes particularly evident whenever international decision organs, in order to fulfil basic community tasks, are endowed with decision competences which severely restrict — as in the cases of the International Civil Aviation Organization (ICAO) or the Inter-Governmental Maritime Consultative Organization (IMCO) — possibilities for alternative decisions by individual member states. In both cases decisions by the organization are of a binding character for each member, provided it does not declare its rejection of a decision within a specified period. In ICAO a declared rejection of a decision even entails the exclusion of the respective member as a contracting party (so-called 'contracting out' or 'opting out').

IV

If the assumption is true that norms of international law state only to a very limited degree specific forms of behaviour, but that their primary function — today even more than in the past — is to define elementary needs to be satisfied for the larger part of global society, then one may *hypothesize* that the *most significant changes in the substance of norms can be expected to occur in those areas where the norms affect the shaping of economic conditions as well as in areas where basic existential needs of states are in question.* These are also those norms within the international legal structure which are presently most seriously disputed, viz.

- norms pertaining to economic affairs in general and trade in particular, which were over a long period — or still are — biased in favour of the industrial development of 'the North' (or the so-called 'civilized countries') and which, therefore, are considered as elements that have contributed, or continue to contribute, to the emergence and persistence of extreme economic and social inequalities within the community of states;
- norms which still allow the threat or application of force in international relations and which, therefore, are regarded as decisive elements in supporting the continued existence of socio-economic imbalances, for armaments attract major shares of national products at the expense of peaceful progress;
- norms concerning fundamental human rights, the realization of which for individual persons is considered by an increasing number of states as a constitutive and inseparable element of any order of peace, and likewise of any socio-economic change and development.

The intensity of changes in international law differs in each of the areas referred to, and the necessity for changes was also felt differently at different times. Thus, normative changes in the sphere of interstate armed conflict during the sixties were much more significant than in any other area. They were caused by the growing risks in the East–West conflict (Suez crisis, Congo crisis, Vietnam conflict) and induced the superpowers to concentrate efforts on developing new forms of behaviour in order to prevent the possibility of a sudden and accidental nuclear clash (bilateral détente agreements USA/USSR, test stop, nonproliferation treaty, seabed treaty, SALT I, and others). Against this background it also became possible for the first time to succeed in giving a restrictive definition to the notion of aggression which found the approval of the majority of states.

Since the beginning of the seventies, however, the international discussion has been dominated by global socio-economic problems. Specific attention was given to the development needs of the Third World and their peace-threatening implications. This discussion has initiated normative changes which may be considered as expressions of more fundamental changes in both attitudinal orientations and modes of behaviour. The reversal of priorities has come about since traditional categories of international trade, and of world economic relations in general, are increasingly perceived not only as obstacles to further development, but also as a threat to the status quo and the continued functioning of the international economy as such.

More or less simultaneously with this reorientation, another international discussion began, which focused on how to achieve a stronger foundation of individual human rights in state practice. The tendency to be observed in many states of seeking solutions to domestic difficulties by violent and terrorist actions against individuals caused strong reactions calling for a more effective international protection. This development does not only reflect a broadly based international concern about, and recognition of, the necessity for a humanization of those environmental conditions of life typical for present-day technological-industrial societies. It also takes account of the experience that political aspirations which are related in whatever form to violence and terror spill over into the international domain with detrimental effects on the climate of inter national security. The explicit discussions of human rights problems during the seventies, following the first promising results achieved by the human rights conventions of 1966, thus led to a number of international activities which, indeed, turned human rights into a category of international security (CSCE Final Act, numerous UN Resolutions condemning racial separation in South Africa, the unanimous condemnation of policies in Chile after the demise of Allende). However, this international recognition does not yet imply that the observation and promotion of human rights is fully ensured. On the one hand, there is still a clear priority attributed to (*a*) securing external peace as it exists, *de facto*, in East–West relations and as it is envisaged similarly for the Near-East conflict, and (*b*) increased efforts towards the Third World's economic and social development. On the other hand, human rights are, indeed, considered by many states more often than not as a direct or indirect threat to their domestic order whenever more than mere verbal action is asked for. Despite these reservations the discussion of human rights has initiated a move towards changes in attitudes (and spectacular events such as the dissident movement in the Soviet Union are symptomatic in this regard), which is likely to have an impact on interstate relations in a long-term perspective.

V

Which substantive norms of international law, then, primarily reflect these changes? It appears that one has to consider, in the first place, some of the *legal consequences from interpretations of the principle of equality*. This principle is one of the most fundamental rights of states, and it prohibits any legal differentiation based on the size or political significance (power) of a state irrespective of any factual inequalities that may exist. It is only the legal equality which makes it possible to arrive at legally binding compromises among states. However, formal norms aiming at an equal treatment often have discriminatory effects if economically less-developed countries are confronted with developed countries. This is not so much the result of a consequent application of the principle of equality as such, but rather of the consequences that developed from a long-standing European and American state practice in the interpretation of the principle at the expense of Third World countries.

For, as has already been stated by the Permanent International Court of Justice in an advisory opinion in 1935 (minority schools in Albania), the right to enjoy equality does not allow any different treatment except in those cases where it is the explicit objective to bring about a balance between different initial conditions.

It became, therefore, a central concern of the new states after having achieved independence to correct the most important causes of imbalances already at the normative level. Their efforts were directed towards *eliminating* existing discriminations, in particular those that had evolved in international trade relations as a consequence of equal treatment in mere formal terms, and to *substitute them by respective privileges for LDCs*. These efforts showed some success when a Part IV (Trade and Development) was inserted into GATT in 1965, whereby the most-favoured-nation treatment as well as duties of reciprocity were formally cancelled for relations between LDCs and DCs. However, though facilitating the LDC's access to the markets of DCs, this action eventually proved to be insufficient. Privileges for LDCs in GATT were therefore soon replaced by a more effective system of trade preferences, negotiated and adopted by UNCTAD I–III and thereafter introduced in numerous bi- and multilateral agreements. Both systems have modified the traditional norms reflecting the free-trade principle in terms of formally equal treatment and reciprocity by introducing additional provisions that favour the economically weaker countries whose development potential is threatened.

Further legal consequences, which were derived from the principle of equality, concern the right of foreigners to compensation in cases of expropriation, which belongs to the international legal minimum standard. In its classical form the rule protects foreign property against confiscation. Expropriation is allowed only in exceptional cases if required by public needs, provided that full and effective compensation is granted and if, further, the expropriation does not constitute an unequal treatment of foreigners (prohibition of discrimination). However, in practice this provision implied a number of unfavourable effects for Third World countries, since in general they neither disposed of any capital investments in DCs nor could this be expected to be the case in the foreseeable future. It was this condition which was considered by many states as the most decisive factor responsible for the persistence of underdevelopment. The obligation of full and effective compensation regularly placed a burden on the LDCs which could not be borne without serious complications for their economic capacity and thus made it impossible for them to follow a policy of using capital redistribution and the full exploitation of all existing resources as instruments for socio-economic development, although they possessed, in principle, a general regulatory competence in this regard.

The elimination of the principle of full and unconditional compensation in cases of expropriation thus became a central demand of Third

World countries. Its full realization failed, however, due to the resistance on the part of Western industrialized countries. The continued dependence of the Third World on foreign investments as well as on technical, capital, and trade aid from Western countries led instead to a compromise. It provided that compensation payments should in general be subject to a political settlement. In formal terms the general consensus comprised the recognition by the LDCs of an 'adequate' compensation, but the ultimate authority to determine the terms of settlement remained with the expropriating state. This formula saved the influence, markets, and possibilities of economic activities for capital-exporting countries in regions already open to them at that time. On the other hand, it provided LDCs with the possibility to make the participation of foreign investors in the socio-economic development dependent on conditions which ensured that the interests of the host states were taken into account in more appropriate ways than had been the case in the colonial past. The compromise on the question of expropriation was essentially worked out as part of the negotiations over a suitable operational form for the principle of permanent sovereignty over natural resources (GA Res. 1803 (XVII)). Subsequently, it significantly influenced the state practice and constituted an important prerequisite for the determination of substantial terms of the international law of development as a new category of international law (cf. Art. 2 of the Charter of Economic Rights and Duties of States).

The third important correction of the classical international law in pursuing an adjustment of the principle of equality to demands resulting from imperatives of changed realities concerned the existing Law of the Seas. The traditional legal conception of unrestricted freedom in the use of the seas for all states — as it had still been confirmed by the 1958 Geneva Convention on the Law of the High Seas — was based on the dominating principle of the general prohibition to occupy any part of the high seas. Any use is thereby restricted to the classical freedoms of navigation, fishing, the installation of cables and pipelines, aviation, and research activities. But these freedoms were exercised primarily by a limited number of states with sufficiently high standards of economic and technological development. It goes without saying that the Third World countries considered the principle of the freedom of the seas as an anachronistic legal rule when it became obvious that the exploitation of maritime resources so far untouched no longer encountered any technical problems, but that the accumulation of technology and necessary investment capital in a limited number of countries would again establish disproportional privileges for the developed countries.

In the course of the consideration of these questions in the UN, alternatives for a revision of the traditional rule of the freedom of the seas were advanced. One possible solution provided for the partition of the seas and the sea-bed (as the most important place where natural resources of all kinds could be expected to be found) in favour of respective contiguous coastal states. The other possible solution envisaged the institution of a central agency, independent of national and group interests, for conducting the exploitation either directly under its own authority or by licensing third parties, and for the equitable distribution of profits. In 1970 the UN General Assembly voted for the second option (Res. 2749 (XXV)), which aims at making use of the remaining free resources of the world to improve the economic situation of the least-developed countries (LLDs). However, in the course of the Third UN Conference on the Law of the Seas (since 1973), with 150 states participating in the reformulation of the international law of the seas, the conception of a central maritime agency with a broad range of competences has again become controversial. The idea has lost much of its initial attraction *vis-à-vis* other demands formulated only more recently, among which the delineation of an exclusive economic zone of 200 nautical miles is particularly noteworthy. Though a solution of this question is still pending, it can be expected with some certainty that the substance of the principle of the freedom of the seas will be subjected to considerable modifications and that the LDCs may definitely expect a number of adjustments of the presently existing imbalances.

The tendency to emphasize more strongly social and other common interests in the context of international law, as it becomes apparent in these attempts towards revisions, has received an advance legitimization by certain cautious modifications in the jurisdiction of the ICJ. In the Fisheries Dispute between the Federal Republic of Germany and Iceland over the legality of a unilateral expansion of exclusive fishing zones by Iceland, the Court ruled in 1979 that the determination of fishing rights has, in general, to be made by consensus although the coastal state may enjoy certain forms of preferential treatment. Considering Iceland's specific dependency on fishing industries, the Court held that special circumstances may justify certain modifications of the right of the members of the community of states to equal treatment. However, this ruling did not abolish the principle character of the legal relations between states as determined under the existing dogma of sovereignty; but it must be noted that a new quality of international norm creation has been authoritatively recognized to apply — as explicitly attested by the Court in this case — if relations involve a dimension of specific social relevance.

VI

This leads to the question *what role can still be attributed to the principle of sovereignty* (as the right of self-government in internal affairs, and the right of independence in external affairs) in the context of the common tasks to be solved in the future? The answer depends on the degree of open-mindedness of states in coping with the increasing interdependencies in international trade and in securing a continuous economic development at the level of norm creation, but also on the efficiency with which they are willing to give, in practice, priority to common interests over the pursuance of narrow national goals. A central point of reference in answering this question is the notion of co-operation, which may indeed be considered as a yardstick to measure the capacity and willingess to allow for social change *vis-à-vis* a status quo which has proved increasingly unacceptable. Approaches in these directions are visible, for example, in the various catalogues of principles that were formulated within the UN and laid down, among others, in the Declaration on Social Progress (GA Res. 2542 (XXIV)), the Declaration on Friendly Relations and Co-operation among States (GA Res. 2625 (XXIV)), the Declaration on a New International Economic Order (GA Res. 3201 (S–VI)), the Programme of Action (GA Res. 3202 (S–VI)), and in the Charter of Economic Rights and Duties of States (GA Res. 3281 (XXIX)). All the principles contained in these declarations and programmes aim at providing improved possibilities to promote co-operation which is based on partnership between states without abolishing, however, the traditional categories of sovereignty.

To be successful, co-operation defined in these terms requires as a precondition the general recognition of the necessity of reforming the system of norms, which still privileges developed countries. The report on 'Reshaping the International Order' that a group of experts presented to the Club of Rome in 1976 (Tinbergen Report) states that the general public in the developed countries is well aware, and positively so, of this problem, but doubts are expressed whether this applies also to their governments. The report stresses that governments cannot legitimize a refusal to accept structural changes by taking recourse to public opinion, which is after all influenced if not shaped by their own policies and activities. One of the report's conclusions suggests major efforts to broaden information capacities, since they are presently dominated to a considerable degree by monopolistic and discriminatory practices. Such improvements should facilitate the dissemination of information about the demands, preferences, and needs of the Third World in forms free of ethnocentric prejudices.

If it can be expected that global problems are increasingly treated in terms of a 'domestic policy at global scale' (*Weltinnenpolitik*) such that political decisions will primarily be determined by common universal interests rather than particular self-interests, a new interpretation of national sovereignty will become unavoidable. The increasing transformation of the existing international law into a legal system with more co-operative characteristics, in which a multitude of operative principles or a general treaty similar to the Charter of Economic Rights and Duties of States determine its basic rules, will also increasingly deprive the traditional definition of national sovereignty of one of its constitutive elements, viz., that the primary regulatory competence of states as a function of its territorial character also extends to international affairs. This principle is gradually substituted by elements of transnationality, viz. the functional adequacy of decisions as the only legitimate justification for governmental activities under the regime of a problem-orientated co-operation.

This neither implies that territorial sovereignty will completely vanish in favour of a 'world state' or some similar global political structure, nor that co-operation will ultimately lead to a uniform development of all states based on some general harmony. For both assumptions the prevailing external conditions are much too differentiated and discernible tendencies in present developments do not point in such directions. Also in the future, co-operation is not likely to protect against inequality even if deliberate attempts are made to eliminate conditions of inequality, as it is evident from loan practices and technical aid. Co-operation can be expected to result in inequality whenever one partner in a co-operative relationship fully exploits his actual superiority. Here, the classical principle of sovereignty indeed assumes a new function, viz. as a moderating device in that it allows refusal to enter into or continue co-operative ties whenever they tend to develop in unequal terms or, also, if opportunities for an alternative form of development shall be maintained for a limited period. On the other hand, the principle provides each state with the concrete chance to participate in the exploitation of global resources and of global wealth not yet distributed. In the limited sphere of securing the existence of states (right of self-defence), however, sovereignty will also maintain its traditional significance in the future.

PART IV

MANAGEMENT AND RESOLUTION OF CONFLICTS

11   THE UN IN INTERNATIONAL CONFLICTS
     1946–1976: A NOTE ON RELEVANCE,
     EFFECTIVITY, AND PROSPECTS

RÜDIGER JÜTTE
Institute of Peace Research and Security Policy at the University of Hamburg

The resolution of international conflicts within and by structures of international organization is only one of the modes available for states to settle their differences, 'normal' disputes, more intense situations of crisis, or conflicts involving the use of force. In this article two perspectives will be compared: (1) the general relevance of international institutions for international actors in their attempts to settle conflicts, and (2) in particular the substantive role of the UN in the control and settlement of conflicts once they have been referred to it. The advantage of international organizations as frameworks for the resolution of conflicts is often seen in two factors. First, the combination of a variety of procedures, simultaneously or successively, by which attempts to control, manage, and eventually settle conflicts may be undertaken, and secondly, the international 'supervision' which is expected to influence the conflicting parties to arrive at a peaceful or at least co-operative resolution of conflicting aspirations. One might expect, then, that the greater the relevance of international structures the greater their substantive impact on the course of conflicts and their regulatory control.

1. Relevance

The extent to which international conflicts were dealt with in alternative management contexts provides a suitable indicator with which to assess their relative importance. Table 1 shows the forms in which 246 international conflicts were handled between 1945 and 1974.[1] The three subperiods follow an often used periodization of both the international system and the development within the UN. The first category (*Bilateral*) has to be broadly understood, i.e. no differentiation is made as to whether an active effort to settle a conflict occurred. The following categories all refer to the involvement of a third party. Category *Individual/Concert* comprises conflicts in which an individual state, a group of states, or an individual person exercised some mediating role. Category *Adjudicative/ Affiliative/Functional IO* refers to legal procedures or mediatory roles of both governmental and non-governmental international organizations

Table 1.   Management contexts of international conflicts 1945–74

	Bilateral	Third Parties			
	Parties only	Indiv. State/ Concert	Adjud./Affil./ Funct. IO	Coll. Sec. IO	Total
1945–55	25.8% (17)	4.5% (3)	3.0% (2)	66.7% (44)	100% (66)
1956–62	30.1% (25)	8.4% (7)	6.0% (5)	55.4% (46)	100% (83)
1963–74	14.4% (14)	13.4% (13)	2.1% (2)	70.1% (68)	100% (97)
1945–74	22.8% (56)	9.3% (23)	3.7% (9)	64.2% (158)	100% (246)

Number of cases in ( ).

other than the UN and certain regional organizations (OAS, OAU, Council of Europe, Arab League). These latter organizations constitute the fourth category, *Collective Security IO*.[2]

For both the entire period as well as for the subperiods, a basic relationship becomes apparent. For the whole period, almost two-thirds of the conflicts were introduced into the UN or one of the regional organizations. Together with the other institutional forms this share rises to nearly 70%. Only about 23% have remained exclusively a matter between the parties immediately concerned, while another 9% involved some form of non-institutionalized third-party role. Comparing the successive subperiods, it becomes apparent that the role of universal and regional organizations is less important during the second period, but increases again to the highest level during the 1963–74 period with 70%, with respect to both previous periods and the whole period. One notes a further sharp decrease (50%) in conflicts remaining at the bilateral level and a steady increase of non-institutionalized third-party roles. Taken together, these observations suggest a trend towards internationalization, though not exclusively in favour of the institutionalized structures.

The picture is complemented by considering in greater detail the group of the UN and regional organizations (Table 2). The most apparent characteristic is the relative constant referral rate of the UN, above the 70% level through all periods but slightly decreasing. The Arab League and Council of Europe play only a limited role (also in absolute terms). The decrease in referrals to the OAS is somewhat misleading since the data do not reflect the characteristic interaction between OAS and UN, i.e. there is no account taken of conflicts handled in two or even more organizations. Finally, the strong position of the OAU is notable which (immediately after its foundation at the beginning of the third period) became a relatively often-activated forum for the African region.

Focusing on the UN alone we find that the rate of referral to the universal body amounts to about 46% of all the 246 conflicts for the entire period, and close to 50% for the years 1963–74. This reduction

Table 2   Management of international conflicts by global and regional international
organizations 1945–74

	UN	OAS	OAU[1]	Council of Europe	Arab League	Total
1945–55	72.7% (32)	20.5% (9)	–	2.3% (1)	4.5% (2)	100% (44)
1956–62	71.7% (33)	17.4% (8)	–	2.2% (1)	8.7% (4)	100% (46)
1963–74	70.6% (48)	7.4% (5)	14.7% (10)	1.5% (1)	5.9% (4)	100% (68)
1945–74	71.5% (113)	13.9% (22)	6.3% (10)	1.9% (3)	6.3% (10)	100% (158)

[1] OAU founded in 1963.   Number of cases in ( ).

of the role of the UN does not affect the trend towards internationalization
if it is recalled that there is no exclusive domain of the organization, but
rather an intended linkage between the universal and regional levels. A
further breakdown of the distribution of conflicts by qualitative characteristics such as issues, intensity of conflict behaviour, the role of force,
actors involved, etc., would show no remarkable 'exclusion' of the international organizations from specific types of conflicts.[3]

2. Effectivity

So far we have considered the general relevance of international institutions.
The second perspective, specifically focusing on the UN, is then to ask
how the internationalization of international conflicts also translates
into a substantive role for international organization, i.e. the capacity
to exercise conflict-controlling or even conflict-resolving regulatory
functions. Any approach to the question faces the difficulty that there
is no generally accepted standard to evaluate, and integrate, the various
aspects of conflict-controlling activities in a unified measure adequately
characterizing the 'effectivity' of regulatory control of a conflict situation.
For the present purpose of a general assessment, without further analytic
intentions,[4] we use a measure of the effectivity which combines five
aspects of the organization's possible regulatory impact on the course
of conflicts:[5] (1) the organization may attempt *to restrain* the dynamics
of the conflict by narrowing mutual claims of the parties to the conflict
and/or their conflict behaviour. (2) A particular form of restraint is
necessary if the conflict involves the use of force, i.e. it has *to stop and
control direct violence*. While both these aspects constitute a 'vertical'
de-escalation, it may also become necessary to de-escalate a conflict
'horizontally' by (3) *isolating* the conflict from the involvement of third
parties giving support, directly or indirectly, to one or more parties to
the conflict. (4) The *abating* of the conflict may comprise various forms
of establishing or increasing settlement-orientated communication or

co-operation between conflicting parties, and, finally, the organization may (5) contribute to bringing about, formally or *de facto*, a *settlement* of a conflict. In reality these aspects are likely to interact in rather complicated ways; some activity directed to have an impact on the course of a conflict may have effects on more than one of the above dimensions, different conflicts may require different sequences of actions, conflicting parties in a conflict may perceive different priorities, etc. What is of interest here is that these dimensions seem to be related in such a way that a certain achievement in one dimension implies also certain achievements in other dimensions.[6] These relationships allow then to construct an empirically meaningful uniform *measure of effectivity*, which we use here in the form of *four categories*: (1) cases of a complete *failure*, i.e. the organization was not able to exercise any influence in any dimension; (2) a *marginal/low impact*, implying some impact on at least two of the dimensions (including an abatement but without an impact on its settlement); (3) a *moderate impact*, implying some impact on the settlement and also at least some impact on all other dimensions; and (4) a *high impact*, implying a high impact on the settlement, likewise in at least one other dimension, and at least some impact on the remaining dimensions.

Table 3 presents the performance of the UN in 130 cases of conflicts in which it was involved between 1946 and 1976,[7] again for the whole period and subperiods. The 'average' for the 30 years since its foundation is not particularly encouraging: In 60% of the cases it could exercise no impact whatsoever, in 25% of the cases it was 'marginally' or 'moderately' effective in a supporting rather than a decisive role, and in only 5% of the cases was the impact high, i.e. extending also into the sphere of decisive contributions to a settlement. The cases with a high impact are concentrated in the first and second periods. The three cases during the second (Zaïre Independence, West Iranian) and the one case Status of Eritrea, Togo Independence), the same applies to the two cases during the second (Zaïre Independence, West Iranian) and the one case during the third (Ifni Question) period. The remaining cases of the second period (Suez War 1956, Temple of Preah Vihear) are specific phases in which a temporary settlement but no resolution was achieved. If there is one conclusion to be drawn, then it is that only in negative terms did the organization fail to develop an autonomous capacity to influence conflict behaviour under changing international conditions. The colonial cases do not allow sound generalizations, in particular since they belong in part to post-Second World War questions and are all but representative of colonial conflict constellations which were to follow later.

Thus, one is left with the remaining 60% (no impact): 35% (moderate/low impact) split. In comparing the sub-periods some modestly encouraging signs may be drawn from the general increase in supporting roles of the organization from a 24% level during the first period to 50% during

Table 3.   Effectivity of UN conflict resolution 1946–76

	Effectivity				
	None	*Marginal*	*Moderate*	*Low*	*Total*
1946–55	66.7% (22)	9.1% (3)	15.2% (5)	9.1% (3)	100% (33)
1956–62	52.8% (19)	27.8% (10)	8.3% (3)	11.1% (4)	100% (36)
1963–69	64.1% (25)	17.9% (7)	15.4% (6)	2.6% (1)	100% (39)
1970–76	50.0% (11)	27.3% (6)	22.7% (5)	0.0% (0)	100% (22)
1946–76	59.2% (77)	20.0% (26)	14.6% (19)	6.2% (8)	100% (130)

Number of cases in ( ).

the most recent period, while the cases with no impact show a downward tendency, so that in the last period we find a 50:50 split. We have so far treated the UN involvement in conflicts largely in terms of abstract 'cases' without regard for their substantive contours, which in fact vary and combine into a variety of conflict constellations. Accordingly, the organization is confronted with different management tasks, depending on the type of conflict. It would be appropriate here to examine closely what factors make the organization fail altogether in its efforts, and what factors contribute so that it may become, more or less likely, successful in one or more of the dimensions. Does this depend on the *conflict issue*, on the *power relations* between the conflicting parties, on the *intensity* of the conflict, the *international environment* to which the cause or the course of the conflict relates; is it important *when* the organization *intervenes*, with *which type of action* it initiates its involvement, and which *degree of support* is behind its activity? These questions have been addressed in a variety of more or less comprehensive studies, and the different roles which the organization played in specific conflicts as well as which modified or new procedures in the decision-making process and in relations with conflicting parties were developed have found detailed description.[8] What has found less attention in such studies, as well as in the practice of the organization itself, has been succinctly pointed out by Northedge and Donelan in 1971:

The authors of the present study, in their conversations with . . . officials of the UN . . ., were impressed of their zeal, energy and devotion to the task of 'saving succeeding generations from the scourge of war'. However, there was notable in the Secretariat a certain lack of recorded experience of how the UN had fared in grappling with international problems since its foundation, and in particular of an attempt to generalize from this now lengthy experience about what kind of disputes, between what kind of countries and under what conditions, the organization is best and least suited to deal with.

They continue by advocating the value of knowledge for practical purposes

. . . of what the United Nations, on the basis of its past experience, is best fitted to attempt and what tasks it would be well advised, in its own interest, to leave to other agencies.[9]

Though there are by now a number of empirical investigations of the UN's practice which follow this path,[10] some caution seems advisable with generalizations derived from systematic analyses correlating or associating conflict types and constellations with the performance of the organization and related modes of interventions on the basis of the UN's 'complete past'. These seem to vary to a considerable degree with the period during which they were undertaken. Thus, a mode of intervention that proved more or less successful in earlier periods does not necessarily do so in later periods, and there are indications that in particular the late sixties and early seventies are a period where major changes took place which may invalidate earlier experiences, both negative and positive.

3. Prospects

The conclusions that can be drawn are, in the first place, of a negative form. The 'model cases' of the organization (where it could exercise a high impact) seem to be least suggestive for any speculation on future promising approaches. They are typically related to modes of intervention with a high diplomatic-mediatory intensity and/or actions with a strong coercive component and backed by a wide or extensive consensus behind authorizing decisions. This type has apparently, as our data show, seen a marked decline. Apart from the fact that these cases are hardly significant in numerical terms, it has already been noted that they are related to specific issues and decision conditions which are not likely to govern the future. A sizeable portion of the cases in which the UN could exercise some supporting, conflict-moderating role with a moderate or at least marginal impact on the course of conflicts was also related to issues of decolonization with types of relations between the conflicting parties not very likely to appear again in future conflicts. Add to this the inaccessibility to the UN of conflicts which have an explicit relation to the East–West conflict (which may possibly develop a renewed significance). The decolonization process has produced a new generation of states which, as a common characteristic, strongly see that their sovereignty is given primary attention, which is in turn a product of relatively low degrees of internal national integration and/or organization, and of external problems in relations with immediately neighbouring states. 'African issues' demonstrate this most clearly. In fact, interstate conflicts of the more recent past over territorial claims as a consequence of the colonial heritage of artificial borders, interwoven in many cases with ethnic issues or secessionist movements within countries with spill-over effects to interstate relations by other states becoming involved, seem to be the result of incomplete resolutions to decolonization cases in which the UN was earlier involved. The sovereignty to which established regimes take resort is then the guarantee (or at least perceived so) with which to reject whatever claims that may further weaken regime stability. Similarly, though yet still in a *status nascendi*, parts of Latin America seem to be on the verge of breaking up the traditional ties of the 'hemispheric community' under US leadership. Finally, critical regions in Asia are also defined by changes in regimes with fundamental transformations in domestic sociopolitical structures. The reverse of the 'sovereignty coin', which in cases of conflict will become a determinant of the UN's possibilities, seems to be the marked reluctance of states to accept any authoritative decision by international bodies that threatens their standing, either because the decision is influenced by a majority of nations with different value orientations in assessing the conflicting claims and/or because the acceptance of a formalized and visible presence of the UN is considered as incompatible with, possibly even threatening, the sovereign and independent status of one or more of the conflicting parties. Thus, well-known instruments of the past such as fact-finding commissions and commissions of investigation will with some probability meet serious reservations on the part of countries that would have to admit them in the early phase of a conflict.

These observations exclude for the future certain elements of past forms of operations by the UN. What remains are two possible roles which may even be incompatible as mutually reinforcing the moderating management of conflicts. The Security Council and the General Assembly may function as platforms from which a party to a conflict may be condemned. It remains an open question whether such a practice will induce sovereignty-conscious states to comply with such declaratory actions, even if there is a broad supporting majority. There is no reason to believe that this instrument alone will be more successful than in the past. If at all it may constitute a last resort in cases where no other initiatives to accommodate conflicting interests seem at all likely or promising, by the organization itself or in some other form outside the organizational context. The procedural implications of the trend noted above from data on the organizational performance suggest a second role, which is further supported by the observed tendency to introduce conflicts into international frameworks, including the UN. Even if the parties' primary intention is merely to receive support or legitimization, it may form a starting-point for the UN to develop and strengthen a more acceptable role for conflicting parties in terms of 'tacit presence' by its availability for good offices, mediatory, and conciliatory services. More recent conflicts, in Kampuchea and Iran, have demonstrated that it is already difficult enough to have accepted most modest forms of a UN presence, even if restricted to basic humanitarian purposes. Recognizing that the 'police role' of the UN, for which it was originally designed, has with some certainty no prospects and cutting down expectations to supportive functions may seem modest; however, it also implies a considerable potential. The systematic development of these *procedures* into techniques of conflict resolution, with the UN providing and co-ordinating material and intellectual resources, might make conflicting parties gradually more aware of the frequent miscalculations behind enforced settlements or unreflected continuation of conflicts. Mediatory and conciliatory approaches are most suitable to generate partial and stepwise progress and to take greater account of resolving structural, and mostly hidden, factors of conflict which will promote conflict resolutions of greater viability under long-term perspectives. They could contribute to a synthesis of the two facets of peace to be found in the Charter, i.e. not only to 'maintain international peace and security' but also to create its structure. Viable and stable resolutions of conflicts are the prerequisite for the stable conditions under which that economic and social progress and development will become possible which the Charter asserts to form the basis of peaceful and friendly relations.

Notes

1. The determination of the universe of international conflicts is not unproblematic, and definitions adopted will remain unsatisfactory under some aspect. The problem is largely solved 'by definition' if one is concerned with institutional frameworks for dealing with international conflicts. Here the focus is on international conflicts which have as a common characteristic 'political-security' issues. The list of conflicts and data on these conflicts used here are from the data base compiled by Butterworth, R. L. (1976). *Managing Interstate Conflict 1945–74: Data with Synopsis* (Pittsburgh: University of Pittsburgh/University Center for International Studies), in a slightly modified form. Criteria for the selection of cases are presented in Ch. 1.

2. The term 'collective security organization' is used here in a broad sense, referring to organizations which have as their objective the ability to deal with international conflicts without necessarily implying the classical (especially coercive) mechanisms and obligations of members of the system.

3. See Butterworth, R. L. (1978). 'Do Conflict Managers Matter?' *International Studies Quarterly*, XXII. 2: 195–214, especially 201 ff. for a similar analysis.

4. For a detailed substantive and methodological discussion see Jütte, R. (1979). 'The Analysis of UN Effectivity in the Control of International Conflicts.' *Paper (Suppl.), XI. IPSA World Congress*, Moscow, 12–19 Aug. 1979.

5. The organizational impact was evaluated for each relevant conflict by a systematic judicial procedure whether the involvement of the organizations had 'none', 'some' or 'much/decisive' impact on the conflict behaviour of the parties in each of the following dimensions, whereby the control of violence and/or isolation of third-party involvement applies only to a more limited number of cases.

6. Butterworth, 1978 (*n. 3*), 201, reports that the dimensions comprise a Guttman scale. Respective results were obtained from a classification procedure based on information-theoretic (entropy) measures. The procedure is described in Vogel, F. (1975). *Probleme und Verfahren der Numerischen Klassifikation* (Göttingen: Vandenhoeck & Ruprecht), 252–91. The analysis was carried out with the

VGRPG Programme implemented at the Computing Centre at the University of Cologne, cf. the *User's Manual* of the Center, Sect. 6.5.7 (pp. 67–8).

7. This is based on an updated form of the original data base, with ten additional conflicts (up to 1976) considered by the UN, for an analysis of the role of the UN in international conflicts. The differences in the data bases do not affect the observations presented here. Note also that the 1963–74 period is replaced by the two periods 1963–9 and 1970–6.

8. See, for example, James, Alan (1969). *The Politics of Peacekeeping* (New York – Washington: Praeger Publ.), and Raman, K. Venkata (1975). *The Ways of the Peacemaker. A Study of United Nations Intermediary Assistance in the Peaceful Settlement of Disputes* (New York: United Nations Institute for Training and Research).

9. Northedge, F. S. and Donelan, M. D. (1971). *International Disputes. The Political Aspects* (London: Europa Publ.), 201.

10. Representative are analyses by Haas, Ernst B., Butterworth, R. L. and Nye, Joseph S. (1972). *Conflict Management by International Organization* (Morristown, N.J.: General Learning Press) and Butterworth, R. L. (1978) *Moderation from Management. International Organizations and Peace* (Pittsburgh: University Centre for International Studies).

12 NAMIBIA AND APARTHEID: WHAT TYPE OF CONFLICT? WHAT KIND OF UNITED NATIONS ACTION?

FRANZ ANSPRENGER
Free University of Berlin

1. Defining the Problem

Apartheid in South Africa and the destiny of Namibia are two issues of major importance for world politics. It may be somewhat difficult to estimate the percentage of the UN's attention (e.g. in terms of time for their consideration, documents produced) devoted to these two issues. The share is in any case considerable.

Two things are evident, that the world community is faced in both bases, apartheid and Namibia, with a *protracted conflict*, and that the major institution of international organization in the world today – the *United Nations System* – has been involved in this conflict practically ever since it was created in 1945. Furthermore, it is also evident that the two issues belong closely together: efforts to abolish the South African administration in Namibia are part of, and intrinsically related to, the over-all efforts to destroy the socio-political system of apartheid in South Africa itself.

For practical reasons this paper is based mainly on the experience we can derive from the Namibia dispute; problems concerning the international involvement seem to appear somewhat clearer in the Namibia Case – among others because the International Court of Justice (ICJ) has had several occasions to pronounce itself on Namibia. But in broader political terms, most conclusions drawn from the Namibia dispute can easily be transferred to the issue of apartheid.

Many other things remain controversial. This applies especially to the definition of at least two characteristics: What kind of *conflict* are we dealing with? What further problems are inherent in the (possible, desirable, or simply proposed) *solutions* of the conflict?

1.1 *On the Character of the (Namibia) Conflict*

As to the first question, the character of the conflict may be seen under four different perspectives, each having different implications.

(A) Is this an 'international conflict' in the usual sense, i.e. an *inter-state conflict*? One party to the conflict is, indeed, a state actor — the South African government. But what about the other party or parties? Can we see South Africa's opponent as 'the African front line states', as 'the OAU member states', or as 'those UN member-states who regularly vote against South Africa'? This confrontation is obviously part of the conflict — but only a small part. More important is the confrontation between South Africa's *state power*, and the black (or non-white?) people (or peoples, or population?) of Namibia and South Africa.

(B) One way out of the dilemma would be to look at apartheid and (especially) Namibia as *decolonization* conflicts. The liquidation of colonial rule comes under the responsibility of the UN. Already the Charter has expressed some rather vague ideas about 'non self-governing territories' in general (Art. 73), and it has established a special machinery for de-colonizing a few countries selected at historical random: the trusteeship system (Ch. XII). Since December 1960, when the General Assembly adopted Res. 1514 (XV), all UN institutions involved have made com-bined efforts for the pursuit of decolonization, in most cases with active support of the formerly colonial powers. Namibia is clearly a territory under colonial rule; concerning South Africa, it is only logical to analyse the political system as one of 'domestic colonialism' in order to justify UN intervention. The programmes of the South African Communist Party (SACP) and the African National Congress (ANC/SA) as presented by Slovo[1] are indicative in this regard.

But decolonization cannot explain everything. It remains a voluntary decision to regard *XY* as a situation of colonial rule and *YX* as nothing of the sort (Bretagne; Baltic countries; Kurdistan; Western Sahara).

(C) There remains a third possibility: to regard the apartheid/Namibia conflict as a (potential? actual?) *civil war* situation with established power structures — like the Spanish Civil War 1936–9. This option explains the insistence on 'armed struggle' on the part of African liberation move-ments, and their advancement (however slow and incomplete) towards a 'permanent observer' status in the UN. The logical conclusion of this approach would be to proclaim new ('black' or multi-racial) govern-ments. But governments-*in-exile* have difficulties in being acknowledged as parties to a civil war. In fact, no government-in-exile has ever been proclaimed during the process of Africa's liberation (decolonization) after Roberto's ill-fated GRAE.[2] Rapid success, however, followed the 1973 proclamation of a PAIGC[3] *government-in-liberated-territory*, in Guinea-Bissau: this action, indeed, set the pace for take-overs not only in Guinea Bissau itself, but in all former Portuguese colonies (except Angola) after 1974. Liberation movements in Namibia and South Africa must have had their own reasons *not* to follow this example. Is it predominantly their military weakness?

(D) One thing is clear: *a revolutionary situation* in South Africa and/or

Namibia, perceived as an outcome of *class struggle*, could never explain or justify an involvement of international organizations in the conflict. Even extremely oppressive regimes containing revolutionary situations in their respective countries are accepted as members of the UN without any challenge, and without serious efforts to regard their policies as international conflicts.

1.2. *On the Character of Possible Solutions*

If Option B (Decolonization) from the preceding section is adopted as a perspective for the predominant character of the conflict, as it is, indeed, conclusive for Namibia, the solution would have to be *self-determination by the people* concerned. This leads, of course, to the old question of what constitutes a 'people' entitled to a rightful claim to self-determination and self-government? In my opinion it is *not* possible to answer this question in objective terms. Historically, however, the question has been answered for Africa during its process of decolonization: a people entitled to self-determination, and self-government, is defined as all the inhabitants of a given administrative territorial unit, within the borders drawn by the colonial governments as they exist immediately prior to the moment of self-determination. This well-known 'OAU principle'[4] is only controversial, at present, for the Western Sahara, not even for Eritrea (there, it could only be argued whether or not the Eritrean people really did determine their future in the process of joining Ethiopia; 'second thoughts' are not admitted under the OAU principle). On Cabinda, the principle has correctly been applied by handing over this enclave to Angola, prohibiting separate self-determination of its inhabitants. Applied to Namibia, the principle without doubt *excludes* Walfish Bay from Namibia, and *includes* Eastern Caprivi (which, under all other considerations, should be attached to Zambia, as Walfish Bay should, of course, be attached to Namibia).

If Option C (Civil War) from the preceding section is adopted as a valid perspective, the character of a possible solution would be much more difficult to define: The UN Charter ignores civil wars as objects for organizational actions, and the historical record of UN dealings with civil wars is in fact not impressive: the UN has strictly *ignored* the Vietnam civil war over many years (a logical policy under the Charter, but not very helpful for the Vietnamese people), as well as the Nigerian (Biafran) and the Southern Sudanese civil wars; they have *muddled through* the Congo (Zaïre) civil wars between 1960 and 1964; they again *ignored* the civil war in Lebanon until Israel became involved.

In one civil war situation which was brought to the UN early in its history — the question of Palestine — the General Assembly voted for territorial partition as the conflict solution. The power of the General Assembly to decide this issue has been questioned, but never really challenged. The decision has been only partly realized (creation of the state of Israel, not, however, of the Palestinian Arab state). The conflict has *not* been solved.

For Namibia, a formula of *territorial partition* has for some time been envisaged by the South African government. This has always been rejected most categorically by the UN as well as by SWAPO with reference to the above-mentioned OAU decolonization principle.

It remains an open question if territorial partition, for the UN, can remain a potential solution for the apartheid conflict in South Africa itself. Developments in Namibia suggest a negative answer, as does the Congo (Zaïre) experience of the UN. But the fate of Germany, Korea, Israel/Palestine, and (for a time) Vietnam show that there is still a tendency alive in favour of territorial partition as a solution for civil-war type international conflicts. In fact, some writers are already busy drawing maps of a future South Africa divided into a *Black State* and some kind of Homeland for the white Africans (and their brown stepchildren) around the Western Cape.

There remain some final considerations as regards possible solutions. If we exclude territorial partition of South Africa as a solution of the apartheid conflict, and if we continue to approach this conflict as a civil-war situation, we must conclude that the desirable solution (for the UN) is to help *replace the present bad/intolerable government by a better/ more tolerable one*. But this is, in itself, no answer to the question of how to define the character of a possible conflict solution. Two alternatives are open: first, replacing the existing bad/intolerable government by the other civil-war party, i.e. by the 'authentic representatives of (the true aspirations of) the people . . .', meaning SWAPO in Namibia (without the words in brackets), or ANC/SA and (!) PAC in South Africa (with the words in brackets)[5] or, secondly, replacing the existing intolerable apartheid government by an entirely new structure, without a clear-cut victory of the other party to the civil war.

The alternative to *peace by unconditional surrender* or *peace by negotiations* leading to a *compromise* poses a dilemma which is not entirely new for wars of the nineteenth and twentieth centuries, whether civil wars or others. There are encouraging historical examples for both formulas: the end of the Second World War by German surrender; the solution of the Trieste conflict by compromise; the American Civil War was ended by a surrender which was then turned into a compromise. But, unfortunately, there are also other examples for both types of solutions without encouraging results: the Vietnam compromise formula of 1954; or the 'surrender' (total defeat) of Republican Spain in 1939.

There are no definite conclusions. No formula for the solution of a conflict of the civil-war type is convincing by itself. The material character of the parties to the conflict must be considered, and the outcome can only be an *ad hoc* formula for this particular conflict (was it, perhaps, a wise decision not to include civil wars in the UN Charter?).

2. Review of UN Efforts to Solve the Namibia Conflict: The Time Perspective.

The purpose of this review is not, of course, to repeat the calendar of events, which can be traced much better by consulting one of the many handbooks,[6] but rather to focus on and to find out the systematic problems inherent in the successive approaches of the UN to cope with the situation in Namibia.

2.1. *The Trusteeship Approach*

Immediately after the creation of the UN, indeed already during the process, a majority of member-states' governments pressed for an inclusion of South West Africa into the trusteeship system. In other words, they wanted South West Africa ultimately to become a 'self-governing' or 'independent' territory — 'as may be appropriate . . .' in the words of Art. 76 of the UN Charter, but implicitly *excluding* its annexation by or incorporation in South Africa.[7] At that early time, and continuing up to 1974, South Africa's case rested on the contention that South West Africa was not prepared for separate independence *The case against South Africa* was based on the opposite contention. The UN majority would have liked to debate the issue in the framework of trusteeship, as it had been set up under the Charter. But this would have anticipated the outcome of the debate and South Africa consequently refused. However, Fieldmarshal Smuts's government, in power until 1948, 'signalled' a possible readiness to *compromise* by actually submitting a *Report* to the UN Trusteeship Council for the year 1946. But no compromise was reached. The UN (or some UN delegates) hoped to press South Africa from compromise to surrender (viz. by an acceptance of a trusteeship agreement) by, in the words of the Mexican delegate,[8] '. . . an aroused world public opinion (which) would compel the Union of South Africa to take that step . . .'. South Africa, in due course, reacted with the election of a Nationalist Government under Dr. Malan, who closed the potential road towards a compromise by the refusal to submit further reports.

The dispute was then brought before the International Court of Justice — still in accordance with the machinery set up in the UN Charter for settling conflicts, but no longer as a specific decolonization conflict. The ICJ Advisory Opinion of 1950[9] tried again to achieve a solution by compromise, or more precisely, to keep a future chance open for compromise by postponing a solution: the substance for a compromise that was offered in the ICJ Advisory Opinion was purely negative in that it affirmed the General Assembly's claim in so far as nothing should be changed unilaterally by South Africa; and South Africa's position was accepted in so far as *no* obligation existed to enter into a trusteeship agreement with the UN. These negative roots for a possible compromise (holes into which roots perhaps could have been planted) were neglected — foremost by South Africa whose government refused to continue the 'dialogue' with the UN.

This deadlock in developing a conflict resolution for South West Africa (Namibia) seems to be free of any links with the apartheid problem, which could be raised in the UN only after the coming to power of a South African government that promoted apartheid as its declared policy, viz. after 1948. But this is only superficially true: in substance, *South African policies of racial segregation and discrimination* are, of course, older than the nationalist government. In the concrete actions concerning South West Africa in 1945–8, concern about the racist approach did play an important role.

When South Africa (under Smuts) pretended to consult South West Africa's population about their political future, it did so under racist auspices: chiefs and headmen alone were asked to sign a pro-South African memorial on behalf of their respective 'tribe'.[10] Already at that time, the UN did not recognize such a procedure as an act of popular self-determination (though the British delegation then was still prepared to do so).

2.2. *The Legal Approach (for Namibia only)*

Attempts to solve the Namibia conflict by legal action, resulted in several decisions of the ICJ:

Advisory Opinions in 1950 and 1956.[11] The political substance of the 1950 Advisory Opinion has just been characterized as keeping a door open for a future compromise between the parties, by postponing a solution. In 1955 the ICJ authorized the General Assembly to adopt resolutions on South West Africa (thereby confirming the character of the conflict as an international one); in 1956 the ICJ authorized the General Assembly to grant oral hearings to (anti-South African) petitioners from South West Africa. The political result of these two statements, therefore, can be seen as *strengthening the anti-South African party* in the conflict.

The next step of the legal approach, however, ended with a defeat for the anti-South African coalition in the UN. The attempt of *Ethiopia and Liberia* in 1966 to obtain a binding ICJ judgement to the effect that South Africa was under an obligation to submit South West Africa to UN supervision was rejected by the court on the ground that the two states (the only African member-states of the defunct League of Nations except South Africa itself) had no legal right or interest in the case.[12]

This famous statement of the ICJ 1966 is of continuing political interest in so far as it sets tight limits for a conception of the conflict as an interstate conflict (South Africa v. OAU member-states).

The legal approach was continued with the Advisory Opinion of the ICJ of 21 June 1971,[13] recognizing (1) the illegal occupation of Namibia by South Africa and defining (2) certain obligations for all states of the world, whether UN members or not, in the struggle against this illegal situation.

Politically, this 1971 Advisory Opinion has so far been the culmination point of legal action against South Africa in the Namibia issue. The ICJ endorsed the position of the UN majority, and practically *summoned South Africa to surrender*. This action by the ICJ was considered in South Africa as a political volte-face after the 1966 judgement, and mainly explained by changes on the judges' bench in the ICJ.

But this suggestion does not hold water. In fact, the new trend of the 1971 Advisory Opinion follows from the political 'legislative' action, which the UN General Assembly had undertaken immediately after the 1966 ruling: the revocation of the South African Mandate to administer Namibia embodied in Res. 2145 (XXI) of 27 October 1966.

It is, of course, open to discussion, and has been heatedly discussed, whether the General Assembly has the right to 'legislate' in such a way in an international conflict. But the ICJ had always confirmed this opinion, and specifically so in its 1966 South West Africa decision, which was politically favourable to South Africa.

The court had suggested that the question of whether or not the Mandate had been violated, should be decided by a political and not a legal institution. And it is obvious that such supervision is a responsibility of the General Assembly, not of the Security Council (where a draft resolution to revoke the South African Mandate, at least in 1966, would probably have been vetoed by one or more permanent members).

2.3. *The Legislative Approach*

It is true that in the UN General Assembly, on 27 October 1966, 114 states voted in favour of Res. 2145 (XXI); only Portugal and South Africa voted against it, and three delegations abstained (France, Malawi, and the UK). But the voting behaviour of the Great Powers is not necessarily the same in the General Assembly (where mainly recommendations are passed) and in the Security Council (when exercising whatever executive authority the Charter provides for the UN).

Did certain Western powers, then, *underestimate* the 'legislative' importance of Res. 2145 (XXI) at the time of the voting? Strictly speaking, as is well known, the General Assembly is not a legislative body, and this is the main reason why the UN as a whole is by no means a government for the international community. But the *revocation of the South African Mandate must be considered as a kind of legislative measure*, in the same political context as the power of most national parliaments to ratify international treaties is part of their legislative authority. The revocation of the mandate brings an end to a treaty relationship between South Africa and the League of Nations (the UN acting as a legal successor to the League) on the ground of fundamental breaches in the treaty, effected by South African policy towards Namibia.

It is not necessary to go into material details. South Africa, of course, denies that any of its policies, apartheid or whatever they have been called, was inconsistent with the fundamental humanitarian principles of the old Mandate. The rest of the world is more or less convinced that this is just the case. In academic circles the discussion of apartheid under this perspective, whether or not it violates basic human rights, should be closed. It is the *formal question* of a successful attempt of the General Assembly to 'legislate' for the UN which is of interest to us today, because such an attempt may be renewed in some other conflict. Can the General Assembly exercise this right only in matters of decolonization (as, indeed, it had already been done in the case of Palestine in 1947), or is it a general power notwithstanding and beyond the main function of the Assembly, viz. to give recommendations?

For many years the General Assembly has tried in vain to put into effect its resolution of 1966. New institutions within the UN system were created for this purpose, in particular the UN Council for Namibia and the UN Commissioner for Namibia, as a kind of provisional government-in-exile of the territory. For more than 10 years, all the reports and multi-formous activities of these bodies (publications, conferences, etc.) seemed to be of no consequence for the solution of the conflict. But that was only the surface of the real political evolution. In depth, the General Assembly's resolution of 1966 prepared solid ground, not only for the ICJ to give its Advisory Opinion in 1971, but mainly for the Security Council to establish step by step a procedure which has finally been effective in nearly compelling South Africa to leave Namibia. For this reason adoption of the 1966 resolution should in fact be considered a 'successful' attempt of the General Assembly to 'legislate' on Namibia.

2.4. *The Persuasion/Conciliation Approach*

In the years of interlude and doubt about the effectiveness of General Assembly 'legislation', the UN tried yet another approach for solving the conflict: conciliation or persuasion through the offices of the Secretary-General. The Namibia issue is also of general interest from the point of view that practically all UN organs have been involved in it, with markedly different degrees of success.

In July/August 1972 the Security Council empowered the Secretary-

General, Dr. Waldheim, to '. . . continue his contacts with all parties concerned, with a view to establishing the necessary conditions so as to enable the people of Namibia . . . to exercise their right to self-determination and independence . . .'.[14] By prescribing the outcome of the contacts in this manner, the Security Council opened a road tending more to persuasion than to conciliation, the latter implying compromise. Dr. Waldheim appointed a Swiss diplomat, Ambassador Aldred Martin Escher, as his personal representative for this mission.

Reading the Escher Report[15] today, one cannot but feel, however, that it was not persuasion, but rather conciliation that Ambassador Escher tried to achieve. He clearly suggested a *compromise* between apartheid (in this case, homeland) policies and the UN objectives for Namibia, when he wrote under para. 5 of his conclusions:

> The Prime Minister (Vorster) believed that experience in self-government was an essential element for eventual self-determination and that such experience could be best achieved on a regional basis. However, when I made it clear that simultaneously an authority for the whole territory would have to be established, he agreed to certain measures involving the 'Territory as a whole'. This would appear to be in line with the aim of maintaining the unity of Namibia.

The offer to compromise is contained in the word 'simultaneously': Prime Minister Vorster had changed South Africa's basic policy for Namibia in 1974, no longer insisting on the deadlocked status quo, but preparing 'self-determination' of a plurality of Namibian 'peoples' according to the South African Bantu-homelands model. The UN could not agree to this offer of the Secretary-General's envoy. The Security Council, therefore, in December 1973, discontinued the Waldheim–Escher mission.[16]

2.5. *The Executive Approach*

Over the years following 1973, the UN Security Council engaged in executive action in order to materialize UN policy in terms of taking over the actual administration of Namibia for a transitional period, and guide it to independent statehood as a single entity.

In December 1974 the Security Council for the first time obtained concurrent votes of the three Western permanent members (USA, UK, and France) to adopt a relatively strong resolution on Namibia.[17] It asked South Africa ultimately to accept the UN policy by 30 May 1975. Prime Minister Vorster, of course, did nothing of the sort. His answer was a proof of tactical flexibility, not an offer to achieve a compromise. He dropped his former 'pluralistic' line and pushed forward the Turnhalle policy instead; in other words, he agreed to the indivisibility of Namibia's territory — provided South Africa could determine who was going to rule it. When the Security Council considered the situation in

June 1975, it fell back into its old dilemma. The three Western powers vetoed a draft resolution which could have imposed a mandatory arms embargo on South Africa under Chapter VII of the Charter. But this was only a temporary drawback; in a more general view, the Security Council was now on its way to proceeding by 'two steps ahead, then one (only) in retreat'.

On 30 January 1976 the Security Council unanimously adopted Resolution 385, calling (*a*) for a transfer of power in Namibia to the UN, and (*b*) the holding of free elections in Namibia under UN control. Implicitly, all the member-states of the Council at that time committed themselves to make active contributions to the implementation of this policy, i.e. to accept some degree of political or technical responsibility for the success of UN transitional government in Namibia. October 1976 witnessed again the 'one step backward' in the progress of UN policy. The arms embargo proposal, based on the contention that South Africa's behaviour in Namibia constituted a 'threat to the peace' in the meaning of Art. 39 of the UN Charter, was again vetoed by the three Western permanent members.[18]

But on 4 November 1977 the stalemate was broken, and the UN Security Council reached a working compromise among its own members on future executive action against South Africa.[19] Unanimously, the Council strengthened the already existing arms embargo, and *expressis verbis* it acted 'under Chapter VII of the Charter . . .'. This action was not directed towards Namibia alone, but towards the over-all policies of South Africa in confronting (unfriendly) neighbouring states. As it happens, the (in the words of Security Council Resolution 418 of 1977) '. . . military build-up and persistent acts of aggression by South Africa against the neighbouring states . . .' do take place mainly on the northern border of Namibia — against Angola and against Zambia, never (so far) on the borders between South Africa itself and Mozambique, Botswana, Swaziland, or Lesotho. Indeed, 'a threat to the maintenance of international peace and security' is mentioned in Res. 418 — *not*, however, in relation to these acts of aggression, but only to 'the acquisition by South Africa of arms . . .' (operative para. 1). The aggression, according to the preamble of the resolution, does simply '. . . seriously disturb the security of those states'.

Art. 39 of the UN Charter (which opens Ch. VII) describes a sequence of escalation of conflicts: threat to peace, breach of peace, act of aggression. Res. 418 seems to reverse this sequence: or is a 'disturbance of security' considered to be the very same thing as a 'threat to the peace'? Something has been done to save the Western Powers' faces, I imagine.

There is a good reason here to repeat a general question already asked earlier: do UN policies against South Africa pre-determine strategies in other, future conflicts? More concretely: will the UN Security Council see 'threats to peace' simply in the acquisition of certain weapons by a state whose domestic policies have been condemned? And will we hear more about 'disturbances of security' when armed forces of a state practise what their government may call 'hot pursuit' or — more candidly still — a 'measure of correction' (as in the China vs. Vietnam dispute)? We can only question and leave the answer left open. We had better return to the Namibia case.

We know that Western Powers, among them non-permanent members (the Federal Republic of Germany and Canada), obtained a mandate from the Security Council in 1978 to prepare the next steps of action. The Council adopted the plan of this 'Gang of Five' later in the same year (in July) with only two abstentions — from the USSR and the CSSR. We know that this Western plan endorsed by the Council means a *sharing* of administrative power in Namibia, for the transitional period, between the South African officials and the UN Commissioner.[20]

This plan has not yet worked. A new dispute has arisen exactly where it could have been expected: who will demonstrate *dominating military power* at the crucial moment of internationally supervised elections? South Africa obviously hopes that as long as South African soldiers remain present close to the polling stations, a majority of the people will vote for the pro-South African candidates of the DTA. SWAPO soldiers in the open, of course, means a SWAPO electoral victory. It is not possible to reach a compromise by bringing into Namibia a UN force: for too long the UN have identified themselves with SWAPO's aspiration to rule alone in an independent Namibia.

In conclusion, we note that the Namibia conflict has put the UN back on its original track. The Charter envisages an organization (centred around the Great Powers) which will maintain peace, in the form of policies debated and *recommended by the General Assembly*, and *executed by the Security Council*. The temptation to sidestep from this given deadlock by handing over to the Secretary-General more authority than the Charter wants him to have — and therefore a degree of authority too heavy for any Secretary-General to handle (the 'Hammarskjöld-Congo–Temptation') has been avoided (with difficulties) in the Namibia conflict. South Africa, as stubborn as its government and white people may be, has been compelled to retreat, at least tactically. This shows how strong the UN still can be in world politics, if only it would follow its own constitutional (Charter) provisions.

3. Types of UN Actions

This would now be the place to analyse, in more detail, what types of action, employed at different moments by different UN organs and other institutions, have been shown to be most efficient in influencing the development of the Namibia conflict. For reasons of space such an analysis cannot be fully developed here, but I will give an outline of its major steps.

It would be necessary, for this purpose, to analyse in detail relevant materials. From within the UN system, these would have to comprise (1) the resolutions of various UN organs, reports of the UN Council for Namibia, and information material issued under the auspices of the UN Centre Against Apartheid, the Council for Namibia, etc., (2) further sources would have to be conference papers, e.g. from the Lagos World Conference for Action against Apartheid (August 1977); and, of course, (3) texts from the counter-actions and counter-information provided by the South African authorities.

Possibly, such an analysis could be divided as follows:

(1) *Establishment of formal UN responsibility for Namibia.*
(2) *Establishment of formal UN responsibility for apartheid, i.e. for the struggle against apartheid.*
(3) *Apartheid and Human Rights.*
(4) *Apartheid as a prevention of popular self-determination, especially in Namibia.*
(5) *The breakdown of political freedoms and democratic institutions under apartheid (i.e. follow-up of the fate of opposition groups, free press, church institutions, etc.).*
(6) *Action Proposals type A: encouragement of resistance.*
(7) *Action Proposals type B: encouragement of armed struggle.*
(8) *Action Proposals type C: calls for economic sanctions, arms embargo, etc.*
(9) *Action Proposals type D: calls for active intervention from UN and UN member-states.*
(10) *Action Proposals type E: preparing for an independent Namibia.*

It is likely that the result of such an analysis would be somewhere on the line of 'splendid information work, inconsistent action proposals'. In particular, the Decree No. 1 of the UN Council for Namibia, enacted in 1975 and meant to 'protect the Natural Resources' of Namibia, would become subject to criticism. This decree threatens Western companies that raw-material exports from Namibia could be liable to confiscation by the UN Council for Namibia. It did not achieve the result of stopping the exploitation of Namibia's mineral resources.

4. Remaining Crucial Problems

Political scientists might suggest investigating some of the following questions for further studies of the conduct of different actors in the Namibia conflict.

4.1   *The Voting — and other — Behaviour of the Great Powers*

I have suggested above that some Great Powers (perhaps other states as well) tended to express their vote differently in different UN organs, in particular in the General Assembly and in the Security Council.

Another question is the *consistency*, in logic and in time, of the policy of individual states. For the Federal Republic of Germany, for instance, I suggest that there exists a consistent but unrealistic wish to be 'everybody's darling' and therefore to avoid taking sides in the conflict. This policy was later eroded by the overriding interest to do something positive for its international standing by making use of its membership in the UN General Assembly, and later on in the Security Council. At present, the position of the Federal Republic appears as one of a 'reluctant anti-imperialist'. All these developments did occur under the SPD/FDP administration Schmidt/Genscher; before this the Federal Republic did not have a policy conception for Namibia or apartheid.

With regard to the USA,[21] it is customary to distinguish policies according to administrations, and this may be a useful tool of analysis for the cases of Namibia and apartheid: Carter and his advisers brought a quite different approach from that of Nixon and Kissinger. But this change cannot explain everything. The changing general posture of the USA in the world economy, and therefore in world politics, must cast some reflection on American policies regarding Namibia and apartheid. Given the high degree of American investment in South Africa, and the complicated relationship between gold production there, the capitalist world monetary system in general, and the role of the dollar in particular, this may not be an easy task for a political research.

China's position will be comparatively much easier to determine. According to the words of Chinese delegates in the UN, the present Peking government subordinates all and every development in the international arena to her confrontation with the Soviet Union. China has veto power in the Security Council, but at present it lacks any real power — military or economic — to influence events in Southern Africa. Chinese support for liberation movements, in particular, is no longer specific (since its Angolan disaster) and purely verbal.

The Soviet Union, on the other hand, can rely on a long and successful policy of valuable support for a precisely defined group of *liberation movements* from Southern Africa. In Angola and Mozambique, these movements are now in exclusive command. For Zimbabwe/Rhodesia and Namibia, they are recognized by the OAU, and therefore by the UN, as true representatives of the black peoples.[22] Only with regard to South Africa itself is the situation less clear, as the PAC (an old adversary of Soviet and Communist influence in African liberation policies) still enjoys international recognition, and the split within the ANC (precisely on the same problem) is ignored by the OAU and UN.

But the voting behaviour of the USSR regarding Namibia raises another question: to what degree is the Soviet government prepared to channel its *intervention through the UN system?* For many years since the anti-Soviet turn of the UN Congo Operation in 1961, USSR delegates showed distrust of any practical UN activities, e.g. in Namibia. In 1972 the USSR joined the UN Council for Namibia (no Great Power from the West has ever become a member); but this step did not commit the Soviet government to much action. It is obvious that the USSR gave the 'green light' for the Western powers in the Security Council to bring about a Namibia solution in 1978; why the USSR did not insist on participating in this venture is less clear and difficult to answer. Will the USSR — directly, or through one of her trusted allies — take part in the transitional UN administration of Namibia?

4.2 SWAPO and its Armed Struggle

Late in 1973 the UN General Assembly recognized SWAPO as '. . . the *authentic representative of the Namibian people* . . .', thereby exceeding the honourable nomenclature of the other OAU-recognized African liberation movements as '. . . sole and authentic representatives of the true aspirations . . .' of their respective peoples. But the UN always stopped short of recognizing the existing SWAPO leadership as some kind of legal government(-in-exile) of Namibia: this role remained reserved for the UN Council for Namibia and the UN Commissioner. Consequently, an African move in the UN in December 1976 to obtain *permanent-observer* status for SWAPO (as enjoyed by non-member-states like Switzerland and the Vatican), was turned down already at the low level of considerations by legal experts. There is another consequence, i.e. the Lusaka-based Institute for Namibia — the most important training centre for administrative personnel of a future independent Namibia — is a UN institution, and among the eleven members of the Institute's Senate, there are only two SWAPO officials.

When the UN Council for Namibia reports annually to the General Assembly about, among other things, the 'Participation of the Representatives of the Namibian People in the Work of the Council', nobody except SWAPO is mentioned. But *in* the Council, SWAPO is an associate member only. And wherever Namibia as a country has become a member of an international governmental organization in the UN system — e.g. as a full member in FAO, and an associate member in WHO and UNESCO — it is the UN Council which represents Namibia. However, SWAPO delegates usually 'accompany' the delegates of the Council who may be citizens of any member-state.[23]

Such formalities may not be very important. Sometimes one reads that there is a lot of infighting among different UN institutions who feel responsible for Namibia. More important, politically, is the UN attitude to the basic policy of SWAPO.

Armed Struggle is the basis of SWAPO's claim to be the sole and authentic representative of the Namibian people, and therefore the sole political authority of the future independent Namibia. The commitment of SWAPO to armed struggle has been the decisive element for the recognition of this party as the one and only liberation movement for Namibia by the Organization of African Unity (OAU) back in 1963. In theory SWAPO has been waging an armed struggle in Namibia since 1965 — in practice it has done so since 1974.

The UN Charter is silent about the legitimacy of a 'people's war'. But the OAU has always tried to establish justifications for armed struggle waged by recognized liberation movements. Occasionally, African diplomats have even claimed a *ius ad bellum* for those movements. Certain privileges have been claimed, accordingly, for guerilla fighters in the Geneva Conference on Humanitarian International Law and have been included in the revised Geneva Red Cross Conventions.

The UN tends to follow suit with the OAU in matters of African liberation policies.[24] This includes the *explicit approval of armed struggle* waged by liberation movements. There is a majority for this approval in the General Assembly; but the minority speaking up against it is more impressive than in many other issues concerning southern Africa.

On 4 November 1977 the General Assembly adopted a resolution dealing with the 'Situation in Namibia Resulting from the Illegal Occupation of the Territory by South Africa'.[25] The resolution states that the General Assembly

> *Supports* the armed struggle of the Namibian people, led by the SWAPO, to achieve self-determination, freedom and national independence in a united Namibia.

The *vote* was 117 in favour, none against, but 24 abstentions: all 9 EC countries, the USA, Japan, Canada, Austria, even Sweden, Spain, 4 states from Latin America — 5 states from Africa: Botswana, the Central African Empire, Ivory Coast, Lesotho, and Swaziland. The Swedish delegate explained that '. . . only a decision by the Security Council to designate the situation as a threat to peace, could form the basis for Sweden's explicit endorsement of armed action'. The speaker from the Ivory Coast said his government '. . . supported the efforts of the SWAPO militants who were waging a relentless war against the support of apartheid, but it believed that the United Nations had other means for achieving the same end'. Australia, a member of the UN Council for Namibia since 1974, voted in favour of the draft but declared that she '. . . could not endorse violence in the pursuit of the UN objective . . .'; similar reservations were expressed by delegates from New Zealand, Finland, and other countries.[26]

One year earlier, still in November 1976, the nine EC countries, the USA, and Canada had voted against a General Assembly draft resolution affirming '. . . the legitimacy of the struggle of the oppressed people of

Southern Africa, and their liberation movements, by all possible means, for the seizure of power by the people . . .'. In the historical context it must have been obvious that by 'all possible means' reference is made to armed struggle.[27]

There is not much information, in the UN documents or periodicals, on the actual pursuit of the armed struggle. Very little is published on SWAPO military achievements; in the UN Council's quarterly *Namibia Bulletin*, there are just three pages in all the four issues of 1977. And the 1976 Report of the UN Council on Namibia refers to the killing of Chief Elifas (Prime Minister of the Owambo Bantu homeland) on 16 August 1975 as an 'assassination'. It is true that SWAPO never claimed the merit of this violent action, neither did they accept responsibility for the later killings of other Namibians collaborating with South Africa — Toivo Shiyagaya and Clemens Kapuuo. But no independent observer can avoid the impression that such killings are logical ingredients of any people's war.

An important issue which is completely ignored in the UN information materials, and in resolutions of UN organs, is the *internal political development of SWAPO*, or, for that matter, of any other recognized liberation movement. This is hardly understandable if the impressive international status accorded to those movements is meant to be meaningful. On the other hand, the UN follow closely internal political developments in South Africa and Namibia, and comment upon them in official or semi-official publications.

It is common knowledge that SWAPO lives with strong internal debates, conflicts, and showdowns at least since 1976. No Congress has been held since 1969. The leading group, with the President Sam Nujoma at its head, has to defend its rule against bitter opposition. Andreas Shipanga, SWAPO Secretary for Information, has been 'convicted' by the Nujoma group of a '. . . revolt . . . plotted, masterminded and executed by South African-Imperialist (particularly West German) interests, using reactionary, opportunistic, ambitious, and disgruntled elements within SWAPO' and sent to prison in Tanzania.[28] Many more Namibians in exile are held captives of SWAPO as enemy agents, and when SWAPO presented its proposals for negotiation to the Western members of the Security Council, on 10 February 1978, it included an offer to release eleven 'counter-revolutionaries' from prison in exchange for the Namibian political prisoners held by South Africa. Nothing on these developments has reached the public through UN information media.

This paper is not the place for a detailed study of SWAPO. We know that the South African government speaks of SWAPO, especially of the external leadership under Sam Nujoma, in terms of 'communism' — but this does not mean much in the political language of white South Africa. We know about the consistent support for SWAPO from the USSR. We have read in a Zambian paper, in February 1976, that '. . . the

Soviet Union has offered SWAPO large amounts of military aid . . . if SWAPO agrees to scale down, and eventually phase out, the support it receives from China . . .'.[29] A South African (white) journalist who made a name for himself as an expert on Namibia, Hennie Serfontein, concludes from the analysis of a Constitutional Proposal, that SWAPO published in 1975, that SWAPO '. . . *has remained free from the grips of communism* — ideologically and organisationally . . .'.[30] On the other hand, we read in the political programme adopted by the SWAPO Central Committee in July 1976 with reference to SWAPO's tasks:

> To unite all Namibian people particularly the working class, the peasantry and progressive intellectuals into a vanguard party capable of safe-guarding national independence and the building of a classless non-exploitative society based on scientific socialist ideals and principles . . .'.

This paragraph is quoted as proof of 'a significant advance, and a further ideological maturing can be confidently predicted . . .' by the London-based journal *The African Communist*.[31] In the negotiations with the Western members of the Security Council, SWAPO is supposed to have agreed to free elections. In a more recent article on 'One-Man, One-Vote in Namibia', *The African Communist* reminds readers that '. . . by themselves elections are not a mechanism for the transfer of power . . .', and accuses SWAPO's rival — the Democratic Turnhalle Alliance — that '. . . if the racists have their way, Namibia's first one-man one-vote election would also be its last. Events in Zimbabwe and Namibia make it clear that one-man one-vote elections planned by the racists and imperialists are not a device for transferring power but for consolidating the power of the ruling class.'[32]

This, and likewise similar texts, are the basis from which we could at present analyse the political character of SWAPO. We cannot do it here. The UN does not seem to care anyway. Perhaps they cannot do otherwise, as the term 'class struggle' has no place in the idealistic world of the UN Charter.

5. A Perspective on the UN, from the Namibia Conflict

In conclusion, I advance two hypotheses:

(1) *The United Nations see it as their purpose, not only to keep the peace, but to change the world order.*

This is a quote from a South African pamphlet criticizing the 1971 ICJ Advisory Opinion, and it comes originally from a dissenting opinion by Judge Fitzmaurice, who wrote '. . . it was to keep the peace, not to change the world order, that the Security Council was set up.' This is no longer true. In other words, the *concept of peace* implied in UN actions on Namibia is no longer the traditional, negative concept of peace as a situation of non-war between sovereign states. It has developed into something more positive. It remains an open question into what concept of peace precisely, and with what kind of possible consequences for other areas and situations in today's world.

(2)　*Any effective action on the UN presupposes unanimity of the Great Powers, or at least active support from one (or some) such Power(s) and voluntary abstention from others.*

This is not new. But we can go one step further and say that under these circumstances:

An effective UN action promoting peace (under the new concept) is equivalent to open intervention by at least one Great Power into the internal affairs of a sovereign state.

If the Security Council should compel South Africa to pull out of Namibia, by further pursuing the approach adopted in 1978,[33] this will mean massive intervention of the Five Western States not only into South Africa's conduct of her colonial – or mandatory – policy in Namibia, but into South Africa's internal policies of military defence, of race relations, of Bantu homelands, of electoral matters, etc. The Namibia operation must reflect on these internal South Africa affairs, and it has indeed always been meant by its promoters in the UN to reflect on them: the struggle for Namibia is an integral part of the struggle against apartheid.

Will this become a general rule of world politics? Or is it already one? Does the USSR abstain from active participation in the UN Namibia operation because her government views it as an example of a 'reversed Breshnev doctrine' – the USA and four of her closest allies intervening in a country of the American sphere of influence[34] – just as the USSR intervened in the CSSR in 1968?

Notes

1. Slovo, Joe (1976). 'South Africa – No Middle Road' in Davidson, Basil, *et al.* (1976). *Southern Africa: The New Politics of Revolution* (Harmondsworth: Penguin), 106–210.
2. GRAE = Government-in-Exile for Angola, proclaimed in Kinshasa in 1962. GRAE won OAU recognition for only a short period.
3. PAIGC = African Independence Party for Guinea and the Cape Verde Islands.
4. For the policy of the OAU in the liberation process see Ansprenger, Franz (1975). *Die Befreiungspolitik der Organization für Afrikanische Einheit (OAU) 1963–1975* (München: Kaiser and Mainz: Grünewald); with English summary.
5. This is in accordance with the distinction introduced by GA Res. 3111 (XXVIII) of 12 Dec. 1973 and the subsequent UN practice to consider SWAPO as the 'authentic representation of the Namibian people', while all other African liberation movements are (only) considered as the 'representatives of the true aspirations' of the respective people.

6. As references see Dugard, John (1973). *The South West Africa/Namibia Dispute* (Berkeley–London: Univ. of California Press); Serfontein, J. H. P. (1976). *Namibia?* (Randburg/RSA: Fokus Suld Publ.); Slomim, Solomon (1973). *South West Africa and the United Nations: International Mandate in Dispute* (Baltimore–London: Johns Hopkins Univ. Press); the most important periodicals as sources for on-going developments are *Africa Research Bulletin* (Political Series, Exeter); *The African Communist (London, publ. by SACP); Informationsdienst Südliches Afrika* (= Information Service Southern Africa, Bonn); *Namibia* (formerly *Namibia Today*, London, publ. by SWAPO); *Namibia Bulletin* (New York, publ. by the UN Council for Namibia); *Notes and Documents* (New York, publ. by the UN Centre Against Apartheid), *UN Chronicle* (formerly *UN Monthly*, UN, New York).

7. In 1946 South Africa had requested the General Assembly to terminate the Mandate established under the League of Nations and to incorporate South West Africa as a province of the Republic (UN Doc. A/123). The General Assembly rejected this request and recommended the conclusion of a trusteeship agreement to replace the Mandate (GA Res. 65(I), 14 Dec. 1946). South Africa did not accept this proposal and the status quo remained unchanged.

8. Quoted by Slonim (1973) (*n. 6*), 94.

9. *ICJ Reports 1950*, 128.

10. *African Communist*, 74 (1978).

11. *ICJ Reports 1950*, 128; *ICJ Reports 1955*, 67; *ICJ Reports 1956*, 23.

12. *ICJ Reports 1966*, 35.

13. *ICJ Reports 1971*, 16.

14. SC Res. 319 (1 Aug. 1972); the involvement of the Secretary-General to become active on behalf of the Security Council was initiated by the Council's decision in February, see SC Res. 309 (4 Feb. 1972).

15. UN Doc. S/10832, 15 Nov. 1972.

16. SC Res. 342 (11 Dec. 1972).

17. SC Res. 366 (17 Dec. 1974).

18. See UN Doc. S/12211, 15 Oct. 1976.

19. SC Res. 418 (4 Nov. 1977).

20. For the proposal of the five Western Council members see UN Doc. S/12636, 10 Apr. 1978. The Council adopted the plan by SC Res. 432 (27 July 1978), in conjunction with SC Res. 431 (27 July 1978) empowering the Secretary-General to appoint a Commissioner for Namibia to prepare and carry out further steps.

21. For an analysis of US policy towards South Africa see Czempiel, Ernst-Otto (1977). 'Die Südafrika-Politik der Vereinigten Staaten 1970–1975' in Ansprenger, Franz and Czempiel, Ernst-Otto (1977). *Südafrika in der Politik Grossbritanniens und der USA* (München: Kaiser and Mainz: Grünewald), 65–164, with English summary.

22. In Rhodesia Soviet support for many years went to Joshua Nkomo's party, now the Zimbabwe African People's Union (ZAPU). It constitutes only one of the two wings of the Patrotic Front. To what extent the Mugabe organization (ZANU) has rallied to Nkomo's pro-Soviet position, and deserted the Chinese camp, which it belonged to some time ago, is unclear.

23. For this form of representation see GA Res. 3031 (XXVII), 18 Dec. 1972.

24. See Ansprenger (1975) (*n. 4*).

25. GA Res. 32/9 (4 Nov. 1977), Sect. D, para. 11.

26. For the vote and statements by individual states see *UN Chronicle*, XIV. 11 (Dec. 1977), 33 ff.

27. GA Res. 31/6 (9 Nov. 1976), Sect. I, para. 4.

28. Quoted from the *Report of the John Ya Otto Commission of Inquiry*, 4 June 1976. After his release from a Tanzanian prison, in 1978, Shipanga returned to Namibia and formed his own party, called SWAPO-D (*D* for Democrats).

29. *Africa Research Bulletin* (Feb. 1976).
30. Serfontein (1976) (*n. 4*), 173.
31. *The African Communist*, 68 (1977).
32. Ibid. 74 (1978).
33. Following the breakdown of negotiations and subsequent dissolution of the Western group in terms of joint membership in the Council, negotiations have been resumed in 1979 to find solutions to the critical issues referred to earlier, *above* 191.
34. It should be noted that the Western initiative was no isolated move, but rather a continuation of the more active concern of the USA with African affairs (beginning with the Kissinger speech, Lusaka, 1976) towards 'containing' a perceived influence of the USSR in the region. What is noteworthy is that the initiative was then operationalized within the UN framework, by partially reversing, or at least modifying, earlier positions and by co-ordinating its execution with prevailing majority attitudes in the organization.

13 CONFLICT RESOLUTION IN AFRICA: WHAT ROLE FOR INTERNATIONAL ORGANIZATION?

NOSA-OLA OBASEKI
Nigerian Institute of International Affairs, Lagos

1. Introduction

In the recent past we have witnessed in Africa a rise in the number of conflicts which have become manifest and at the same time pose as threats to the long-term stability of the continent — not only in terms of the relationships between the states in the region, but also in terms of the likelihood that the superpowers become involved. Such escalation provides the opportunity and might accordingly be used to implant amongst African states the extremes of their competing ideologies, with interests then no longer being tied to economic and development needs, but becoming functions of the ability to pursue policies which seek to undermine efforts to attain and maintain an acceptable degree of independence.

Whilst there were those who viewed the reluctance of one or the other superpower to intervene in support of a weaker side (which adherents of classical balance-of-power expected) as timidity or appeasement, it must be recognized that such reluctance or outright rejection of the option of intervention has contributed to the relatively favourable degree of stability within the region. The questions one might therefore pose are: (*a*) Was the non- or de- escalation accomplished mainly by superpower co-operation and restraint, and/or did a more adverse reaction on the part of the regional states prevent these conflicts from escalating any further? (*b*) What specific measures can one identify which stand out as those which were reinforcing the de-escalation process and acted as accelerating agents to subsequent efforts aimed at providing permanent solutions to the conflicts? and lastly (*c*) What factors have impeded the resolution of the conflicts?

A number of factors may have been responsible for such restraints and thus for accelerating the de-escalation process. As to the first question, some impact certainly flows from the general climate of *détente* between the superpowers in which there is a tacit understanding that efforts must be geared towards 'preserving the peace'. Though the meaning of this is all but clearly defined, it comprises a recognition of areas in which superpower co-operation could be further extended or enhanced as well as implicit definitions of each other's 'sphere of influence'. The moralistic leanings of the US President in his definition of foreign policy determinants restricted, at least initially, US response to non-military action and reduced or curtailed to an extremely low level the amount of subversive acts that could undermine whatever gains their adversary had made.

The more important factor, however, was the adverse reaction on the part of member-states of the Organization of African Unity (OAU) by which foreign intervention and superpower interference in the affairs of the continent were unequivocally condemned. Attempts to manipulate local conflicts to suit the designs of the major powers would only lead to further escalation and could threaten the maintenance of peace and security in the region. Control of these conflicts, whether directly or indirectly, was therefore essential.

But up to the present, conflicts have not been totally resolved. While some specific measures prevented further escalation, their resolution is still being impeded. The possibility of partisan intervention has loomed in the background, and expectations of support from extra-African powers still lurk in the corners, thus undermining the search for solutions to conflicts. The point here is whether a collective voice of condemnation and superpower restraint, rather than an exclusion of major powers, are enough to encourage negotiations by those directly involved to resolve their conflicts.

In this article possibilities for mediation roles by international organizations for conflicts in the African region will be explored. While there will be no attempt to give a descriptive account of the involvement of international organizations in the past, full regard will be paid to pragmatism under the prevailing conditions. Certain characteristics of the conflicts in the region determine the preoccupation with conflicts which — though basically of an internal nature — become *externalized* such that the peace and security of the whole region, if not the international system, are threatened. Before considering international organizations' roles it will prove useful to outline some of the peculiarities of conflicts in the African setting which define the tasks to be met by attempts to control them.

2. Peculiarities of Conflict in the African Region

2.1. *Forms of Interstate Conflict*

Certain types of conflict have been prevalent in the region over the last two decades. Whilst the degree of occurrence of some specific forms has changed since the 1970s, some basic characteristics have continued to be determined by circumstances over which people have little or no control.

The conflicts were and are mainly characterized by racial and colonial questions, boundary and territorial problems, ideological differences of leadership or personality divergencies, charges of subversion and external intervention/involvement in domestic disorders, and, finally, disputes arising out of non-recognition of a government attaining or seizing power by a *coup d'etat*.[1] Table 1 gives a survey of interstate conflicts and their major characteristics. Indications as to the OAU's role in attempts at solving them will be referred to in the subsequent discussion.[2]

Immediately after African countries achieved their independence in the 1960s, the majority of conflicts were bound up either with colonialism itself or the heritage of colonial rule.[3] The most threatening factor was the artificiality of existing boundaries, which created avenues for exploitation of ethnic differences. The numerous territorial or boundary conflicts were thus related to colonialism, either in its original form or in its contemporary state. The changes in the pattern of African conflicts from structural impediments of the immediate post-colonial era (reflected in the perpetuation of earlier ties and relationships) to conflicts directly related to 'issues' and therefore bound up with the present international system of states,[4] have brought to the fore the continued manipulation of leadership, not only by external forces but also by intrinsic characteristics as depicted by basic human weaknesses.[5]

Foreign policy in Africa is strongly influenced by leadership, and the personality of individuals has therefore acquired a prominent position when discussing interstate conflict.[6] Consequently, we can identify an increase in the number of personality clashes related to ideological differences, broadly covering cases of charges of subversion, non-recognition of a government coming to power by a *coup d'état*, and in some cases refugee problems. The Shaba Conflict (Zaïre–Angola), the conflicts between Uganda and Tanzania, Libya and Egypt, and Libya and Tunisia are examples which to some extent reflect such constellations.

If it is accepted that 'sovereignty' was well guarded by relatively recent independent nations,[7] and as it is also true that a lot of attention was devoted to the 'day-to-day business of building and holding power in a specific state',[8] it may therefore have been necessary for conflict to have been displaced. Where internal cohesion remained a goal which still had to be achieved, a certain amount of 'unreal' conflict may have been encouraged.[9] Nevertheless, potentialities for 'real' conflict did, and still do, exist.

2.2. Basic Conflict Characteristics

Thus *racial conflict* still remains the main source of instability in southern Africa. Where the system of *apartheid* is practised and encouraged both directly and indirectly by external forces, the connection between support and the basis on which it depends becomes very important to the conflict-resolution process and procedures adopted by international organizations.

Table 1   African intra-regional conflicts and OAU involvement 1963–79

Conflict/Parties	Issue	Role of OAU	Outcome
Algeria/Morocco (1963–5)	Territorial	Legitimization of cease-fire Establishment of contacts Providing neutral place for negotiations	Bilateral settlement
Dahomey/Niger (1963)	Territorial	None (considered by UAM)	Settled by UAM mediation
Ethiopia/Kenya/Somalia (since 1964)	Territorial	Call for cease-fire (1964) Providing neutral place for negotiations (1967) Good Offices Committee (1973)	Continues
Ghana/Upper Volta (1964–5)	Territorial	Attempt to mediate Pressure on Ghana	Settled (Withdrawal Ghana)
Equatorial Guinea/Gabon (1972)	Territorial	Assistance in negotiations Border Commission	Situation 'calmed down'
Ghana/Neighbouring Countries	Subversion	Attempt to mediate (1965)	Terminated by *coup d'état* in Ghana
Rwanda/Burundi (1966–73)	Subversion	Attempt to mediate Mediation Committee (1973)	'Calmed down'
Ghana/Guinea (1966)	Arrest of diplomats	Investigation by Council of Ministers Pressure on Ghana	Release negotiated by three Heads of State

Guinea/Ivory Coast (1966–7)	Subversion	Legitimization of mediation attempt/President Tubman	Settled
Guinea/Senegal (since 1971)	Subversion	Mediation Committee (1971)	'Calmed down'
Tanzania/Uganda (1972)	Subversion	Providing neutral place for negotiations (1973) Support for Somalian attempt to mediate	Settled
Nigeria (Biafra) (1967–70)	Secession	Support for Central Government Attempt to mediate	Terminated by military victory
Sudan (1964–71)	Attempt secession	None	Settled (partial mediation Ethiopia)
Kenya/Uganda (1976–7)	Territorial	Mediation	'Calmed down'
Angola (1975–6)	Struggle for political power	Special Summit Meeting	Settled by military victory
Western Sahara (since 1977)	Territorial	Mediation; also by OAU Commission	Continues
Zaïre (Shaba) (1977–8)	Riots and uprising	None	Latent continuation
Egypt/Libya (1977)	Territorial	Attempt to mediate	Bilateral settlement

Table 1 *continued*

Conflict/Parties	Issue	Role of OAU	Outcome
Chad (1977–9)	Civil war	Assigned mediation under Nigerian Chairmanship	Settled
Upper Volta/Mali (1977)	Territorial	Mediation by OAU Commission	Settled
Sudan/Ethiopia (since 1977)	Territorial	Formation of Commissions	Continues
Uganda/Tanzania (1979)	Territorial	Mediation	Settled by military victory
Southern Africa (since late sixties)	Independence	Support for nationalist movements	Eventual achievement of independence by all; except at present Namibia and the blacks of South Africa

Similarly, the creation of *artificial boundaries* in the past encourages conflict as *self-determination* becomes incompatible with the continued sustenance or maintenance of 'sovereignty' and the 'territorial integrity' of a state. The most important factor for the present, however, is *structure* — both internal and external. There is the reluctance of ruling élites not only to relinquish power, but also to grant certain rights to the ruled, and to encourage the establishment of a more equitable or egalitarian society. The threat perceived by the élites to their positions, and ownership in providing basic requirements to their fellow citizens, is disguised under the cloak of interpretations of such actions in terms of ideological drift. Preservation of positions of dominance becomes a very important consideration, and the means to preserve and guarantee such positions comprise arsenals of repressive machinery and persistent patterns of dependency relationships.[10]

The racial conflict in South Africa involves both these factors and their effective utilization. In other contexts neo-colonialism, and consequently foreign interventionist support for leadership definitions of a conflict, may be the real obstacle. Two major areas of concern therefore are (*a*) non-satisfactory performance of leadership role obligations or duties, the concomitant of which is demand for change, and (*b*) absolute resistance to change and preference for the status quo.

3. Scope of the Conflicts

The direct and immediate effects of just and legitimized solutions to these conflicts, which have indeed a great deal of black African emotion attached to them, would go a long way towards stabilizing sub-regions normally considered inherently unstable.

International organizations become more actively involved in conflicts which are in transition between the initiation and escalation stages of the conflict process. This is one of the criteria that can be used to determine the conflicts where organizations may exercise some function. Another criterion is that at least two of the parties involved in the conflict, directly or indirectly and in an active capacity, are 'legally' constituted governments that have jurisdiction over internationally recognized territories and frontiers. This criterion reflects the problems created by the principle of non-interference in the internal affairs of states as enshrined in Art. III of the OAU Charter, as well as the provision reflected in Art. 2 (7) of the UN Charter. While it is difficult to identify a clear line of demarcation between purely internal affairs and international dispute, one might take into consideration motives which could make a conflict one of great concern internationally. This provision could be further related to that of Art. XII of the Protocol of the Commission of Mediation, Conciliation and Arbitration of the OAU, which forms an integral part of the OAU Charter, specifically allowing for its jurisdiction *only in disputes between states.*

How does the scope of the types of conflicts discussed above relate to the question of determining a more specific role for international organizations in resolving such conflicts? Why not leave those directly involved in these conflicts to settle their problems on their own? One realizes that this is the most preferred approach, but are they prepared to get together on their own accord? Assuming they are, the nature of the conflict is such that certain inhibitory agents (cognitive and affective) referred to earlier on become real obstacles to the adoption of co-operative postures on the part of one or more of the parties to the conflict. Where there is a principled recognition of the desirability of negotiation, the actual coming together of parties is prevented or delayed unnecessarily by the introduction or application of bargaining strategies detrimental to the process of conflict resolution.[11]

The preconditions usually set by the competing parties normally hold back the convening of conferences where negotiations can take place, and even when the parties decide to get together, one or more of them engages in precursory manoeuvres aimed at outwitting an adversary so that when the discussions begin bargaining is done from a position of strength. The 'exploitation of potential force'[12] is effectively utilized and becomes reflected in the outcomes of such negotiations — where coercion is applied so as to influence results, 'settlements' are arrived at in which the underlying forces of the conflict are not resolved, or, on the other hand, stands may be taken during negotiations which precipitate stalemates, and/or one of the parties abandons the exercise because it is regarded as not capable of yielding fruitful results.

Third-party mediation normally initiates negotiations and sustains them for longer periods more efficiently than the parties directly involved can between themselves. While it does happen that a third party's mediating initatives could be sought by any of the parties involved in a conflict, the question of the legitimacy of the mediator usually rears its head. This becomes a stumbling block even if the party expressing a genuine desire to mediate professes impartiality. Although third-party mediation outside the auspices of organizations still takes place, what has evolved over the years is a preference for international organizations as mediating agents.

Even if, as has been stressed, third-party mediation has a much better chance of success, this will be more so if the legitimacy which is attached to an international organization is related to both its generally accepted role in world society and the scope of the conflict.[13] In most of the conflicts a discernible feature is that they all are basically internal. The consequences of these conflicts include, in particular, the inflow of refugees into surrounding states, creating extra problems with burdens they cannot bear, as well as the possible extension of such conflicts into surrounding areas and inevitably the entire region.

This externalization of conflicts becomes an absolute possibility in the absence of restraints on the part of the major powers seeking to exploit such openings for their benefit. In the event of an externalization of the conflict, serious problems are created for the state directly involved as it is now confronted with the real threat of total devastation or destruction; also looming in the background is the threat to the entire region from the escalating confrontation between the now totally committed external powers. It is the escalation which constantly poses threats to the region that points to the need for an identification of the appropriate institutions for dealing with such situations.

Whilst the surrounding states are faced with the refugee problem and the threat of an extension of the conflict, legitimacy problems are bound to arise with regard to their mediation capacity, because a real or imagined discovery of the partiality phenomenon is usually made, by either of the actors, one or more of the surrounding states, or even observers (active or passive), in their intentions or policies. International organizations as entities do not have such acute legitimacy problems confronting them in their attempts or efforts to act as mediators. The general conception of international organization as neutral and independent actors devoid of the 'weaknesses' of states does enhance their legitimacy status. The scope of the conflict must therefore be a determining factor in assigning to an international organization the responsibility or role of acting as a mediating agent in the conflict resolution process.

4. International Organizations as Legitimized Mediators

4.1 *UN and OAU*

One can only identify two international organizations which may exercise an acceptable mediation role; the United Nations and the Organization of African Unity. The role of the UN in solving African disputes, is, however, limited.[14] While its legitimacy extends to all regions of the world, at least legally, certain practical and procedural problems restrict its area of manoeuvre and its status to act as a legitimized mediator.[15]

The composition of the UN and the weight accorded to the votes of certain members in the organization's Security Council, on which primary responsibility for the 'maintenance of international peace and security' is placed (Art. 24 UNCh)), are in fact major factors preventing regions from according it that legitimization. It is presumed that conflict within regions could be exploited by the major powers and converted into bloc conflicts in which the interests of those directly involved become subsumed within the 'greater interest' of protecting and extending spheres of influence — a minor dispute could be transformed into major antagonisms assuming such proportions that the primary source of conflict eventually becomes secondary.

Chapter VIII of the UN Charter deals with the connection between the UN, its Security Council, and regional arrangements in respect of the maintenance of international peace and security. This reflects a tacit recognition of the practical limitation of the UN's effectivity in this area: Provision is made for regional arrangements or agencies to deal with such matters relating to the maintenace of international peace and security *as are appropriate for regional action*, provided that such arrangements or agencies and their activities are 'consistent with the purpose and principles of the UN'.[16] Although under Art. 52 of the UN Charter the members of regional arrangements are to seek pacific settlements of local disputes, such specifications are not strictly adhered to. What is important here is that as long as the exercise of extra powers by the regional arrangement does not extend to actions inconsistent with the purpose and principles of the UN, the regional arrangements can take whatever non-violent steps are deemed necessary to resolve disputes (or conflicts) without consultations with the UN.

While we realize that the members of the OAU make up a sizeable proportion of the UN membership, the world organization takes on an appearance of detachment from the regions' problems since the majority of its members are not capable of accurately analysing these problems. *Effective distance*[17] limits their capacity for a proper understanding of the nature and causes of such conflicts as may occur in Africa, and this is an obstacle to its total and unqualified acceptance in the mediation role by the Africans. The provisions of Chapter VII of the UN Charter must therefore be viewed as an essential element in this context: it establishes the terms formally governing the relationships between regional arrangements and the UN, but the OAU — whilst reaffirming its adherence to the Charter of the UN and such instruments as the Universal Declaration of Human Rights as well as registering its Charter in conformity with Art. 102 of the UN Charter — has not made itself an instrument of the UN in precise legal terms. Though legal capacity is extended to the UN by Arts. 104, 105 of the UN Charter there is no close collaboration based on firmly laid-down rules. What does exist is based on convenience.

Therefore, over the years we have witnessed a reluctance on the part of the UN to become actively involved in mediation duties connected with disputes within the African region. There is a tacit acceptance that the interests of those involved in the conflict would best be served, and the dispute managed, by a regional organization since it would be more appreciative of the issues involved than the world body itself. As most or all of its members face similar problems, they can draw on similar backgrounds and shared experiences and relate their solutions for the conflicts with the wider interests with which they all can identify, in other words, 'matters appropriate for regional action'.

4.2. *Constraints on the Conflict-resolving Capacity of the OAU*

Considerations in favour of stressing the regional context also in terms of regional action should not preclude recognition that the OAU's ability to effectively resolve conflicts is itself subject to limitations. As will be discussed later in greater detail, the organization relies on peaceful or non-coercive means of resolution for conflicts over which its legitimacy is unquestionable. There is a total dependence on the complete identification with the organization's purposes and principles by all its members which in turn means that there is the expectation and confidence that its members will heed the demands placed on them. Unity, or the 'we-feeling', is thus the binding factor and consequently the choice of a state to remain a member of the organization, or community, is an expression of a value preference as opposed to a probable ostracization based on disrespect for its decisions, principles, and/or purposes.

The question then is how much appreciation there is for this warm welcoming attitude of the organization to member-states of the continent. If the value attached to membership and general regional reception into the fold is very high, then such peaceful means of conflict resolution should be very successful without compromising other important principles; but where it is not high, we can expect that the organization would expend more energy, under the circumstances, in retaining the membership and thus compromising its duties regarding the issue of resolving conflicts. Inactivity may, then, be the order of the day and expressions of condemnation of external involvement or intervention by foreign powers wherever and whenever they occur may be ridiculed as mere rhetoric.

Coercive measures may be more appropriate under the circumstances for guaranteeing an eventual resolution of conflict. Although provision is made for the institution of collective measures (as reflected in the need to create an African High Command under the OAS's Defence Commission) a number of factors will inhibit its successful establishment and deployment. These include: (1) the level of dependence of individual member-states on major powers generally and on the two superpowers in particular. We can expect that the more dependent a member-state is on a foreign power, the less it will appreciate the need for the formation of such a force as extremely essential. It will prefer instead to have its security guaranteed by a metropolitan power, and of course is encouraged in thinking in this direction by such powers. (2) Limited financial resources for the funding or maintenance of such a force, especially where there may not be envisaged any actual situations under which such a force will be used. (3) No general acceptance of the defined real threat. For example, what occasions or circumstances would warrant the deployment of such a force? A general agreement will be hard to come by, especially where superpowers and other allied penetrators have successfully imparted to dependent states their divergent definitions and interpretations of the 'real' threat.[18] (4) A constant fear that such a force could be used to serve the purposes of particular states, and accordingly an unwillingness to compromise one's 'sovereignty' whenever provisions of the UN Charter and the OAU Charter relating to non-interference appear as not being adequately guaranteed and provided for any more.

With these obstacles to the application of collective measures, peaceful measures will have to be more preferable, and it may be presumed that member-states will value continued membership only to the extent that the organization in its activities gives due regard to these attitudes and expectations.

5. The OAU's Organizational Role and Conflict-Resolution Procedures

5.1. *Charter Provisions on the Mediation Role*

Abstention from coercive strategies, both in the past and very likely so in the future *vis-à-vis* the attitudinal obstacles referred to, is the major characteristic of the OAU's approach. In the preamble of its Charter there is an affirmation of adherence to the UN Charter. As the evolution of both bodies is related to the prevailing conditions immediately preceding their creation, one notices from the Charter of the OAU the relatively few provisions, as opposed to that of the UN, regarding the mechanisms for the maintenance of peace and security. This may also be ascribed to the mutually reinforcing nature of the provisions of both charters and a preference for legitimized modes.

As far as the UN is concerned this latter aspect is reflected not only in the general emphasis in the UN-Charter provisions to give responsibility to settle their disputes to the parties themselves and to empower the Security Council to direct efforts towards a peaceful resolution only after they have failed to do so. The 'last resort' role thus assigned to the Security Council has also been put into practice; one observes that parties to disputes in Africa have regularly been referred to seek solutions through the OAU as the regional entity most properly constituted to resolve their problems.

The few provisions in the OAU Charter relating it to the UN are to be found in Arts. III, VI, and XIX. Among the principles of the OAU we thus find provisions which discourage actions prejudicial to the stability and security of the region (Art. III (2, 3)) and encourage the peaceful settlement of disputes by negotiation, mediation, conciliation, or arbitration (Art. III (4)). Art. VI is related indirectly to the maintenance of peace and security by specifying rights and duties of member-states, whereby they pledge to observe scrupulously the principles enumerated in Art. III of the OAU Charter.[19] Finally, Art. XIX provides for the Commission of Mediation, Conciliation, and Arbitration, by which 'member-states pledge themselves to settle all disputes among themselves by peaceful means . . .'.[20] Thereby the Charter establishes a legal obligation binding all member-states to settle their disputes peacefully. As an integral part of the Charter, the Protocol on the Commission of Mediation, Conciliation, and Arbitration restricts the choice of the parties in dispute to mediation, conciliation, and arbitration only. What is relevant is the implicit assumption that both parties will submit their disputes to the Commission for consideration. If they do not, the Council of Ministers, after deliberation, can only formulate recommendations which are of no binding character. There is no provision for sanctions if a state refuses to abide by the ruling of the Commission.

One can gather from the above provisions that the role assigned to, and intended for, the OAU regarding mediating efforts is *more legitimized than legalized*. Further evidence in this regard is the fact that Art. XIX has never been invoked for the settlement of disputes; what has in fact evolved from the OAU's approach to the peaceful settlement of disputes is the moral obligation on the conflicting parties to settle their disputes in the interest of African Unity while searching for compromise — an African framework which has tended to exclude external interference. The collective conscience which the OAU constitutes has mitigated the intensity of conflict within the region. Because the emphasis has been clearly placed on negotiation rather than on the rule of law,[21] we find that 'disputes among the OAU members have been settled through direct negotiations between states, good offices offered by third parties, *ad hoc* committees composed of heads of state, and diplomatic negotiations conducted during sessions of the Assembly of Heads of States and Government'.[22]

5.2. *'Role Demand' and 'Role Performance'*

The contours emerging from these observations as to the institutional and procedural strength of the OAU differ significantly from the common understanding of international organization. The apparently moderate consensus-based capacity of the organization is reflected in the low degree of formalization such that initiatives actually taken are regularly strongly determined by the concrete circumstances prevailing in a concrete situation. It will therefore be useful to evaluate the role of the OAU and the available procedures for the resolution of conflicts in the context of certain general observations on the place of international organizations in international relations. In the background of these considerations is the question whether the constraints under which the organization has to operate should be considered as deficiencies or whether the restrictions merit a more positive assessment under a broader perspective.

The basis of international organizations' existence determines, or is synonymous with, their 'role' through which 'the major responsibilities for managing the political affairs of the group are exercised'. The executive organs are 'characterized by special capabilities they possess to mobilize the resources and energies of the members of the system and bring them to bear upon broad or specified objectives'.[23] An international organization's existence is contingent upon an identified range of interests shared by its members, and the benefits to be derived by each member-state through a pledge of allegiance. The organization is granted a legitimate status under those conditions where an explicit recognition is made of the need to safeguard state sovereignty in exchange 'for operation at the level of consent, recommendation, and cooperation'.[24] The facilitation of co-operation by an organization is then a very important source of its legitimacy. However, certain responsibilites can and do limit the role of international organizations regarding conflict resolution on an extensive scale, some of which have already been referred to earlier. Thus, major limitations on the UN's mediating role include the veto, the lack of funds for peacekeeping operations, as well as such constitutional provisions encouraging states to settle their disputes themselves and restraining, at least temporarily, possibilities to intervene.[25] As to the shared interests, the disruptive bipolar context has constantly reduced potential effectiveness. In fact even the UN's absence from an arena of conflict often becomes a requisite when, depending on the parties involved, an intervention might imply an escalatory effect rather than resolving a local conflict. Its authority and legitimacy is therefore definitely restricted to areas which prove to be neither too divisive nor too demanding to be handled by the limited means available nor amenable to be treated primarily by or shunted to some other organizational context.[26] Thus there are glaring disparities between the 'role demand' (as laid down formally in its constitutional documents) and its actual 'role performance'. As a consequence, a set of means has been developed which, while not actually resolving conflicts by formal settlements, nevertheless helps to 'freeze' or isolate them, or impose controls on their violence.[27] One of the limitations placed upon the UN in performing the role assigned to it in maintaining international peace and security is the near-total opposition of local interest within regions to the externalization which such a performance might encourage. On the other hand, there are also similar disparities between 'role demand' and 'role performance' on the side of those very regional organizations that could be expected to fill this gap — one example being the OAU.

One might counter, though, that in the case of the OAU the founding fathers never made provisions for instruments, and in particular legal sanctions, that could serve as substitutes for those of the UN and discourage disruptions of the stability and security of the region. The 'collective conscience' in terms of the moral obligation provided the deterrent basis. The choice not to incorporate recourse to international law and the ICJ in its machinery of peaceful settlement meant that the emphasis was to be placed on negotiations devoid of acrimonies.

The goal of African Unity which the OAU has always affirmed meant that all other values had to be subservient to it. Though this unity has often been threatened, the OAU remained a centre from where it could again be consolidated. This was often only possible by deliberately restrained actions on the part of the organization, and the unity was thus formally maintained. However, it should be taken into account that the OAU in fact represents the only 'continental forum', and its preservation as the focal point to represent unity *vis-à-vis* open conflicts as well as attempts of external influence deserves priority. One must accept that the demands upon the organization in its mediating role have not been proportionally related to the actual provisions that were made for performing such a role, hence the constant barrage thrown at it for its failure to resolve most conflicts. The organization accepts and realizes that, as any entity constituted by sovereign states, all its decisions have to be based on a voluntary consensus. Where this is absent, then its hands are tied. Nevertheless, if escalation creates a situation of crisis, one can expect *that* solidarity — which usually resides in the background — to create conditions beneficial to the peace process. As with the UN, though to a lesser extent, it has been useful to each of the competing groups eager to get not only a forum for their views, but also diplomatic reinforcement for their policies. This role may indeed remain paramount for a while.

5.3. *Conflict-resolving Procedures*

What are, then, the procedures for the resolution of conflict both open to the organization and actually followed, and how to evaluate them taking into account the actual 'role demand' as derived from the documentary evidence considered? Theoretically, conflict resolution procedures fall into two broad categories,[28] coercive or accommodative (including concessions) — though the extent to which the former of these categories is in fact conflict-resolving is open to question. K. J. Holsti suggests six theoretical modes of behaviour and outcomes embraced by these categories and available to parties seeking to achieve or defend incompatible goals, values, interests or positions: (1) avoidance or voluntary withdrawal: (2) violent conquest; (3) forced submission or withdrawal; (4) compromise; (5) award-arbitration or adjudication; and (6) passive settlement.[29] Which of these alternatives is eventually chosen is the result of bargaining, and it is in this area that international organizations have openings for performing a role to guide choices in the direction effectively contributing to peace-promoting resolutions of conflicts. Burton identifies three elements important for the process of arriving at a resolution of conflicts: the degree of third-party coercive intervention, the degree of participation by the conflicting parties, and the degree of communication between the parties.[30] I have pointed out the significance of problems of (mis-)perception and (lack of) communication as a consequence of the conflict relations and constellations typical for conflicts in Africa. Hence the mediating role of international organizations should primarily be in terms of bringing parties together to solve their problems through negotiating processes, i.e. mediation being in terms of *guiding negotiations* towards success as opposed to *demanding* a 'positive' outcome of the process. Some may argue that initiatives by an international organization that seeks to get the negotiating process going constitute, by implication, coercive intervention in that there exist sanctions which may be applied if one or more of the parties refuses to go to the negotiating table, either legal and/or material (as within the UN framework) or psychological, i.e. by an ostracization for ignoring the collective conscience reflected in recommendations of a body like the OAU. Even if such an interpretation is accepted as correct, as long as this 'coercion' does increase, or makes total, the degree of participation of the conflicting parties and the degree of communication between the adversaries, such mediation efforts are acceptable.

The OAU Charter provides for the Commission of Mediation, Conciliation and Arbitration and therefore recognizes that solutions are not to be found in legally enforceable decisions in which the participation of the conflicting parties is restricted, or almost totally non-existent. While both the UN Charter and the OAU Charter specifically state a preference for mutual agreement between adversaries, the UN's powers under certain conditions do extend to explicit coercive measures. The OAU has definitely placed the emphasis on negotiation towards conflict resolution, and in practice its formal role has been in the realm of providing a forum (since the services of the Commission have never been utilized); informally it has been active in exploiting the arena of *ad hoc* procedures.

6. Conclusions

In the foregoing analysis I have shown not only the conditions, but also the limitations for the role of international organization in African conflicts. Focusing on the latter, some may be tempted to dismiss international organizations in general, and the OAU in particular, as bodies which may not be able to get results felt necessary, especially in the absence of a full commitment by its membership. However, we have also shown the difficulty of genuine solutions to conflicts in a region where conflict constellations involve a variety of unfavourable conditions related to continuing effects of the colonial period, struggles over political power, renewed efforts of extra-regional influences, and strong tendencies that essentially domestic conflicts become externalized. The OAU's effectivity, in abstract terms of conflict-resolution successes, is highly restricted under such circumstances. If it comes to the question whether the organization should be strengthened by providing additional coercive deterrence or compellance mechanisms, caution seems to be advisable. It can be well argued that the organization's conflict-resolving role should not be enhanced by legal or constitutional provisions for putting at its disposal a more 'efficient' machinery whereby the coercive instruments are increased and utilized to force parties in conflict to obtain settlements. It is, indeed, questionable whether such machinery would be more successful than that which already exists, for it is the will of states that makes for the effectiveness of such provisions, in the past and very likely also in the future. Preference should therefore be given to roles and procedures to influence the attitudes of states and to work for voluntary consent of the parties involved in conflicts. When mediation does take place it must aim at bringing parties to the negotiating table and guiding negotiations along lines of substance, as well as providing supportive forms of communication. In relating its role to conflict resolution procedures, the OAU has successfully charted a course which should be given greater attention in generally defining and determining the role of international organization in the resolution of conflicts under the given conditions and state of international relations. International organizations must not be neutral, as this amounts to disinterest, but they can and should be both involved and impartial.

Notes

1. See Matthews, Robert O. (1970). 'Interstate Conflicts in Africa: A Review.' *International Organization*, XXIV.2: 335–60, and Červenka, Z. (1977). The Unfinished Quest for Unity: Africa and the OAU (London: Julien Friedman).
2. This survey has been taken from Tandon, Yashphal and Mathews, K. (1979). 'Die Organisation der Afrikanischen Einheit in der Phase der Konsolidierung' (The Organization of African Unity in the Phase of Consolidation). *Europa-Archiv*, 4 (1979); 113–22 (Appendix) and was updated to take account of recent developments.
3. Useful in this connection are Oliver, R. and Fage, J. D. (1972). *A Short History of Africa* (Harmondsworth:Penguin), Ajala, Adekunle (1973). *Pan-Africanism: Evolution, Progress, and Prospects* (London: Andre Deutsch), and Davidson, Basil ([3]1971), *Which Way Africa? The Search for a New Society* (Harmondsworth: Penguin).
4. This distinction is made by Käkönen, J. (1979) in a discussion paper prepared for the 8th Nordic Conference on Peace Research, Turku, 11–13 Jan. 1979 on 'Trends in African Conflict Development — Some Notes on the Changing Pattern of African Conflict'.
5. This factor is directly related to the personality of the leader. Ambition seems to be the more important as opposed to what we may call the positive purposes and goals of the role occupant. See the discussion by Burton, J. W. (1979a). 'The Role of Authority in World Society.' *Journal of International Studies* (Milennum-Issue), VII. 1 (Spring). The illusion demonstrated in the 'role performance' of leaders as related to their 'role conception' is a perfect illustration of the manner in which the 'role demand' may be disregarded in order to fulfil certain desires. On types of 'roles' cf. Greenstein, R. I. and Lerner, M., eds. (1971). *A Source Book for the Study of Personality and Politics* (Chicago: Markham).

6. Greenstein, R. I. (1971). 'The Impact of Personality on Politics: An Attempt to Clear away Underbrush.' *American Political Science Review*, LXI.3, suggests conditions under which personality may be very influential in decision-making and most of these conditions prevail in the foreign policy decision-making process in the African region. The impact of personality on the foreign policies ot African States is supported by Aluko, O. ed. (1977). *The Foreign Policies of African States* (Kent: Hodder & Stoughton).

7. See Hazelwood, A. D., ed. (1967). *African Integration and Disintegration* (London: Oxford Univ. Press), especially the Introduction.

8. See Hosky's contribution in Hazelwood, ed. (1967) (*n. 7*).

9. On displacement and unreal conflict see Coser, L. (1956). *The Functions of Social Conflict* (London: Routledge & Kegan Paul).

10. On the issue of dependent relationships we may talk of the interdependence between the scarce and strategic resources much needed by the West, and the preservation of the despicable systems or regimes by various forms of support. For the hinderances posed to real development in Africa see Ajala (1973) (*n. 3*), and Axline, W. A. (1977). 'Underdevelopment, Dependence and Integration: The Politics of Regionalism in the Third World.' *International Organization*, XXXI.1: 83–105.

11. More traditional as well as more recent conflict-resolution procedures are discussed by Parkinson, F. (1977). *The Philosophy of International Relations* (London: Sage Publ.). Whilst he seeks to be very critical regarding new methods, one should consult works by Burton, see Burton, J. W. (1969), *Conflict and Communication* (London: Macmillan); (1972), *World Society* (London: Cambridge Univ. Press), and more recently (1979b), *Deviance, Terrorism, and War. The Process of solving Unsolved Social and Political Problems* (Oxford: Martin Robertson); 1979a (*n. 5*) as well as a discussion of his 'controlled communication' approach between C. R. Mitchell and R. Yalem, see Mitchell, C. R. (1973). 'Conflict Resolution and Controlled Communication: Some Comments.' *Journal of Peace Research*, X.1–2: 123 (Rejoinder to Yalem R. 'Controlled Communication and Conflict Resolution.' *Journal of Peace Research*, VIII.3–4: 263–72.

12. See Schelling, T. C. (1960). *The Strategy of Conflict* (Cambridge: Harvard Univ. Press).

13. The concepts of legitimacy and legitimization are discussed by Kelman, H. C. (1968). 'Education for the Concept of a Global Society.' *Social Education*, XII.2, and by Burton (1972) (*n. 11*) and (1979a) (*n. 5*).

14. See Matthews (1970) (*n. 1*).

15. In relation to the South African conflicts the UN will be the most appropriate organization for tackling the problems associated with the region because South Africa is not a member of the OAU. In addition, there is a relatively high degree of involvement of external actors, especially by Western Powers which have interests in the economy and the military complex in southern Africa, and strategical interest in propping up the regime. The OAU's role here is limited to providing moral and material support for the prosecution of a liberation struggle.

16. See Goodrich, Hambro and Simons ([3]1969). *The Charter of the United Nations. Commentary and Documents* (New York–London: Columbia Univ. Press), 35 ff.

17. On the concept of 'effective distance', see Burton (1972) (*n. 11*), 47.

18. Certain inherent weaknesses of the OAU are dealt with by Tandon and Mathews (1979) (*n. 2*) and some of these are reflected in the present analysis.

19. Červenka, Z. (1968). *The Organization of African Unity and its Charter* (Prague: Academia Nakladatelství Československe Akademie Věd).

20. See Ibid.

21. This issue is discussed by Bozeman, A. B. (1976). *Conflict in Africa: Concepts & Realities* (Princeton, N.J.: Princeton Univ. Press).
22. See Červenka (1977) (*n. 1*).
23. The definition used here is borrowed from Easton, D. (1965). *A Framework for Political Analysis* (Englewood Cliffs, N.J.: Prentice-Hall), see also the definition of role by Burton, in particular as given in Burton (1979a) (*n. 5*).
24. See Bennet, Ale Roy (1977), *International Organizations: Principles and Issues* (Englewood Cliffs, N.J.: Prentice-Hall).
25. See Holsti, K. J. (1967). 'Resolving International Conflicts: A Taxomony of Behavior and Some Figures on Procedure.' *Journal of Conflict Resolution*, X.3: 272–6.
26. See Hoffmann, St. (1970). 'International Organization and the International System.' *International Organization*, XXIV. 3: 389–413, for these views.
27. See Holsti, K. J. (1967) (*n. 25*). These means comprise, for example, cease-fire agreements insisted on, dispatch of truce supervisory forces, and peace-keeping forces to separate combatants.
28. See Luard, E. (1968). *Conflict and Peace in the Modern International System* (Boston: Little, Brown).
29. Holsti, K. J. (1976) (*n. 25*).
30. Burton (1972) (*n. 11*).

THE AUTHORS

FRANZ ANSPRENGER is Professor of Political Science (African Politics and International Organization) at the Free University of Berlin and head of the African Politics Research Unit. Since 1970 he has served as a member of the Board, and later of the Council, of the German Society of Peace and Conflict Research. He was one of the principal investigators of the research project 'Conflict in Southern Africa', sponsored by the Iustitia-et-Pax Commission of the Catholic Church in the FRG and co-editor of the seven-volume series *Studies on Conflict in Southern Africa* (1975/7; in German, with English summaries). He wrote or co-wrote volumes on The Politics of Liberation of the OAU, 1963–75, and Policies of Great Britain and the USA towards South Africa; other publications include *Politik im Schwarzen Afrika* (1961), *Kolonisierung und Entkolonisierung in Afrika* (³1979), and *Auflösung der Kolonialreiche* (1966; new edn. forthcoming).

JAN BIELAWSKI is Assistant Professor at the Institute of International Economic Relations and International Law at the Central School of Planning and Statistics, Warsaw, where he also received his doctorate. A specialist in multilateral economic co-operation and international trade, he served in Polish delegations to various UN bodies and has been nominated as Polish expert to the UN. He is an active member of the Polish movement for the UN and presently on the Board of the Polish UN Association. Most recent publications include *EEC Integration and its Impact on Industrial Co-operation with CMEA Countries* (1978), *Soviet Initiatives of All-European Economic Co-operation* (1979), and *Exports of Manufactures from the Developing Countries and the New Protectionism* (1979).

KLAUS BURRI is assistant at the Institute for Foreign Relations at the University of Zurich where he also completed his postgraduate education in political science and international relations. His research interests are in North–South relations and UN voting. He is the author of *UNO-Abstimmungsverhalten und Bilaterale Beziehungen* (1977).

RAJENDRA CHANDISINGH presently pursues research for a study on the theory of non-capitalist development at the University of Hamburg. He studied international relations at the London School of Economics and peace and conflict research at the University of Lancaster. Following work as a civil servant and teacher in England, he was Lecturer in Political Science at the University of Guyana, Georgetown, 1974–7.

ROBERT W. GREGG is Professor of International Studies at the School of International Services of the American University, Washington, D.C. He is presently associated with the UN Institute for Training and Research, New York, as Project Director of a project on the institutional framework for the NIEO. Among others, he was consultant to the UN for the organization of the UNDP (1964) and Special Advisor for International Organization Policies to the US Department of State (1977). Publications include *The UN System and its Functions* (ed., with M. Barkun, 1969), *The UN Regional Commissions and Integration in the Underdeveloped World* (1968), *The International Control System for Narcotic Drugs* (1974), and *The Apportioning of Political Power in the UN* (1977).

ANNEMARIE GROSSE-JÜTTE holds a degree in social sciences from the Ruhr-University Bochum and has been a Research Associate in the Institute of Peace Research and Security Policy at the University of Hamburg since 1973. Her research interests are in the fields of political systems of Eastern Europe, Yugoslavia, theory and politics of non-alignment, and North–South relations. She co-edited *Europe: From Detente to Peace* (1977), other publications include *Peace and the Structure of East–West Conflict* (1977), *NIEO and Self-Reliance: The Institutional Development of Non-Alignment* (1978), and works on the domestic and foreign policy of Yugoslavia.

MARJO HOEFNAGELS holds a degree in political science from the Free University of Brussels and is presently Research Associate of the University's Polemological Centre. Her main fields of interest are structures of the international system, political violence, and international organizations. Most recent publications include *Repression and Political Violence* and (ed., 1977), *Interdependence in the International System* (1978, in Dutch), and *International Conflict Structure, Repressive Violence, and Peace Research* (1979, in Dutch). She is presently engaged in a study on multilateral diplomacy.

RÜDIGER JÜTTE has been a Research Associate in the Institute of Peace Research and Security Policy at the University of Hamburg since 1972. He studied political science and international relations at the Free University of Berlin and the University of Pennsylvania, Philadelphia. His research interests are in international organization, international conflicts and East–West relations. Since 1975 he has been teaching courses in these fields in the Inter-University Centre of Postgraduate Studies, Dubrovnik. Publications include *Konflikt und Internationale Organisation — Kybernetische Konzepte und Modelle* (1974), *Detente and Peace in Europe* and *Europe: From Detente to Peace?* (ed. and contributor, 1977).

NOSA-OLA OBASEKI is a Research Associate in the Nigerian Institute of International Affairs, Lagos. Following a social science education, he completed his graduate studies in international relations at the University College, London. His research interests are in regional integration and development, African international relations, and regional conflicts.

M. S. RAJAN is professor of International Organization, School of International Studies, Jawaharlal Nehru University, New Delhi. From 1965–71 he was Director of the School and editor of its *International Studies* (1963–73). Since the end of 1974, he has also been editor of *India Quarterly* and *Foreign Affairs Reports*, published by the Indian Council of World Affairs. Apart from many contributions to learned journals in India and abroad on Indian foreign policy, Commonwealth affairs, United Nations affairs, and non-alignment, his own books include *United Nations and Domestic Jurisdiction* (^{2}1961), *India in World Affairs 1954–56* (1964), and *Sovereignty over Natural Resources* (1978).

KATARINA TOMASEVSKI is presently associated with the Institute for Social Research of the University of Zagreb. She studied Law at Zagreb University and Harvard University and subsequently became Assistant Professor of International Law at the University of Rijeka. Her research interests are in the regulation of violence in the international community, including terrorism and irregular warfare, and international economic law and development. She is presently engaged in a study on the development of human rights in Yugoslavia since 1945, and collaborates in a project on development of science in the country. Apart from contributions to journals, she is the author of *The Challenge of Terrorism* (1978, in Croatian).

HERMANN WEBER is a Research Associate in the Institute of International Affairs at the University of Hamburg and Lecturer in International Law in the Law Faculty. His research interests are in the fields of the application of international law in international conflicts, legal, aspects of East–West relations, and the evolution of norms for an international law of development. In addition to many articles in these fields he is the author of *Der Vietnam-Konflikt — bellum legale? Rechtspflichten der Staaten unter dem Gewaltverbot der UN-Charter* (1970) and of a textbook on international law (1977).

INDEX